THE IMPORTANCE OF VISUAL SUSTAINABILITY IN URBAN DESIGN STRATEGY

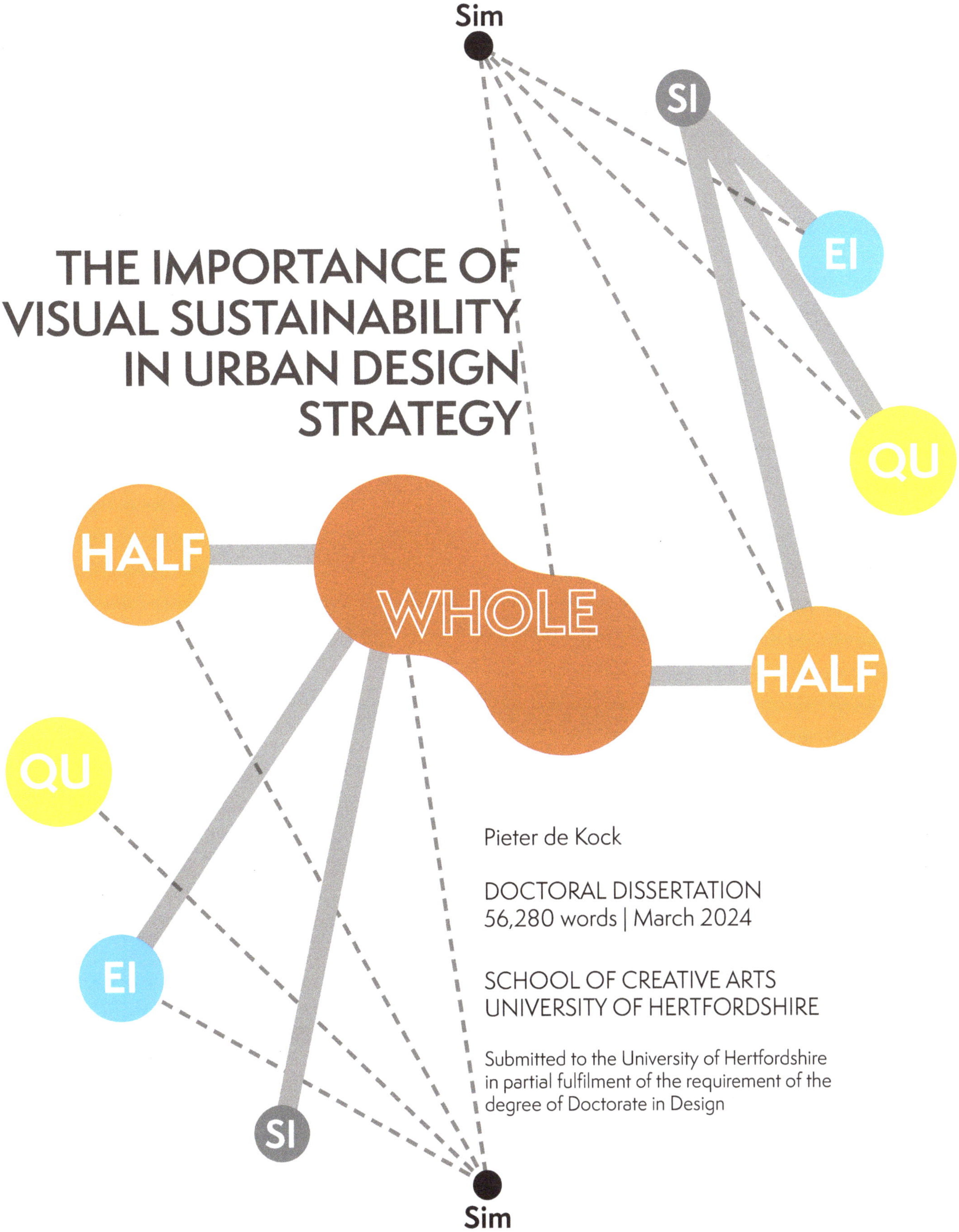

Pieter de Kock

DOCTORAL DISSERTATION
56,280 words | March 2024

SCHOOL OF CREATIVE ARTS
UNIVERSITY OF HERTFORDSHIRE

Submitted to the University of Hertfordshire in partial fulfilment of the requirement of the degree of Doctorate in Design

THE IMPORTANCE OF VISUAL SUSTAINABILITY

Author's Declaration

This study is the result of my own work and includes nothing which is the outcome of work done in collaboration except as declared in the preface and specified in the text.

ISBN 978-1-0686586-7-9
© 2024

IN URBAN DESIGN STRATEGY

ABSTRACT

This research addresses interactions in urban environments—when defined as interaction types and used as a metric—as they provide an effective strategy for understanding the relationship between urban heterogeneity and how we are visually sustained through engagement with our surroundings. With most of us now living in cities, the importance of visual sustainability in urban design strategy should not be underestimated. Interaction type analysis is key to bridging the gap in knowledge which lies in the challenges posed by the levels of subjectivity inherent in how we see, what we see, and the difficulty in measuring visual sustainability. The aim of this study is to explore the philosophy behind how we are sustained by what we see and its relevance to urban design. By using a mixed methods approach, the research shows how a practical application of Bergson's philosophy can be reconciled with urban design at a strategic level to establish an operational logic for understanding urban environments, one which does not require us to identify the meaning or even what it is people have looked at. The findings suggest that urban density plays less of a role than we might expect and what is more influential are the elements that hold people's attention, in other words, levels of urban activity. The variables comparison points to the proposal that interaction types have a role to play in urban design strategy. To understand visual sustainability better we need to understand three things. Firstly, the role duration plays in the types of interaction we have with our surroundings. Secondly, how elements that we cannot see exist on every site, and are important in understanding not only existing conditions properly but the potential for development. Thirdly, that these elements that we cannot see are valid, real structures—as real as the physical structures which act as proxies for them. The main finding of this study is the suggestion that visual interaction types are the building blocks of visual sustainability when considered in the context of urban design strategy. What difference this makes depends on the level of analysis—whether student or practitioner, commercially oriented, in terms of spatial health and well-being, or at a more abstract level, in personal development and growth. But the overarching consideration is that interaction types are able to reveal where the real city lies and by real city is meant the city we pay attention to. The emphasis going forward must be on an effective implementation of urban design strategy by including interaction type because, as city dwellers, it is we who stand to benefit the most.

THE IMPORTANCE OF VISUAL SUSTAINABILITY

Table of Contents

PART ONE

INTRODUCTION — 1

§. 1 *Introductory statement* — 1

§. 2 *Summary of research* — 2

§. 3 *Investigation overview* — 6

§. 4 *Key expressions* — 6

Chapter One — 11

SEEING AS INTERACTION — 11

§. 5 *Seeing by interacting with our surroundings* — 11

§. 6 *Theoretical premise* — 16

§. 7 *Theoretical framework* — 16

§. 8 *Literature review* — 17

Chapter Two — 35

UNIFYING OBJECT WITH EXPERIENCE — 35

§. 9 *Object versus Experience* — 35

Chapter Three — 51

THE INVISIBLE CITY — 51

§. 10 *Invisible City versus Visible City* — 51

PART TWO

Chapter Four — 63

METHODOLOGY — 63

§. 11 *Bergson and mixed methods* — 63

§. 12 *Research philosophy* — 70

§. 13 *Research approach* — 77

§. 14 *Research design* — 77

§. 15 *Data collection* — 80

Chapter Five — 85

FINDINGS — 85

§. 16 *Data* — 85

THE IMPORTANCE OF VISUAL SUSTAINABILITY

§. 17 *Hypothesis test*	89

PART THREE

§. 18 *The dataset in its entirety*	95
§. 19 *Reciprocity in data*	102
§. 20 *The building block*	108
§. 21 *Commercial application*	124
§. 22 *Findings summary*	135

CONCLUSION 147

§. 23 *Measuring our temporal urban*	147
§. 24 *Response overview*	149
§. 25 *Outcomes*	151
§. 26 *Future research*	153
§. 27 *Study limitations*	156
§. 28 *Final word*	158
Bibliography	159
List of Figures	169
List of Tables	173
Appendices	175
Appendix A	177
Survey strategy and survey form	177
Appendix B	193
Interviews	193
Youtube: Larry And Janet Move Out	206
Appendix C	221
The sound of data	221

IN URBAN DESIGN STRATEGY

ACKNOWLEDGEMENTS

It is better to have meaning

Special thanks go to my supervisors
Silvio Carta and
Lubo Jankovic

What is seen
was not made out of
what was visible
—Hebrews

THE IMPORTANCE OF VISUAL SUSTAINABILITY

IN URBAN DESIGN STRATEGY

DISSEMINATION OF THIS RESEARCH

Chapter Two of this study references UNIFYING OBJECT WITH EXPERIENCE: HERITAGE IN A TEMPORAL SETTING presented at the AMPS Prague–Heritages conference held in June 2023 (proceedings ISSN 2398–9467 published in 2024). I am the first author on this paper and responsible for the written content. However, I received advice on shaping the argument for its intended audience from my main supervisor, Dr Silvio Carta.

Chapter Three in this study references a paper called ARCHITECTURE: HURTLING TOWARDS AN IRRELEVANT CONCLUSION; OR SKILFULLY SHIFTING THE PARADIGM? presented at the ArchiDOCT conference held in July 2023 (proceedings ISBN 9781912319084 published in 2024). I am the sole author of this paper. I was introduced to this conference by Dr Lubo Jankovic (my second supervisor).

Chapter Four references a published article called TROJANS OF AMBIGUITY VS RESILIENT REGENERATION: VISUAL MEANING IN CITIES, which was written jointly with Dr Silvio Carta (whose contribution was section 3.2 Sidewalk Labs' Quayside, Toronto).

In addition, excerpts are taken from several more manuscripts, of which I am sole author, and which were written and submitted as pre-prints to Figshare, an online open-access repository. These include:

- Joyful vs joyless expenditure: relevance, real estate, & the voice of urban data. 2023 | Preprint DOI: 10.6084/M9.figshare.23834781.
- The importance of visual sustainability in urban design strategy. 2022 | Preprint DOI: 10.6084/M9.figshare.21311427.V1.
- Visual Sustainability Manifesto. 2022 | Preprint DOI: 10.6084/M9.FIGSHARE.19165931.V1.
- Visual sustainability– hypothetical synopsis. 2022 | Preprint. DOI: 10.6084/m9.figshare.18526436.v1.
- Visually dissecting sustainability. 2020 | Preprint. DOI: 10.6084/m9.figshare.13095578.v2.

THE IMPORTANCE OF VISUAL SUSTAINABILITY

IN URBAN DESIGN STRATEGY

PART ONE

INTRODUCTION

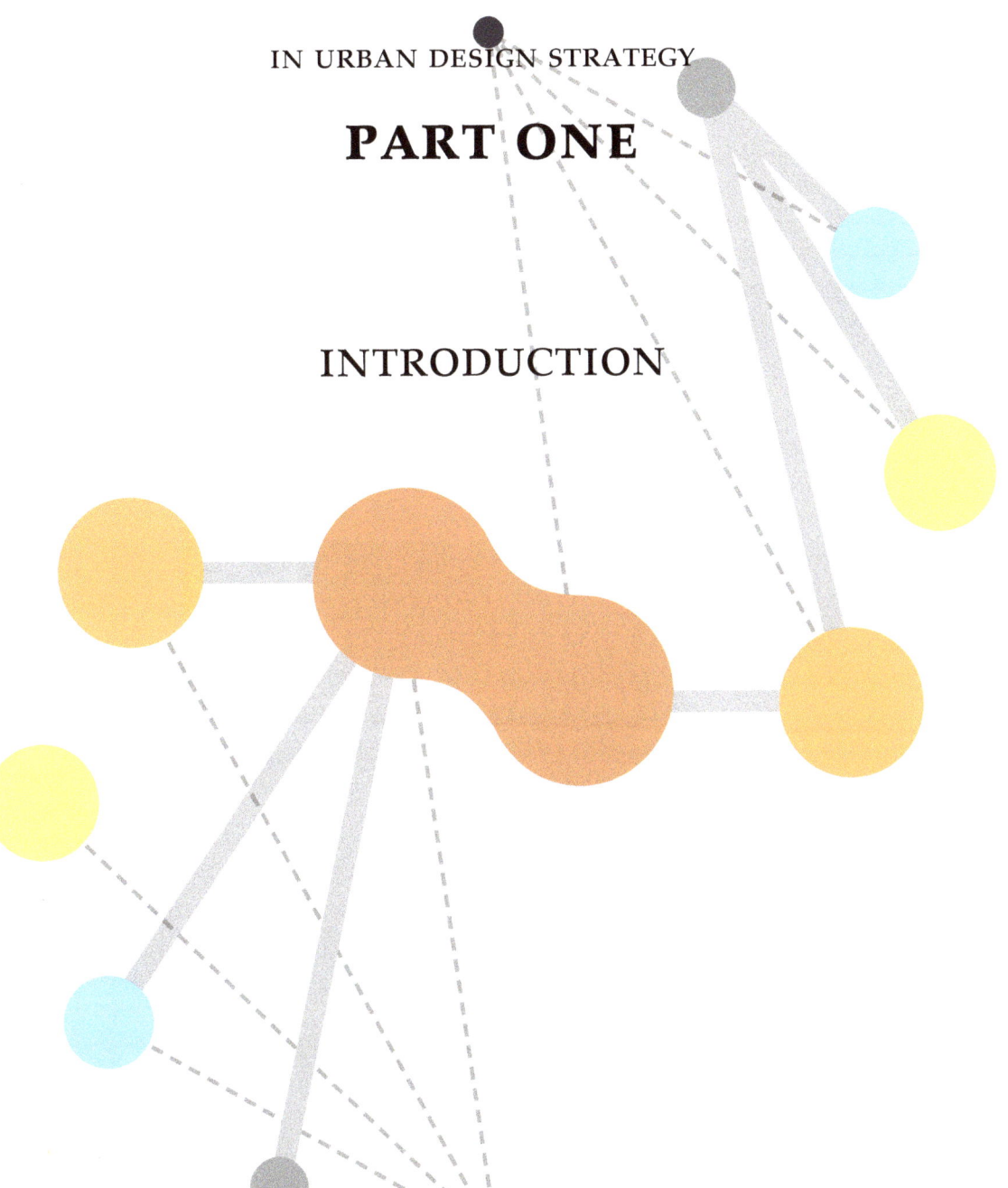

§. 1 *Introductory statement*

If there is one thing I would like the reader to take from this study, it is the idea that *VISUAL INTERACTION TYPES are the building blocks of visual sustainability. Where we once relied on photography because photographs never lie, they now can, they often do, and often we expect them to. Instead, a true reading of our urban may be evidenced by the visual interactions we demonstrate in the exchanges we have with our environment—transactions we pay for every day with our attention—and which form the bedrock of our understanding of visual sustainability. Our interactions with the environment do not lie, and **until they do, these VISUAL INTERACTION TYPES must be collected and analysed to enhance our understanding of the reality of the surrounding invisible city.

*Also referred to as interaction type(s)

**In the context of the ongoing debate about artificial intelligence, see, for example, Narayan et al., 2023.

THE IMPORTANCE OF VISUAL SUSTAINABILITY

*See Chapter Three on page 51.

Because an *invisible city is proposed in this study, one which straddles the city we see, the main thrust of my argument (developed in Chapter Three "Visible versus invisible city" on page 58) is that this invisible city is more important than the visible because of what it is we 'see', namely, our own reflection. The invisible city which I am about to describe in this study is a reflection pool. It reflects the physical city, but not only that, it reveals the true nature of the things and events we interact with.

When we look up towards the sky, we see the galaxy through its visible parts. At night it is the stars that guide and direct our senses. But there is more than meets the eye because what we do not see is dark matter. Now imagine the view back down towards earth. Again, we see stars, but of a different kind, in the lights of our cities. And my argument is that there is also dark matter in amongst these lights which we do not see. Urban dark matter. The dark matter in this view is what my research seeks to understand more about through the premise that it is not only the 'lights' from the visible cities that matter but also the 'constellations' that describe 'invisible cities.' I will argue that these invisible cities are formed from the interactions we have with our surroundings and, when defined through interaction type and used as a metric, provides an effective strategy for understanding more about the relationship between urban **heterogeneity and the way we engage with our surroundings.

***Heterogeneity*: the quality or state of consisting of dissimilar or diverse elements (Merriam Webster Dictionary, 2023).

There is therefore more to this research than meets the eye because it is directed towards looking at urban dark matter and builds a case for why doing so is important in urban design strategy. And why, both the invisible and urban design strategy are important to how we are visually sustained. Which describes the topic of this research: the importance of visual sustainability in urban design strategy.

§. 2 *Summary of research*

I have produced several manuscripts in which connections are made and themes generated, that cannot be excluded from this study. Two manuscripts in particular are important. Each is adapted and presented in Chapter's Two and Three respectively and represents the iterative nature of my mixed methods study. Both chapters invest heavily in the formulation of my design premise and hypotheses. They serve to extend the literature review by adding much needed context to the void created by my deliberate omission of architectural and urban design theory. The following summary of chapters provides a roadmap of what lies ahead in the study.

CHAPTER ONE: INTERACTION

Chapter One considers the research question (page 6) through the concept of interaction, namely, our interaction with elements around us and it is our understanding of interaction which will have a bearing on whether the null hypothesis, that there is no difference in the types of interaction we have with our surroundings, can be rejected. If it can be rejected then there is a case for making a claim about 'urban dark matter.' My argument will be that, in any given urban area, INTERACTION directs us towards the code that makes a place unique. Because, if we want to know what makes a place tick then we should look no further than our own interactions for an answer. Interaction is a broad subject, and my intention has always been to inspect the idea of visual interaction from a reality independent of current architectural and urban design theory. Adopting this ontological positioning has made it possible to produce the arguments contained in this study. Which is not to say that I have not referenced snippets of architectural and urban design theory, but these references serve to provide context rather than acting as the driving force behind any of the arguments presented. My decision to *bracket existing architectural and urban design theory is easily made as it allows me to circumvent the associated ambiguity and concentrate my efforts on the main underlying philosophy borne from an ontology which I argue, has been neglected in contemporary research. This underlying philosophy is concerned with the reality of temporal metaphysics, as defined by Bergson's duration (1988), and defended by Robbins (2014, 2023). My study is tasked, primarily using Bergson's philosophy (1988), with understanding more about our interactions in relation to "temporal heterogeneity [where]... qualitative multiplicity defines the duration" (Lawlor and Moulard-Leonard, 2021, pp.8, 9). In other words, how Bergson's reliance on the temporal qualities of our existence helps us to understand the **interactions we have with what surrounds us, both visually and physically—the use we see and how we feel about the use we see. These concepts will be discussed in depth in the first three chapters. In the next chapter, object and experience become the focus of interaction, not only between object and experience, but also in our own interaction with object, with experience, and with both together.

CHAPTER TWO: OBJECT/EXPERIENCE

Chapter Two uses the lens provided by both Bergson and Robbins, to clarify what the terms OBJECT and EXPERIENCE might mean in relation to INTERACTION and urban design strategy. There is the realisation that our perception is composed of pattern recognition (Alexander, Ishikawa and Silverstein, 1977) and regulated by what Robbins (2014) calls invariance structures of events, where each ***invariance structure is comprised of an invariant and

Bracket: to eliminate from consideration (Merriam Webster Dictionary, 2023).

**Interaction*: in this study visual interaction is not only what we see with our eyes. It embraces both physical use and visual use, i.e. embodied interaction as well as sight. Therefore, visual interaction refers to what our body does when we look at something *as well as* what our eyes tell us about what's seen.

***See Figure 8 on page 43.

THE IMPORTANCE OF VISUAL SUSTAINABILITY

transformation. In this chapter object and experience are merged into what is, in effect, a temporal event. A data–driven visual artefact is also proposed, which draws on Bergson's theory of qualitative multiplicity. The underlying message throughout the chapter is that we are right to concern ourselves with the TYPES OF VISUAL INTERACTION we have with our surroundings, especially in *the ordinary. In the next chapter, I have taken interaction, object, and experience and made a case for why they belong together in an ontologically relevant construct called the invisible city. And why this is relevant to urban design strategy.

*See page 48.

CHAPTER THREE: INVISIBLE CITY

The notion of an invisible city inhabited by us through our location, is a natural continuation of the debate from the previous chapter, about how we relate to object and experience. A step is taken in the direction of what is proposed as the visible and invisible variables active or dormant in the qualities which reveal levels of urban (visual) heterogeneity. Bergson provides inspiration through his concept of qualitative multiplicity (1988) and this is expressed through his example of "notes of the musical scale" (Bergson, 1988, p. 203). In this study, NOTE refers to the time values of sounds and are used to define interaction types by their duration (categorical data) as well as provide a set of continuous data (seconds) which are useful in the statistical analysis. The signs in people that direct us towards the invisible city can be found in what I propose to be THE BUILDING BLOCK OF VISUAL SUSTAINABILITY, namely, the VISUAL INTERACTION TYPE. And the argument is taken a step further, by focusing in on THE MIX of visual interaction types. In the next chapter, we go on to discuss the strategy for revealing more about the invisible city and the best approach to take to examine and test the nature of its presence in relation to the physical city we are used to interacting with.

CHAPTER FOUR: METHODOLOGY

Chapter Four looks at interaction as a measuring device using Bergson's concept of temporal heterogeneity. While in the previous chapters I will have alluded to several research techniques, in Chapter Four these are laid out in more detail as part of the mixed methods approach. In order to understand interaction type I needed to understand urban alienation. I did so by analysing the effect of urban rejection and repulsion through the effect of estrangement on former residents of an abandoned inner city residential housing estate. I found this strategy easier than trying to understand the concept I am really interested in—visual sustainability—because the devastating effects of alienation on people is more palpable. It is also unapologetically broadcast by the communities themselves and thus provides excellent data to work with. But I also needed a simple device to categorise these subjective data, which could be robust enough to serve both qualitative and quantitative analysis. I found what I was looking for because I was able to free myself from the inherent bias of my professional training as both architect and urban designer, having situated myself in an ontology which lies outside generally accepted built environment theory. The videos (Figure 18 on page 69 and Figure 19 on page 69) describe the device and its use. The next chapter is all about testing for signs of life in my research question, which is: *In thinking about the philosophy behind a concept such as visual sustainability, how may it be possible for visual sustainability to, in some way, play a role in urban design strategy?*

CHAPTER FIVE: FINDINGS

Chapter Five addresses how the strategy of using interaction type as a measuring device helps us understand more about the relationship between urban heterogeneity and how we are visually sustained through engagement with our surroundings. The findings suggest that the visual health of any urban area can be recorded with a degree of accuracy because the methods used are resistant to the kind of ambiguity and subjectivity that has confounded traditional attempts at stitching together meaning in urban patterns and, more importantly, trying to convey that meaning to others. Where we were once confused by the empirical value of 'feelings,' my argument is that it is now possible to understand feelings as TRANSFORMATION, in the sense of the invariance structures proposed by Robbins. And transformation is a record of time, which, in this study, is represented by NOTES. It is the device used to categorise the duration of engagement people have with their surroundings. Interaction type therefore presents itself as the unique building block which can be used to measure the impact on us of the objects that surround us. I also introduce another artefact in this chapter which describes, in a simulation, the commercial reality of strategic urban design.

CONCLUSION

In the conclusion I summarise the key findings in the context of my setting out point, namely, the ontology identified through Bergson's theory of qualitative multiplicity. The key finding is that if we are able to understand more about what the invisible city means and represents, then we can look forward to building those structures simultaneously with the physical city. Our future depends on the things we cannot see and, as this study I hope will demonstrate, it is possible to see the invisible if we look in the right place. The right place is not a place but a state of mind, one that opens our eyes to

THE IMPORTANCE OF VISUAL SUSTAINABILITY

the potential of being sustained and enriched in daily life. The suggestion is that when we are visually sustained *we see more* and this is a quality deserving of our attention in cities.

§. 3 Investigation overview

This study is directed towards how interaction with our surroundings appears to determine levels of sustainability through active processes describing the phenomenon we experience: *of memory, virtual action (Bergson, 1988), **redintegration, temporal metaphysics (Robbins, 2014), affordance, ecological perception (Gibson, 2015), enaction (Varela et al.), and tacit knowledge (Polanyi & Grene, 1969).

*See "Philosophical inspiration" on page 53 for a detailed look at the relationship between the four main theories in this study.

**Redintegration*: the law of redintegration in Gibsonian terms would be: A current event, E' redintegrates a previous event, E, when E' and E share the same invariance structure. Derived from "a term coined already in 1732 by Wolff, a disciple of Leibniz, in his Psychologia Empirica. It is defined roughly as "a part of a current event retrieves the whole of a past event," or as Klein (1971) puts it, a pattern in a current event retrieves a past event with a similar pattern" (Robbins, S. E., 2021, p.21).

UNDERLYING RATIONALE

The purpose of this study is to understand more about how we are visually sustained in the urban environment (which I elaborate more on in "§. 5 Seeing by interacting with our surroundings" on page 11).

Aim

To explore the philosophy behind how we are sustained by what we see and its relevance to urban design.

Objectives

The aim is addressed through the following objectives:

1. To establish an operational logic for understanding urban areas, one that does not require us to identify the exact meaning or even what it is people interact with.
2. To produce a mixed method approach which can be replicated.
3. To demonstrate how the practical application of Bergson's philosophy can be reconciled with urban design at a strategic level.

Research question

In thinking about the philosophy behind a concept such as visual sustainability, how may it be possible for visual sustainability to, in some way, play a role in urban design strategy?

§. 4 Key expressions

The following definitions describe the intended meaning in this study, unless otherwise noted in the margins.

Alienation: is the absence of what we hold dear (cf. VISUAL SUSTAINABILITY). It is described by a lack of engagement with our surroundings as evidenced through interaction type (cf. INTERACTION TYPE).

Digital tapestry: is a visual artefact I have produced from these data which accurately represents these data and describes emergent properties, as a MIX of INTERACTION TYPES at block and zone level, using Bergson's theory of QUALITATIVE MULTIPLICITY (see also Figure 46 on page 123 and Figure 56 on page 222).

Duration: is a certain length of time which is indivisible for its entire length (cf. QUALITATIVE MULTIPLICITY). It is a concept of temporal metaphysics and is used by Bergson in his 1896 'Matter and Memory' to describe an experience made up of a multiplicity of interpenetrating moments (Bergson, 1988; Robbins, 2023) (cf. time–extended event). One way to understand duration is by the effect of the melody in music on us, as described in Bergson's 1922 'Duration and Simultaneity' (1965, p.44, p.49). It is the effect of "multiplicity without divisibility and succession without separation" (Bergson, 1965, p.44) (cf. NOTE).

Event: describes an occurrence, in an engagement with our surroundings, which lasts for a length of time. An EVENT interacts with an invariance structure to produce a PATTERN (cf. PATTERN). See also "Figure 8. Use patterns premise, adapted using the concept by Robbins of patterns as invariance structures of events, to describe the environmental transaction between PHYSICAL USE and VISUAL USE (De Kock, Pieter, 2022, p.21)." on page 43.

Experience: is argued in this study to be an intangible manifestation of TRANSFORMATION (feeling).

Interaction: is argued in this study to represent our embodied engagement with a surrounding OBJECT or EVENT.

Interaction type: is the full description of the metric used in this study which describes what I have called a NOTE (a sound used to account for how long an interaction lasts). There are six INTERACTION TYPES that are categorised as sounds. Each interaction type can also be converted into continuous data using their duration in (parts of) seconds. The primary role of INTERACTION TYPE *as a sound* is to test for emergent qualities using Bergson's theory of QUALITATIVE MULTIPLICITY when these sounds are considered as a MIX of interactions, at the level of blocks or zones (cf. digital tapestry). The primary role of interaction type *as a time value* (continuous data) is to test the statistical relevance using regression analysis methods.

Interpenetration: is a condition state which "when characterized as indivisible, as melodic, as interpenetrating, permeating "instants," is a form of memory per Bergson" (Robbins, 2023, p.10).

Note: is a sound which I have used as a metric. Each NOTE describes a separate interaction type by the way it accounts for how long the interaction lasts. It is related to "notes of the musical scale" (Bergson, 1988, p. 203) that have an interpenetrating quality (Robbins, 2023), but in this study is not intended as music, merely as a sound effect or groups of sound effects. When considering the MIX of interaction types I am looking for emergence (in a non–linear sense) based on the analogy of interpenetrating sounds, in the same way that DURATION describes interpenetrating melody (cf. DURATION).

Object: The argument in this study is that objects are typically components of the physical city we look at but they can also be components of intangible elements There is a difference in this study between *looking* at an object and *seeing* an object.

Patterns: are recognisable objects or events having a certain similarity of appearance or effect in the environment. In this study we do not look at patterns, we *see* patterns.

Physical Use: The use that we see when we define an object (cf. VISUAL USE).

Qualitative multiplicity: describes temporal heterogeneity of multiple psychic states merged indivisibly in time (Lawlor and Moulard-Leonard, 2021).

Rhythm: is an alternative metric to sound and useful for understanding the effect of energy or liveliness in an urban environment (see "Tempo or Energy" on page 83).

Structural invariant: is something which never changes in a time–extended event for the duration of that time–extended event. Something can be a structural invariant in one event but may not be in another. In other words, in one event it may be unchanging while in another it may act as transformation when engaged with by an observer (for examples, see "Chapter Two" on page 35).

Time–extended event: is "an event extending into the "past"" (Robbins, 2023, p.8). An event which has the properties of an indivisible series of moments in time where it has reached a condition state in which the whole is more than the sum of its parts.

Transformation: is feeling in the context of Robbins' analysis of invariance structures. My argument is that to feel is to be transformed i.e., feeling is transformation.

Visual Use: How we feel about the use that we see, when we are defined by an object through TRANSFORMATION (cf. PHYSICAL USE).

Visual sustainability: is the process by which we are sustained and enriched in daily life through the visual relationship we hold dear to our surroundings (De Kock 2019, p.72).

THE IMPORTANCE OF VISUAL SUSTAINABILITY

Chapter One
SEEING AS INTERACTION

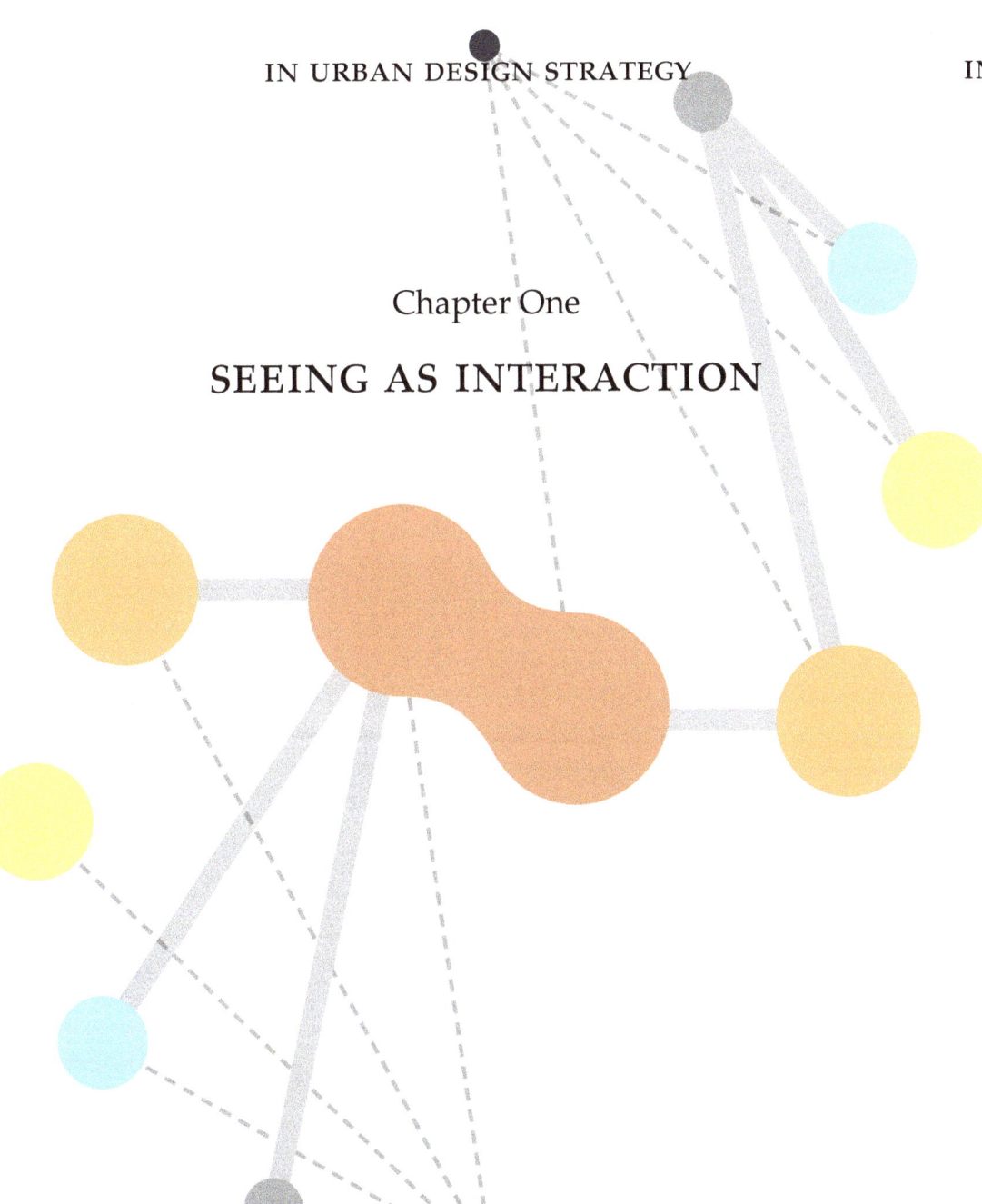

§. 5 *Seeing by interacting with our surroundings*

If the act of seeing is reasonably understood to be the result of interactions we have with our surroundings, then we should be able to measure *visual sustainability using these interactions. And until now, it seems, the only way we have been able to measure levels of *visual sustainability is through a complex mental negotiation within a maze of complicated theory (see, for example, Table 1 on page 15). In this chapter I will look at the concept of interaction with a view to uncovering whether existing literature reveals a difference in the types of interactions we have with our environment, or whether the null hypothesis is true. It appears to be the case that interactions are associated with the visual and rarely documented as embodied experiences.

Visual sustainability: the process by which people are sustained and enriched in daily life through the visual relationship they hold dear to their surroundings (De Kock, 2019, p.72).

CHAPTER 1   THE IMPORTANCE OF VISUAL SUSTAINABILITY

And it is this act of 'seeing,' of the visual, which has been a very ambiguous, fluid concept (Ballantyne, 2007; Berleant, 1997; Lefebvre & Nicholson-Smith, 2011; Makin, 2018; Ramachandran & Hirstein, 1999; Rapoport, 1990; Rodaway, 2011; Scarantino & de Sousa, 2018; Scruton, 2007), in the sense that there appears to be little consensus, in theoretical terms, about the mechanics of it all. In an urban context Brenner, for example, points out: "Rather, we concur with Leitner and Sheppard's (2016: 230) recent injunction "to take seriously the possibility that no single theory suffices to account for the variegated nature of urbanization and cities across the world" (2018, p.577). There can also be said to be little in common between how we are sustained by our visual world, and how we are sustained by modern-day sustainability. This claim is supported by two arguments which are partially competing. The first is that of a visual world in which perception is subjective, unscientific, and messy (Merleau-Ponty, 1968; Polanyi and Grene, 1969; Rose, 2007; Kromm and Bakewell, 2010; Mirzoeff, 2010; Designed to Hesitate: Consciousness as Paying Attention, 2010; Haun et al., 2017). In this visual world we are immersed in visually oriented reflexive behavioural patterns that we do not quite understand but which work in a very heuristic way (Moustakas, 1990; Gigerenzer, 2000). In contrast to this experience, the impression we have of modern-day sustainability can be said to be quite different from the fluidity of what we see and how we feel about what we see. The second argument manifests itself along an objective, scientific route. It presents itself to us in a more prescriptive manner: as a science-based recipe for the preservation and judicious harnessing of earth's valuable resources. The difference between the two approaches stems from the existence of dualism which describes two categorically different forces at work (Robinson, 2020) under the guise of the same or similar terms.

*"This loop refers to the ambiguity of theory in relation to what we see being produced. I refer to these mixed messages as *"confused meaning* [where]... The threat lies specifically and ultimately in the betrayal of an expectation or expected outcome." (De Kock and Carta, 2020b).

**Visual attraction and repulsion, see also Salingaros (1999).

Interaction: rhetorical statement, problems, and presuppositions
There is then the question of the impasse in *the loop between *theory* (i.e., the 'messiness' from the first argument), and *strategy* (which poses as modern-day sustainability and the solution in the second argument), and how these two are complicated by the ambiguous nature of both **visual attraction and visual repulsion. It is the contradiction of life and why "artists only create in order to survive, to gain a little more breathing space…Otherwise I don't think artists would kill themselves by living as they do" (Something Rich and Strange: The Life and Music of Iannis Xenakis, 2022, 00:48:30). The struggle that artists have is the struggle that we all want to share in because that is human nature. My argument therefore is that the struggle we all have in some way or another with the finite is the struggle of classic metaphysics.

It is in ambiguity, that we appear to seek the richness we crave to validate meaning. Ambiguity appears to be the conduit for the incomplete interactions with surrounding elements. We seem to act differently when confronted by *theory* as opposed to *strategy* and this difference in interaction is the impasse that traps us. In a sense, we trap ourselves with intellectual impossibilities. But for Bergson, richness exists in *time*, free of confused meaning. Through his concept of qualitative multiplicity, ambiguity becomes irrelevant and the resulting intellectual impossibility therefore becomes irrelevant. The idea behind qualitative multiplicity is best explained by Bergson's example of "notes of the musical scale" (Bergson, 1988, p. 203) or "sounds of a bell" (Bergson, 2001, p.86). He explains how we can never tell where one sound stops and the other starts and so for the duration of a ringing bell, we think of it as one event because it is one indivisible moment. It is a time–extended (Robbins, 2014) event. As far as Bergson is concerned, we have got it wrong because relevance is temporal in its quality and exists in memory. Relevance represents experiences which are difficult to identify properly and often impossible to describe due to their phenomenological characteristics, existing much like *qualia. This is true also of urban design strategy, in that our cities rely on solutions that are invariably heavily influenced by a single theory (or a narrow range of complementary theories), which is then used as the yardstick to retrospectively validate and underpin the quality of our built environment. *But if those theories, that have constructed our urban, are used to evaluate the completed works, what then does that say about the success of urban space?* It is, in many respects a self–fulfilling prophecy if what we build is validated by what we build. What is needed is a metric which can be unbiased and independent of the process of creation.

Qualia: as described by Robbins (2004, 2013) and in more detail by Ramachandran and Hirstein (1997).

Measuring our urban

So, in this research I will argue that we cannot successfully measure urban space using the same theory that constructed those spaces in the first place. What we should be doing is finding a way to measure an urban construct in a less biased way. By this is meant, that we might be able to understand our levels of comfort in an urban environment in the same way we might understand a child's progress at school through their school report. The report is the metric which describes a child's activity. The activity has already occurred and the report can not create the activity, it just reports it. My proposal is that the code found in Robbins' interpretation of urban PATTERNS: as invariance structures of events (2014) gets us to the starting line in understanding more about how we report i.e., measure our urban. And one way to understand how the act of seeing sustains us, is to identify where it appears to be absent.

CHAPTER 1 THE IMPORTANCE OF VISUAL SUSTAINABILITY

*Excerpts from my preprint: The importance of visual sustainability in urban design strategy (2022a).

Gap in knowledge

In the second argument, for *modern–day sustainability (the objective, scientific route) the norm is that we take care of ourselves by managing the earth's resources. But there does not appear to be any room for taking care of ourselves by caring for our visual world. By visual world is meant what we see and how we feel about what we see. And by what we see and how we feel is meant the whole notion of embodied perception as articulated and contextualised by Varela et al. (2016). It is notable that the concept of being visually sustained is absent from **modern–day sustainability which is defined by the 1987 Brundtland Report (World Commission on Environment and Development, 1987) and successive policy documents described by the United Nations (UN), the World Economic Forum (WEF), and related Sustainable Development Goals (SDGs). The emphasis of this study will be to consider the notion of sustainability from a wider perspective, thus shifting weight from physical and tangible elements, towards our visual world. It aims at exploring the idea of visual sustainability as a cognate definition to traditional sustainability. The gap in knowledge has been made discoverable in broad terms by the absence from modern–day sustainability of a concept of visual sustainability. But there is a more granular approach that I intend to follow which focuses on visual interaction type. The gap in knowledge that interests me is not that there is no regard for visual sustainability in modern–day sustainability but that it appears that modern–day sustainability does not know how to *measure* visual sustainability. This research will address this gap in knowledge, about how to measure visual sustainability, by proposing a solution that engages with the idea of VISUAL INTERACTION TYPE. Because only then will we be able to counter, what appears to be, the prejudice in modern–day sustainability against perceived impossible levels of subjectivity in the act of seeing.

** "In 1987, the United Nations Brundtland Commission defined sustainability as meeting the needs of the present without compromising the ability of future generations to meet their own needs." (https://www.un.org/en/academic-impact/sustainability).

How we are visually sustained through interaction

This study is about how we are visually sustained and what that looks like in philosophical terms through the lens of design. It is a mixed methods study within the domain of design studies which hopes in its conclusion to point out some practical ways by which to produce documented networks of meaning. ***Networks of meaning can be understood in a physical sense to mean those related assemblages (De Landa, 2006) that make up a particular physical built environment—peculiar to a group of engaged and invested people who are evidenced through the concept of territorialization (De Landa, 2006). Together, these physical environments, attached as they are to their communities, are networks with meaning, the meaning of which, it is

***See also Community, Heritage, and Meaning as a major network of meaning on page 36

		Levels of scale	
		Strong centres	
		Thick boundaries	
		Alternating repetition	
		Positive space	
		Good shape	
		Local symmetries	
		Deep interlock and ambiguity	Alexander's 'Fifteen Fundamental Properties'
		Contrast	Biophilia
		Gradients	Complexity
Path	The description of space	Roughness	Convex space
Edge	The theory of natural movement	Echoes	Design patterns
District	Cities as movement economies	The void	Fractals
Node	The simultaneously multi-scale city	Simplicity and inner calm	Scaling coherence
Landmark	The dual grid	Not–separateness	Symmetries
1960	1983	2001	2010
Lynch	Space Syntax	Alexander	Salingaros

Table 1. An example of the complexity in and between just four architectural theories.

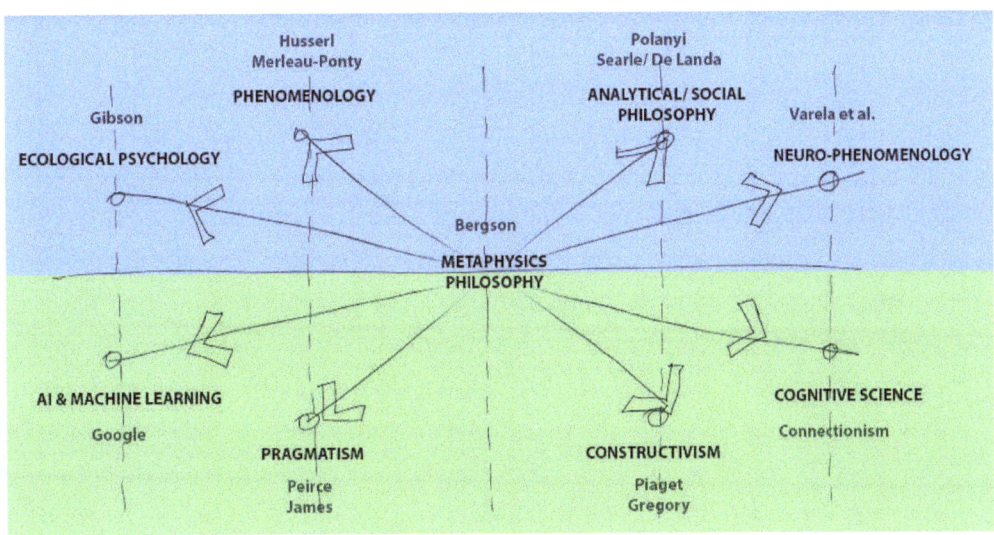

Figure 1. Theoretical premise. This diagram illustrates the connection between Bergson's temporal metaphysics and epistemological approaches from other domains of knowledge pertaining to the visual world (De Kock, 2022a, p.18).

proposed, can be recorded in a unique way; and updated on a regular basis. These documents and artefacts are envisaged as collateral that can be used to protect sensitive urban nodes for future generations.

§. 6 *Theoretical premise*

In this urban design perspective on the act of seeing, I will focus on the ontological and philosophical relevance of how we see, what it is we see, and how and why we consume visual elements around us. I do so by borrowing from my central figure in continental philosophy, Bergson (Figure 1 on page 15) who was the pivot in a sense between analytical philosophy in the style of his contemporary Russell and the phenomenology of Husserl, another contemporary. Bergson was not a phenomenologist, but he was instrumental, through his leaning towards the concept of intuition in a metaphysical sense, in inspiring the phenomenological tradition. "One might say it all began with Henri Bergson" (Merquior, 1987, p.11).

§. 7 *Theoretical framework*

*See also Figure 16 on page 65.

*To uncover more about the act of seeing, this study has adopted Bergson's temporal metaphysics as an investigative tool over classic metaphysics in exploring the concept of visual sustainability of our urban because I wish to understand more about our interactions as a consequence of their temporal qualities, which are not based on Euclidean principles of planes and solids. Bergson, in the English translation of his 1896 Matter and Memory (1988) provides what can be argued as a coherent theory for temporal metaphysics, specifically through his concepts of DURATION and QUALITATIVE MULTIPLICITY, which are discussed in more detail the next section. Through these two concepts Bergson explains how we exist not in space but in time. My proposal is to reinforce the relationship between Bergson's philosophy and our experience of urban life today. The premise is that Bergson's theory holds several clues that point to evidence about the way that we interact with our environment, which in turn help simplify the complexity around the act of seeing. It also points us in the direction of how types of visual interactions inform visual sustainability and what that might mean in more precise terms.

§. 8 *Literature review*

If it all started with Bergson then it is fitting for me to start with his theory of Matter and Memory, published in 1896. Bergson was reportedly misunderstood and especially so in his own time by, for example, Einstein and Russell (Robbins, 2000, 2006a; In Our Time: S21/34 Bergson and Time (May 9, 2019), 2019). The emphasis in this study is not to analyse these differences because Robbins, for example, has done so in a thorough and compelling manner. Instead, I would like to understand more about Bergson through his concept of qualitative multiplicity and temporal metaphysics. I would also like to draw from several other key theories which are relevant to a discussion on temporal metaphysics and urban design. But before I take a look at Bergson in relation to the theories of Polanyi, Gibson, and Varela et al., (on page 18) I would like to first address the elephant in the room.

VISUAL SUSTAINABILITY: THE ELEPHANT IN THE ROOM

Visual sustainability may be thought of as a concept which exists by default, through its omission from modern–day sustainability. It is a concept which cannot be contested because we are visually sustained in some way or another by our surroundings. Culture exists because we are visually sustained. It is why there is meaning, because meaning can only be derived from the things that we 'see.' The act of seeing can be said to be about making meaning; making sense of; finding the relevancy in, that which surrounds us.

Because there is no definition available of visual sustainability, my presupposition is that visual sustainability is *the process by which we are sustained and enriched in daily life through the visual relationship we hold dear to our surroundings* (De Kock 2019, p.72). The context of the presupposition in this study lies in its importance in relation to urban design strategy, how we are visually sustained through our interactions, and by extension of the argument, through the types of interaction we have with our surroundings. The argument is not about why such a concept is curiously absent from modern–day sustainability, which, with all the 'bells and whistles' that accompany it, appears to be more aligned with a deterministic, materialistic world view than a pragmatic one. What I would like to do in this study instead, is to directly address my *research question and think about how the philosophy behind a concept such as visual sustainability can, in some way, play a role in urban design strategy. The sense I have is that we can *observe* the role played by visual sustainability by understanding visual interaction and the types of interaction we have with our surroundings. Before I move on to

*See research question on page 6.

CHAPTER 1 THE IMPORTANCE OF VISUAL SUSTAINABILITY

present three philosophical considerations—metaphysical, epistemological, and ethical on page 24, I would like to discuss the search criteria and main search terms of the literature review.

Literature search criteria
For the literature review the word 'visual' in 'visual sustainability' is taken to mean not only what we see and want to use, but through associated qualia, what we feel too. I decided to analyse previous literature which seeks to describe the *entire* transaction: both seeing and feeling. The reason for this decision is that modern-day sustainability appears to focus exclusively on the physical environment, which explains the absence of a concept of visual sustainability. In response, the literature I have engaged with is oriented towards the discovery of a more balanced view, one that incorporates both PHYSICAL USE and VISUAL USE i.e., finding out more about what an object is and its use to us, as well as in how the object makes us feel.

The differences between physical and visual elements

Finding a more balanced view can be explained in terms of the search criteria as follows. In normative terms, what we see is the visual. But as the literature review progressed it became evident that what we see can be described differently. The first point is that in Gibson's case—beyond his theory of reflected light as the reason we see (1983)—what we see can be described as physical use, by way of affordance (1983; 2015). We see the use. But use is not a visual element in a conventional sense. Use is not matter. It is a simulation (of an affordance to act in some way). In this case then, what we see is physical affordance—which I argue is the same as PHYSICAL USE. Secondly, in contrast to the first point, we can infer from Polanyi that the invisible which is inherent in tacit knowledge—that which we feel—is also something that we see. But again, we do not see it in the conventional sense of the word. Instead, we look beyond the object and see its meaning (1969). And, like use, meaning is not matter. What we see in this case is the visual affordance—which I argue is the same as VISUAL USE.

In both cases we see matter first, but for both theories my argument is that the transaction is never complete until we *see* and *feel* the use. The use for Gibson, as well as Varela, is to ACT; and for Polanyi, the use is to FEEL. So, we have PHYSICAL USE and VISUAL USE described. Both conditions are in fact an oxymoron in a sense because WE SEE—BUT WE DO NOT—UNTIL WE DO. This apparent contradiction adds a dynamic new dimension of understanding to the material discovered. Because what we see can be said to be made up of two components of use: physical and visual. So, my argument is that we look, but we only *see* when we comprehend fully the interaction between physical and visual use. Therefore, for the visual world, in addition to seeing physical matter, there is, embedded in the search criteria, the implicit information that points to seeing physical use and seeing visual use. To summarise, it can be said that the term PHYSICAL USE is the use that we see; and the term VISUAL USE is how we feel about the use that we see, which includes embodied experience. The confounding argument around the search criteria into use is that an irreconcilable duality exists between the two concepts. It is as if these two USES are competing. But they are not because they are part of the same conceptual domain, which is interaction. In other words, just as the left arm and the right arm do not compete, so it is with PHYSICAL USE and VISUAL USE. The same for the left eye and the right eye. The one complements the other, to such an extent that my argument is that, in this context, the distinction is irrelevant.

For the discovery phase of the literature review the visual world is therefore not just about what we see and how we feel about what we see; but in the full transaction: about the USE that we see and what we feel about the USE that we see. The proposition is that visual sustainability is a by–product (Frankl, 2003) of the latter condition because visual sustainability is argued from the point of view of use. And the by–product is *emergence through USE. According to Frankl we can not create emergence, it simply exists from the right mix of conditions. I cover the implications of non–linear systems and complexity theory in relation to types of interaction in the methodology on page 70, in the findings on page 96, and in "Interaction mix and non–linear characteristics" on page 112. The relevance of both Gibson and Polanyi to urban design lies simultaneously in the relevance of Bergson and Varela's theory of surrounding objects—because they must have a use to us, either in physical terms (to act) or in visual terms (to feel). For both conditions it is Gibson's direct perception (2015) and Polanyi's intuition (1969) that provide many of the valuable insights into where common ground might exist— between matter and memory. And which ultimately led me in my literature review to the English translation of Bergson's 1896 theory of Matter and Memory (1988).

Main search terms

Alienation

Architecture "can be psychologically manipulative, for better or for worse" (Golembiewski, 2022, p.260). One key feature of my literature review has been to understand the context of urban visual sustainability by understanding

*Emergence can be described in many ways. For Polanyi, it occurs when the whole is greater than the sum of its parts, while in complexity theory it occurs in environmental or human systems and/ or behaviour which do not behave in a linear way. It is non–linear i.e., dynamic, and unpredictable. A well known example is behaviour in flocks of birds, but it can equally be applied to scaling effects, bottom–up processes, and associated phenomenon in cities (See, for example, Batty, 2007, 2012).

CHAPTER 1   THE IMPORTANCE OF VISUAL SUSTAINABILITY

what the opposite effect is. If visual sustainability is able to neutralise the effects of not being visually sustained, then not being visually sustained can be classed as urban alienation. The phenomenon of urban alienation (Alexander, Ishikawa and Silverstein, 1977; Cullen, 1995; Lefebvre and Nicholson–Smith, 2011; Sussman and Ward, 2016; 2017; Sussman and Chen, 2017; Yuill, 2017; Hollander, Sussman and Carr, 2018; Sussman and Hollander, 2018; Bhugra et al., 2019) can be summarised by its definition as: a "psychological or social ill" (Leopold, 2018, p.1). This can be paraphrased to mean the separation from a person (or group of people) of that thing or event that is normally inseparable from the person or group (Leopold, 2018). One way of putting it is that alienation is THE DISAPPEARANCE OF WHAT WE HOLD DEAR. The suggestion is that because alienation separates us from what we hold dear, it can be justified as being the opposite of visual sustainability. My argument is that alienation is really just a transactional dilemma and occurs when trying to 'square the circle'. And these transactions of uncertainty are situated at the crossroads between two different realities: dualism and reciprocity.

Dualism vs. reciprocity: the transactional dilemma

If "our visual world is made up of transactions" (De Kock, 2019, p.72) then duality can be thought of as "transactions of uncertainty" (De Kock, 2020, p.5). This is because we are uncertain about what is happening in the correspondence between what has traditionally been thought of as images stored in our brain, and the things we see around us. A literature review has revealed how dualism has played a role in obstructing our understanding of the world around us. Planning, architecture, and urban design have been beset by *this problem. But for Bergson

*See, for example, analysis provided by Sturzaker and Hickman, 2024.

> ... realism and idealism both go too far, that it is a mistake to reduce matter to the perception which we have of it, a mistake also to make of it a thing able to produce in us perceptions, but in itself of another nature than they. Matter, in our view, is an aggregate of "images." And by "image" we mean a certain existence which is more than that which the idealist calls a representation, but less than that which the realist calls a thing—an existence placed halfway between the "thing" and the "representation" (Bergson, 1988, p.9).

Bergson's argument in favour of the common ground between these two opposites, speaks to the concept of reciprocity. A transaction can be seen as a reciprocal act by way of the interplay between, for example, in a broad sense, an offer and the acceptance of that offer. But *"... how do we compare the transaction of an intangible service or product, with how we experience our urban? ...*

*FOUNDATIONAL AUTHORS: URBAN CONTEXT

Polanyi	Gibson	Varela
Tacit knowledge	Ecological perception	Enaction

The importance of tacit knowledge relates to our lived world and the knowledge we acquire of our urban realm—through experience. Firstly then, in common with the idea of memory (Bergson, 1988), tacit knowing is about things that cannot be described but are learnt through experience (Polanyi and Grene, 1969). And one could say that experience is the main form of urban intelligence. Secondly, the relevance of tacit knowledge in our urban is in how tacit knowledge describes the process of shifting our gaze from local meaning to emergent meaning. From, by extension of the argument, scanning PARTS of an assemblage of architectural components put together in a certain way—to the WHOLE, whose meaning transcends space. Because: "So long as you look at X, you are not attending from X to something else, which would be its meaning. In order to attend from X to its meaning, you must cease to look at X, and the moment you look at X you cease to see its meaning" (Polanyi and Grene, 1969, p.146). This extended meaning can be likened to Bergson's theory of memory in relation to matter. Lastly, tacit knowing is reciprocal in the sense of being "an act of integration… in the visual perception of objects" (Polanyi and Grene, 1969, p.140).

Direct perception or ecological perception is "data–driven processing… [and] begins with the stimulus itself" (McLeod, 2008). For Gibson, as with Bergson, there is no image stored in the brain (Robbins, 2015). The importance of Gibson for how we are sustained by the urban environment lies in an understanding, firstly, of the location of objects: where they are to be found. And secondly, of the importance of objects for action. This refers to the concept of affordance or in Bergson's terms, virtual action. Both these issues are fundamental to how we see, what we see, and how we feel when we look at—and 'transact with'—objects around us.

Enactivist theory aligns with Gibson's theory of direct perception by the rejection of mental representation as the means by which we see things. The brain for Bergson is not a magical entity but simply matter like the rest of the body. The importance of enaction, (where we create our future) for urban design lies in the idea that we act to see; and we see to act. For Bergson (and Gibson) perception *is* action. It is action that leads to seeing with memory. And memory is what arguably binds us to our urban, a bond that, for Polanyi, is realised "… through instances where tacit knowing integrates clearly identifiable elements and have observed the way the appearance of things changes when, instead of looking at them, we look from them to a distal term which is their meaning. Once established, this from–to relation is durable. Yet it can be seriously impaired at will by switching our attention from the meaning to which it is directed, back to the things that have acquired this meaning. By concentrating attention on his fingers, a pianist can paralyse himself; the motion of his fingers no longer bear then on the music performed, they have lost their meaning" (Polanyi and Grene, 1969, p.146). This last statement can be reconciled with how Bergson's qualitative multiplicity (difference by kind) contrasts with space or spatialisation (difference by degree).

*Excerpt from preprint: The importance of visual sustainability in urban design strategy (2022a).

Table 2. This table compares Bergson with three key theories relating to visual interaction, namely, by Polanyi, Gibson, and Varela.

CHAPTER 1   THE IMPORTANCE OF VISUAL SUSTAINABILITY

isn't there something to be said for how we transact and consume surrounding visual elements?" (De Kock, 2019, p.69, emphasis added). It is at this crossroad that the introduction of Bergson provides a level of certainty that has previously been missing from the argument in support of a concept of visual sustainability. Because, at a meta level, a hypothesis for this study can be proposed as follows: THE KEY TO VISUAL SUSTAINABILITY IS THAT A TRANSACTION MUST BE CONCLUDED. If a transaction remains uncertain—if it remains incomplete, if it cannot be closed—then visual sustainability cannot be said to exist. Good urban design should, when seen in this philosophical light, consist of urban environments which produce in us the ability to complete our visually-based transactions. The way to do this is to understand areas where many transactions appear to be completed properly and to emulate these conditions in other areas where this does not appear to be the case. I will make a case for how this may be achieved in a practical sense in the Methodology chapter. It follows, therefore, that an act of RECIPROCITY is a condition for the completion of any transaction. Any process that produces reciprocity invalidates all the contradictory and mixed messages that negatively affect the visual relationship we hold dear to our surroundings (De Kock, 2019). Searle, for example, refers to the fallacy of ambiguity (John Searle on Perception & Philosophy of Mind, 2015) while Lefebvre calls it the "false problem" (2011, p.420). Berleant and Varela et al. value reciprocity in a concept held together by their interpretation of lived experience (1997; 2016). Varela et al. see reciprocity as transparency where things are not opposed but simply less or more transparent depending on context. As one condition comes to the fore the other recedes. But it is only in the irony of going back further still to 1896 that the jigsaw starts to fit together. And it is Bergson who stands out from the crowd, for his Matière et mémoire, which sought to unite spirit with matter, "soul and body" (1988, p.11), with a view to alleviating "the dissociation which idealism and realism have brought about between… existence and its appearance" (1988, p.10).

Many researchers since then have tried using science to deal with dualism. Varela et al. (2016, p.137) introduced neuro-phenomenology in an attempt to reconcile phenomenology with cognitive science. But Bergson had years earlier, chosen to use memory as the tool to unlock the barriers between realism and idealism because "there is no perception which is not full of memories" (Bergson, 1988, p.33). Bergson's view of perception is striking because he asserts that the meaning in seeing is time-related, not space-related. Beinart is a more recent example of acknowledging how "Architecture has a long association with memory" (Beinart, 2013, 00:56:40). "When memory was not available, through television, or through radio, or through telephone, and

so on, it was a very precious commodity" (Beinart, 2013, 00:59:00). For him:
> Architecture serves as a memory system for ideas about human origins, a means for recording and understanding of order and relationship in the world, an attempt to grasp the concept of the eternal cosmos which has no fixed dimension, and neither beginning nor end (Beinart, 2013e, 00:59:18, citing Piere Nora; Nora, 1989, p.8).

Hockney, too, intuitively points out to how we see with memory (David Hockney – The Art of Seeing, 2018, 00:42:18). But it is Bergson's idea in 1896 that paradoxically makes a clean break from the theoretical impasse that still exists today. The 'present,' according to Bergson, is part of continuous motion – instantly a memory. Try catching the precise moment when you feel you are in the 'present' and it is already gone—into the past. And, if you think about it, we can still use 'that which has just passed into memory' to create another 'present.' The past then still exists—is still accessible—as if it were in a parallel condition state in the sense described by De Landa (2016) where for example water is steam as well as ice. And this is one of the many key points offered by Bergson, that there appears to be a reciprocity at work between past, present, and future, which

> ...leads naturally to another [hypothesis]. However, brief we suppose any perception to be, it always occupies a certain duration, and involves, consequently, an effort of memory which prolongs, one into another, *a plurality of moments* (Bergson, 1988, p.34 emphasis added).

This in a nutshell is Bergson's argument for time. *How then, in the light of his argument, should we think of visual sustainability? Is visual sustainability memory? Is memory the defining link between ourselves and the built environment? How does it explain our experience of* "the dynamic progress by which the one [static condition] passes into the other" (Bergson, 1988, p.127)? The answer appears to be grounded in reciprocity. For Bergson there is a certain reciprocity at work. The "object exists in itself, and, on the other hand, the object is, in itself, pictorial, as we perceive it: image it is, but a self–existing image" (Bergson, 1988, p.10). He puts together for us a coherent theory of the relationship between mind and body, insisting that memory is the link between mind (memory) and matter (body) (Ibid. 1988, p.12). Through memory we are "...essentially turned toward action" (Ibid. 1988, p.16). The habits formed in action are oriented towards role–play or, put another way, anticipating an event in the sense of rehearsing for something before the act itself. We mentally test something out to ascertain the level of danger or opportunity IF the action was to be carried out. It is a simulation, carried out in the desire to do something, but before actually doing it, because:

CHAPTER 1 THE IMPORTANCE OF VISUAL SUSTAINABILITY

> ...our perception of an object distinct from our body, separated from our body by an interval, never expresses anything but a virtual action. But the more distance decreases between this object and our body (the more, in other words, the danger becomes urgent or the promise immediate), the more does virtual action tend to pass into real action (Bergson, 1988, p.57).

The way we see, in Bergson's terms, is thus, in the first instance, a form of simulation, which he called virtual action, and which is, after Bergson, commonly referred to as affordance.

In this section we have made a start on a possible connection between visual sustainability and the built environment. That connection is action. One need only think of Salingaros' information field theory (1999) and how we act based on the amount of information available to us—about whether an urban space is an opportunity or threat. For Salingaros alienating urban conditions present a threat, where little or no information makes us want to leave a space (1999). The action, to leave or stay, can be said to be a marker of visual sustainability. It is an outcome of interaction where the transaction is completed (i.e., we stay and complete the engagement) or incomplete (compelling us to leave and discarding the potential for engagement). A key feature of this literature review has been the realisation that thoughts about how we are visually sustained have always returned and settled on the interaction—and more specifically the transaction—between two key implied concepts: PHYSICAL USE and VISUAL USE.

*PHILOSOPHY BEHIND THE CONCEPT OF VISUAL SUSTAINABILITY

Metaphysical

The ontological objects i.e., the different realities at work in visual sustainability, in play for me in this study, when it comes to being visually sustained, are PRESENT and PAST. These objects appear to match Bergson's concepts of MATTER and MEMORY. Matter, because matter is the only evidence we have of being in the present. Memory, because memory is the only evidence we have of *having been* i.e., in the past. In Matter and Memory (1896) Bergson offers us a unique perspective through his theory where, at a metaphysical level, these ontological objects are conjoined by time. *Because how else do we rationalise the existence and purpose of PRESENT, PAST, MATTER, AND MEMORY if not through TIME?*
Since: "memory does not consist in a regression from the present to the past, but, on the contrary, in a progression from the past to the present." (Bergson,

*Includes excerpts from: The importance of visual sustainability in urban design strategy. 2022 | Preprint DOI: 10.6084/M9.figshare.21311427.V1; and Visually dissecting sustainability. 2020 | Preprint. https://doi.org/10.6084/m9.figshare.13095578.

1988, p.239). Therefore, in a metaphysical sense, the reality in this study is that we are dictated to, not by space, but by time, in the sense described by Bergson through DURATION and QUALITATIVE MULTIPLICITY. Because Bergson "… defines the immediate data of consciousness as being temporal, in other words, as the duration (la durée) … [while] qualitative multiplicity defines the duration [which] consists in a TEMPORAL HETEROGENEITY" (Lawlor and Moulard-Leonard, 2021, pp.8, 9, emphasis added). For Bergson:

> THE QUALITATIVE HETEROGENEITY OF OUR SUCCESSIVE PERCEPTIONS of the universe results from the fact that each, in itself, extends over a certain depth of duration and that memory condenses in each an enormous multiplicity of vibrations which appear to us all at once, although they are successive (Bergson, 1988, p.70, emphasis added).

In terms then of my introductory statement on page 1, the relationship between urban heterogeneity and how we are visually sustained through engagement with our surroundings, is actualised by Bergson's concept of TEMPORAL HETEROGENEITY.

Epistemology

The use of the word visual with the word sustainability

At the start of this research, visual sustainability was a term which had not been used in general urban discourse, or at least not in a specific sense, but it is implied in much of the theory and history underpinning architectural and urban practice. A history that Tavernor, for example, highlights for us as follows:

> In a UK context, the "most valued townscapes" are usually a creation of more than one approach to architecture and place making, and townscape quality and character is the outcome of generations, if not centuries of design and planning process (2007, p.3).

It can be argued that it is precisely this diverse array of approaches which has tended to get in the way of a more holistic way of thinking about what it is to be visually sustained by our built environment. One example is the "eco–aesthetic concept of visual sustainability" (Erem and Gür, 2008, p.54, emphasis added) adopted by Guy and Farmer (2001) and represents one of the few discovered uses of the term in the context of our built environment. Guy and Farmer however do not use the term visual sustainability, instead referencing "crystalline forms and fractured planes" (2001, p.144) as evidence of their eco–aesthetic concept. Tavernor, on the other hand, references Sitte and Cullen in terms of the "… notion of a visually sustainable blend of ancient and modern architecture in UK towns and cities" (2007, p.6). This is used in the context of the problem of visual blight of tall buildings in London. He does

CHAPTER 1   THE IMPORTANCE OF VISUAL SUSTAINABILITY

not, however, offer a definition of visual sustainability, instead deferring to "visual boundaries of sustainable urban design" (Tavernor, 2007, p.11) in the context of proposals that are 'not sustainable' when considered in relation to architectural heritage (ibid.: 2007, p.4). Mid–2020 saw another more direct reference to the concept of visual sustainability in the suitably titled paper 'Visually meaningful sustainability in national monuments' (Motevalian and Yeganeh, 2020, emphasis added). Here consideration has been given to morphology, aesthetics, and "visually meaningful sustainability indicators" (ibid.: 2020, p.1). The theoretical framework offered to understand "… Visual Lure…" (ibid.: 2020, p.2) is made feasible by a reasoned argument around two specific drivers: contextual indicators and perceptual indicators. These drivers or "visual indicators" (ibid.: 2020, p.5) defer to, and are reliant on, the prominent architectural theories of, inter alia, Sitte, Lynch, Cullen, Appleyard, Carmona, and Alexander. These drivers are thus bound by the same highly subjective criteria underpinning most urban theory and philosophy. And the level of ambiguity remains unresolved because, it can be argued, the entire analysis is trapped exclusively in architectural thought processes. The notion that elements are "valued according to the views of thinkers and scholars" (ibid.: 2020, p.13) must be challenged because it can be argued (as evident in the conclusion) that the baseline used, of thinkers and scholars, ultimately (and ironically) does little to solve the unreasonably high levels of ambiguity contained in "visual pleasure" (ibid.: 2020, p.19).

The argument around how we make visual sense of the world has been traced from a multitude of disciplines. Visual methodologies (Rose, 2007) offer one perspective into an appropriate methical approach in this study; one that allows us to "make the invisible within a city visible… "seeing" systems and making legible the city" (Altamirano–Allende and Selin, 2016, p.462). The techniques employed vary considerably, ranging from innovative methods about how architectural and urban atmospheres influence our perception in towns (Thomas, 2009), to understanding urban sustainability in the context of green spaces (Anzoise, 2017). There are ideas around enactment—by which is meant the process of creating the future through action (Varela, Thompson and Rosch, 2016)—and these are considered and framed in relation to head movement in my methodology. All these ideas seem to coalesce around the central supporting argument about how "ways of acting in the environment are also ways of perceiving it" (Ingold, 2002, p.9). This two-way process, between seeing and acting, is fundamental to developing an urban concept that speaks to the enduring relationship between two modes of urban consumption: physical satisfaction and visual satisfaction. "By moving around we're actually creating structure" (The ecological approach to perception & action, 2013, 00:37:40; James Gibson – Ohio – 1974 – Part 1, 1974, 00:11:40). There does not appear to be a contradiction between Gibson's analysis of moving around objects to discover them, and the idea floated by Anzoise, "through which meanings immanent in an environment are not so much constructed as discovered" (Anzoise, 2017, p.203). Her view is inspired by the process advocated by Ingold whereby environmental perception is the result of growth, not inborn or through acquisition of skills (2002). This approach can be considered to support Piaget's view that discovery *is* growth. Which in turn supports Gibson's theory of affordance (acknowledged by Varela et al.) and Varela et al.'s own approach "that perception consists in perceptually guided action and that cognitive structures emerge from the recurrent sensorimotor patterns that enable action to be perceptually guided" (Varela, Thompson and Rosch, 2016, pp.200, 203). The construction of our visual world therefore points to how we act in our environment. How we act thus determines the nature of our physical use of objects in the environment, as well as our visual use, or what we consume with our minds. The notion of physical use and visual use must in some way be relevant to Varela's theory of enactment and embodied cognition because it makes sense that we create our own future, as described by the theory of enactment, through a process that requires us to act.

The seeds sown by interaction

These ideas so far are the seeds for a developing argument about interaction in this study: that action/acting can be said to be a physical function; a tangible event. The developing argument is thus: I look at something, which makes me perform an action using my mind, based on the PHYSICAL USE that the object I looked at, affords me. The actions are describable. When however, an object makes me feel something i.e., when an action is internalised, then it is no longer the same describable action. Now it has become an action for which there is no language (Polanyi and Grene, 1969), where we have crossed over into VISUAL USE. Visual use is comprised of intangible processes that act as containers for social and cultural expressions. No action can describe these processes. No physical use can describe these expressions. Because, as Polanyi asserts, these are phenomena for which there is no language. This developing concept of an environment comprised of two things: PHYSICAL USE and VISUAL USE, is similar to that made by Ingold where he describes how it dawned on him that the Cartesian mind–body problem can be solved by adopting Gibson's theory of ecological perception (2015). He offers ecological perception as his answer to the question about whether a link can be established "between the biological life of the organism in its environment and the cultural life of the mind in society..." (Ingold, 2002, p.3). And, for this research into visual sustainability, it can be re–framed into a question about whether the terms physical use and visual use can be substituted for the expressions: biological life and mind in society. The reciprocal nature of (what is perceived as an ambiguous duality) is, as we have seen, evident not only in Ingold's work, but also in Varela's work related to embodied cognition, as well as Searle's work of the mind and language. The idea that people "are carried forward and transformed through their own actions" (Ingold, 2002, p.3) is a compelling one. It speaks to the concept of being visually sustained; where visual sustainability is a litmus test for how people consume and are sustained through both PHYSICAL USE and VISUAL USE.

The four key theories
This study relies on the foundational knowledge of four key authors:

1. Bergson (2001, 1988, 1965; Lawlor and Moulard–Leonard, 2021): a philosopher who challenged the concept of dualism through his theory of matter and memory; as well as introducing the term virtual action.
2. Polanyi (1969): a polymath and philosopher who developed the term tacit knowledge.
3. Gibson (2015): a psychologist and philosopher who specialised in visual perception and who introduced ecological psychology and affordance to the world, and
4. Varela (2016): a cognitive scientist and philosopher who championed the concept of an embodied mind, cognition in relation to lived experience, and enaction.

The theories of these four authors do not explicitly reference urban design and are scarcely recognised or addressed in contemporary urban design literature. The one exception in the field of urban design is a contemporary of Bergson, Poëte (1866–1950) who, in 1919, championed the pedagogical relevance and philosophical urban application of Bergson's concept of duration. This was first applied to Paris and later disseminated through French town planning (Terranova, 2008; Periton, 2018). During these years there is a proliferation of ideas around memory and non–linearity in urban design theory. Poëte's interpretation of Bergson however leaned towards a concept of the city as organism (Terranova, 2008; Periton, 2018)—which can be argued to deflect from Bergson's central idea of qualitative multiplicity. The emphasis in this study is on the application of how these four authors, combined, can add to the contemporary discourse on cities and sustainability through the lens of the types of interaction we have with our surroundings (Table 2 on page 21). Of the four, it is Bergson (1859–1941) who provides what is arguably the most comprehensive philosophical analysis for how we see, what we see, and why (Robbins, 2002; 2004; 2006; 2013). He focuses on both physical use at a metaphysical level where the brain acts as a re–constructive wave in a vast interference pattern of intersecting waves (Robbins, 2015); and visual use, through how we see with memory. Polanyi (1891–1976) focuses on visual use through intuition, or valid sensations for which there are no words to describe. By contrast, Gibson (1904–1979) focuses on physical use through direct perception. Gibson appears to be well aligned with Bergson's theory especially with regards to virtual action, which Gibson calls affordance and which relates to how we find opportunities in objects and processes that may not have been part of their original intention (2015). Gibson, however, asserts that in the act of seeing "information pickup does not need memory ... it does not have to as a basic postulate, the effect of past experience on present experience by way of memory" (The ecological approach to perception & action, 2013, 00:56:40, citing Gibson, 1979, 254). Varela (1946–2001) attempts to unite physical use with visual use—objective with subjective—through his concept of neuro–phenomenology. His concept embraces lived experience and he is insistent that it forms an indispensable part of cognitive science. All four subscribe to the idea that we act to produce meaning and that meaning is produced through action. For Varela this occurs by way of a process of enaction where we bring forth a world (2016); for Polanyi, through intuition; for Gibson it is through the notion of specifying objects; and for Bergson, it is through the concept of virtual action. The idea of embodied perception is present in all four theories, which in turn is synergistic with the idea of direct perception. Polanyi however is less clear about direct perception, preferring to provide validation through the concept of emergence—where, as in non-linear complex systems, the whole is more meaningful than the sum of its parts, and without which the parts lose their meaning (Batty, 2007; Batty and Marshall, 2012; Reading Ancient Minds: Metaphor, Culture, and Complexity, 2012; Ortman, Lobo and Smith, 2020; De Kock, 2019a). How that happens is less important to Polanyi than the fact that it does. And this is what separates Bergson from the others. Bergson provides what can be argued as a coherent theory for how this happens, specifically narrated through his concepts of duration and qualitative multiplicity. In these concepts Bergson explains how we exist not in space but in time. And according to Bergson we see with memory through a process of virtual action. Bergson's ideas have prompted me to introduce the concept of interaction type as a measuring device because interaction is an action. It promises to reveal more, through our engagement

CHAPTER 1   THE IMPORTANCE OF VISUAL SUSTAINABILITY

with the environment, about the relationship between urban heterogeneity and how we are visually sustained.

We cannot really talk about visual sustainability unless we know what it is we are sustaining. So, *what is the 'visual' we are sustaining*? This study supports Bergson's idea that it is our memory being sustained and, paradoxically, it is being sustained through action. If by using our memory it can be said that we are sustaining ourselves, then this quite literally is 'the meaning in seeing.' We use memory to see. Because, as Bergson asserts, the past melts into the present which leans into the future in one continuous, sequential, indivisible process called duration (1988) because: "The truth is that memory does not consist in a regression from the present to the past, but, on the contrary, in a progression from the past to the present" (1988, p.239). And to sustain our memory—as well as understand what it is we see—the final piece of the puzzle must be to understand "the origin of the image of the external world" (Robbins, 2015, p.i). Because *how else do we complete the puzzle, if we do not know where it is we go to collect the information we need to sustain and enrich ourselves in daily life*? The answer, therefore, in this hypothesis, is that we are sustained by what Robbins describes as the origin of the image of the external world.

It is important to note that in this study I am working off and interacting with four main theories that span a considerable period of time, from the 19th Century (Bergson); the 1980s (Gibson, Polanyi); and recently, 2000 to 2023 (Robbins, Varela). *What then is there to say about the epistemology behind this presupposition of visual sustainability*? *How do we know what we know about being visually sustained*? The knowledge we seek can be found in two main theoretical allies of Bergson, who overlap each another to some degree. Firstly, and most recently, we have Robbins' theory to support Bergson's theory. In particular, it is the rationale behind invariance structures that is valuable and helpful to me. And the overlap here, that both demonstrate, is with Gibson's invariance laws. Secondly, we have Gibson, whose theory is highly valued by Robbins. Gibson's link back to Bergson is through Gibson's concept of AFFORDANCE. Affordance refers to the use an object where the object offers certain uses depending on perceiver and context (Gibson, 2015); a concept which Bergson had earlier termed VIRTUAL ACTION where he describes how "the objects which surround us represent, in varying degrees, an action" (Bergson, 1988, p.144).

The metaphysical and epistemology discussed so far goes some way in effectively addressing the importance of Bergson's theory to my study.

The next question in my mind was: *how can Bergson's concept, of duration, be applied to contemporary urban experience*? I am persuaded that an answer to this seems to lie in the theories of direct perception, affordance, virtual action, and invariance structures, as these all provide a firm foundation to describe how and what we see. I also found that valuable insights in the work of both Polanyi and Varela et al.. For his theory of tacit knowledge, Polanyi is useful for bridging the divide between what we see in the urban and how we feel about what we see. From Bergson's theory, two concepts come to the fore: the physical use we see in objects and events; and the visual use, i.e., how we feel about the physical use we see. And lastly, Varela's embodied mind theory—of seeing with body, as well as with soul— represents a meeting point between the science around a phenomenon and the essence describing that phenomenon. Thus, we have direct perception, affordance, virtual action, tacit knowing, physical use, visual use, and the science of phenomenology— each finding ways to link past with present; and each informing our initial presupposition about visual sustainability. Because for visual sustainability we store in memory that which sustains us over time. Which is exactly where Bergson places the emphasis: on the temporal qualities of what we store and what sustains us. And they all contribute to THE PROCESS. Because the phenomenon of being sustained and enriched appears to me to be a process; one which involves another process, our urban; which can hopefully be captured and measured in some way. The process identifies the 'objects' at work, in other words, it "gives rise to an object" (Complexity Explorer Lecture: David Krakauer. What is Complexity? 2023, 00:17:19). On the other hand, the visual relationship we hold dear to our surroundings, speaks to how this process takes place, of the effect of the urban on us. It points me in the direction as to how we may accomplish effective, durable urban design strategy from the concepts of interaction contained in each of these four main theories.

Ethics

This brings us to the last philosophical consideration, which is, *how does ethics play a role? How does the presupposition mentioned at the start around visual sustainability, sit with values around human conduct and human expression? In other words, how can visual sustainability be known through human conduct or behaviour, and by that, I mean, what are the signs in people that visual sustainability exists*?
It is worth emphasising that our urban is, arguably, already a mild form of simulacrum. Because *do our cities not already produce a mild simulacrum in the present, of past events*? And it is a simulacrum, which, if visually unsustainable, through indifference, becomes alienating. Where buildings borrow from

CHAPTER 1 THE IMPORTANCE OF VISUAL SUSTAINABILITY

billboards and vice–versa, until, further down the line, we are transformed by levels of deception in an increasing escalation of hyper reality. Because, if we think about it... what is being built right now, is not who we are, but who we are becoming. And there is 'the rub' because, true of any simulacrum, matter then defines memory until memory, devoid of its origin, becomes the new reality. *Should we not then examine, not only the effect of the object or event on people; but also, the effect of people on the object or event? Do we not act on an object; and the object act on us?* These thoughts speak in turn to what Robbins refers to as *redintegration (2021) and the role redintegration has to play in urban reality—or in its counterpart: the reality of an urban simulacrum. *Because if reality is, as Searle (1999) asserts, by agreement, which is to say, through collective intentionality and status function declaration, then does it not follow that we can all be tempted to agree to a society visually sustained by technology–driven simulacrum?* In trying to answer this question around human conduct, Varela et al. provide useful context that speaks directly to ethics. Because, while, in opposition to Bergson's theory which acknowledges two realities, Varela et al. gravitate towards life as one single reality. This is evident in Varela's 'The Embodied Mind' which is referential towards human conduct and behaviour. It does so by applying a Buddhist belief system on the relationship between what I have defined as physical use and visual use (which in Varela's terms equates to the special relationship argued for between cognitive science and phenomenology, also categorised by Varela, as neuro–phenomenology). Varela's theory, before he gets to his single reality of 'groundlessness,' also prompts the idea, not of duality, but of complementarity; a dynamic balance where spirit and matter are comprised of endlessly looping reciprocal patterns of energy: between internalised transactions and externalised transactions. You see memory; you see matter, each continuously informing the other, oscillating as it were, like the leaves in a strong breeze—now outward facing/ now inward facing.

*Redintegration: the law of redintegration in Gibsonian terms would be: A current event, E' redintegrates a previous event, E, when E' and E share the same invariance structure. Derived from "a term coined already in 1732 by Wolff, a disciple of Leibniz, in his Psychologia Empirica. It is defined roughly as "a part of a current event retrieves the whole of a past event," or as Klein (1971) puts it, a pattern in a current event retrieves a past event with a similar pattern" (Robbins, S. E., 2021, p.21).

SUMMARY AND CONCLUSION

The three philosophical considerations: metaphysics, epistemology, and ethics drive the underlying philosophy and represents my chosen system of interpretation. *What does this mean in terms of an anticipated research outcome?* What distinguishes Bergson's theory is his understanding of temporal reality. We do not see in space, but in time. Our world is not a spatialised construct, not, at least, in terms of how and what we naturally see. We do not observe in the sense described by classic metaphysics, that is, in a regression of infinite divisibility and alienation of parts. We can, if we want to, pick things apart to examine them; but, as Polanyi points out (Table 2 on page 21), doing so always invalidates the whole, for as long as we are doing so. The observation by Xenakis as he "noticed this frightening thing: houses last longer than human beings" (Something Rich and Strange: The Life and Music of Iannis Xenakis, 2022, 00:49:08) provides a succinct summary of what classic metaphysics represents; and which Bergson's temporal metaphysics disputes. Because far from being less durable, expendable, or unimportant we can, through temporal metaphysics, catch a glimpse of what we are in time. The argument in this study supports the idea that we see in an additive way, through the concept of Bergson's qualitative multiplicity. This rationale is aided by the arguments of Gibson and Robbins; as well as in our performance of tacit knowledge as described by Polanyi; and Varela's pursuit, not of ambiguity, but of reciprocity. If we consider the metaphysical, epistemological and ethical worldviews adopted by this study, our urban can be said to be made up of indivisible experiences that blend past with present—in the same way we experience sound. We can never tell, says Bergson, where one note stops and the other starts (1988). It can be said therefore of our urban experience, that through the sounds we produce, we see—with memory—the 'music' being played right in front of us. Music in this sense is the duration of a temporal event i.e., a time–extended event, and not meant in a literal sense. And that is what I would like to find out more about. In terms of the null hypothesis, it appears from this literature review so far that there is a difference in the types of interaction we have with our surroundings because we experience alienation, often in an indescribable way, and especially so where ambiguity creates conditions of uncertainty. These conditions often appear to be present when, as described by Polanyi, we are focused on the parts and so lose the contextual meaning that exists from understanding the whole. But in terms of Bergson's qualitative multiplicity, *is there a difference in interaction type during a single indivisible event*? It appears so if we take sound as an example of the analogy for a time–extended event. It is one single indivisible experience and yet our interactions in an emotional and embodied sense can be said to vary across the entire temporal event. *What does that say about the use that we see and how we feel about the use that we see*? For an answer to that question, we need to test the null hypothesis. But before we do there are three more concepts to consider: OBJECT, EXPERIENCE, and THE INVISIBLE CITY.

THE IMPORTANCE OF VISUAL SUSTAINABILITY

Chapter Two
UNIFYING OBJECT WITH EXPERIENCE

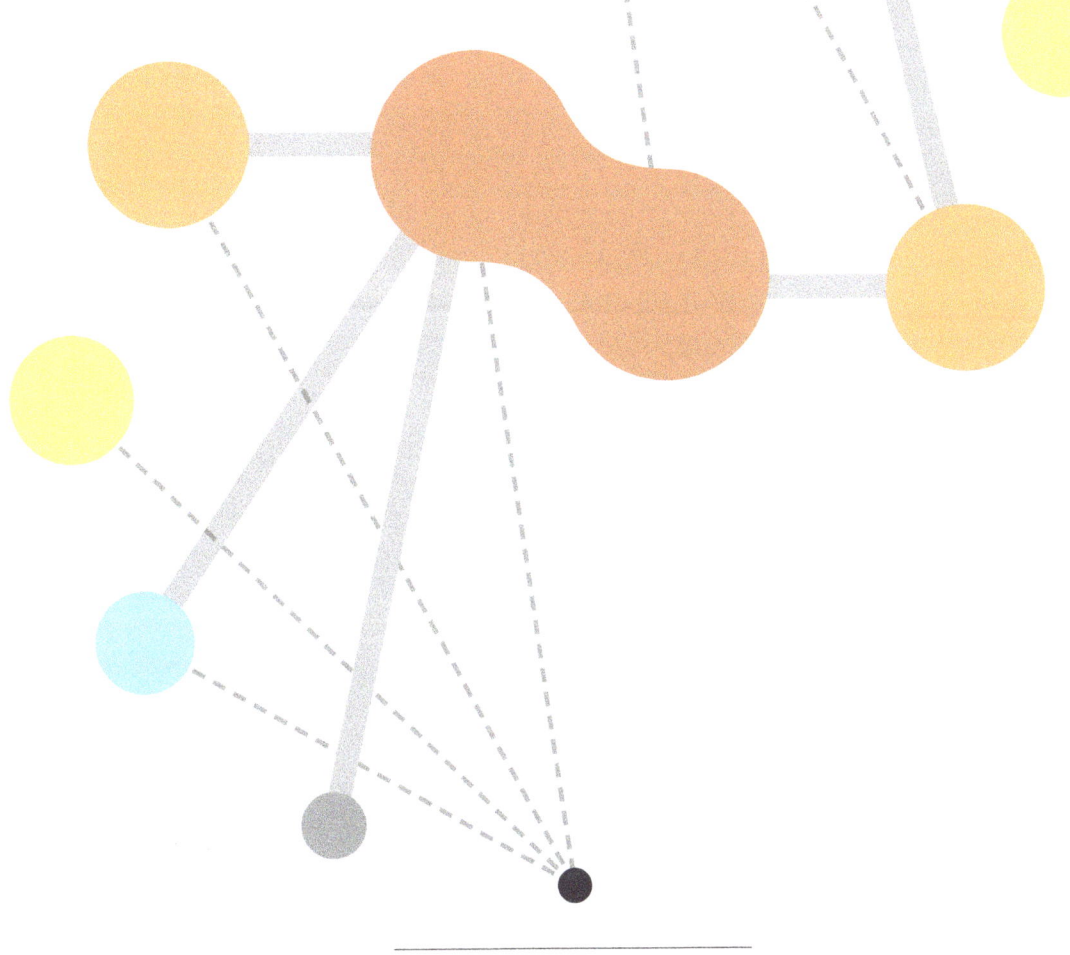

§. 9 *Object versus Experience*

In the last chapter we have looked in broad terms at interaction with the expectation that we might see differences between visual interaction types. In this chapter we are going to keep looking for an answer to that question by paying attention to the kind of 'objects' that might be produced by various modes of interaction. The theories of Bergson, Gibson, Polanyi, and Varela have suggested to me that the way we are able to differentiate between OBJECT and EXPERIENCE, is through INTERACTION. In the next chapter my argument will be extended by introducing the VISIBLE CITY and INVISIBLE CITY, the origin of which is INTERACTION and INTERACTION–TYPE from the previous chapter. And this chapter serves to link the two using OBJECT and EXPERIENCE.

CHAPTER 2 THE IMPORTANCE OF VISUAL SUSTAINABILITY

INTRODUCTION

This chapter is concerned with interactions related to themes that speak to Heritages: Past and Present—Built and Social, all of which can arguably be categorised according to the 'messy' visual world of the first argument in "§. 5 Seeing by interacting with our surroundings" on page 11. It contrasts with the effects of the second argument in which globalization plays a key role. Globalisation is data–driven but data have another dimension shaped by what Robbins calls dynamic form (2004; 2014): that mysterious quality in the built environment that now appears to be missing from what Havel describes as *visible usefulness (2010). In a theoretical exploration, some strategies to uncover the world of experience as data are unpacked in this chapter. Through a methodology underpinned by Bergson (1988), Robbins (2014), and Gibson (2015), I am seeking, in the discussion which follows, relief from what may be called **pseudo–experience. I will be addressing the absence in everyday life of an understanding of the importance of temporal meaning in objects, that is, of meaning—not as a function of space, but of time—because heritage can be said to serve as a link into an intangible world, full of transformation through VISUAL USE and located in the domain of temporal metaphysics. It is a world that can shift the way we think about our built environment because we experience feelings about the use that we see. In this chapter we will look firstly at Bergson's concept of qualitative multiplicity. Secondly, the use a person sees and how they feel about that use, is analysed. And lastly, consideration is given to how data may best represent a person's experience in the context of the following terms: *direct–environment* and *memory–environment*. Also discussed is how a preoccupation with comparatively few iconic examples of heritage, limits our participation in preservation efforts. For if we wish to rekindle our relationship with the intangible and unify OBJECT with EXPERIENCE, then it appears that we need to look no further than Bergson's 1896 theory of qualitative multiplicity to discover the extraordinary in the ordinary. In what follows we will analyse how OBJECT and EXPERIENCE may be identified; then discuss how they appear to be unified; and end with some thoughts about what this might mean in terms of the PHYSICAL USE and VISUAL USE related to ***Heritages: Past and Present—Built and Social.

There are three main parts to this chapter. PART 1 will look at the relationship between architecture, heritage, and people—using the analogy of Buridan's Donkey. PART 2 will look at one person's experience of Prague, what that might mean for understanding the difference between OBJECT and EXPERIENCE in cities; and how this may be different for tourists versus locals. And PART

---

*Visible usefulness is a good term to describe interaction, where a transaction has to be completed to be relevant or useful (see also "Dualism vs. reciprocity: the transactional dilemma" on page 20).

**Pseudo–experience refers here to an effect of simulacrum (Baudrillard, 1983).

***Community, Heritage, and Meaning as a major network of meaning, see also "How we are visually sustained through interaction" on page 14.

3 of this chapter offers some concluding remarks about data, how it might be possible for temporal metaphysics to shift the way we think about our built environment: particularly in the sense that we should unify OBJECT with EXPERIENCE.

Invariance and transformation

In the context of my definition of visual sustainability as "the process by which we are sustained and enriched in daily life through the visual relationship we *hold dear* to our *surroundings*" (De Kock, 2019, p.72, emphasis added) the emphasis in this chapter is on what is dear to us. And because our surroundings appear to gradually resemble conditions of alienation—a reflection, it is argued, of the forces of globalization, technology, and artificial intelligence— architecture has taken on a more object–oriented role, while heritage claims the more experiential ground. My interpretation of architecture as PHYSICAL USE and heritage as VISUAL USE is based on what I argue to be our reaction of these elements, where in architecture these days we often have to define a building first i.e., make sense of it. But in heritage we are most often first defined by what we see i.e., there is more of a transformation in us through our experience. An OBJECT is something that we interpret and define and objects can sometimes act as an invariance as we look for the use to us, in affordance or—in Bergson's terms—virtual action (1988). Modern buildings as manifestations of globalism and elitism are objects that appear to require us to look to their parts in order to define what it represents in its entirety because often we can never be sure what it is, what it represents, what is inside it, and what we are supposed to feel about it. An experience, on the other hand, defines us. It's a transformation and transformation—if nothing else—is feeling. And feeling is never an invariance. It *always* transforms us. Heritage produces experiences because we often immediately look beyond the parts to the meaning (*as suggested by Polanyi's concept of tacit knowing). The suggestion here, for you the reader to think about, is that it may be beneficial to visualize the structure of our surroundings in an altogether different way: as conveying some form of interaction between what Robbins describes as INVARIANCE and TRANSFORMATION (2014, 2023).

*See Table 2 on page 21

PART 1

Buridan's donkey is a tale about a donkey that cannot decide between two identical bales of hay, each the same distance away. It is a story which resonates when trying to describe the role that architecture and heritage play in the built environment (Figure 2 on page 39). The idea behind Buridan's paradox supports the idea of duality and what I have referred to

CHAPTER 2   THE IMPORTANCE OF VISUAL SUSTAINABILITY

* It has been said that: "Architecture is an act of conscious willpower. To create architecture is to put in order. Put what in order? Functions and objects. (Le Corbusier, 1991, p.68).

** Defined as "both material objects and social traditions" with an emphasis today on tangible and intangible together through "The streets on which we live, and the monuments we protect… all connected to the traditions and social groupings we celebrate and preserve—whether physically, socially or, increasingly, digitally [but existing more as] "an open and diverse question" (https://amps-research.com/conference/heritages-prague/).

***Dynamic form: For Robbins "Form is a quality" (Robbins, 2013, p.155).

as "transactions of uncertainty" (De Kock, 2020, p.5). It assumes that what we want—in equal measure—are in two separate locations. In terms of *architecture and **heritage in the built environment, both appear to many of us as two distinct entities. They both look the same, each is the same conceptual distance away from us, and we want both. But if we take the analogy a step further, in unifying object with experience, what the donkey is really looking at is Architecture *and* Heritage; and there is no difference between them, even if it thinks there is.

But now let us suppose they are in the same location. The point being that, in the case of architecture and heritage, there is no difference because they exist in the same location: time. And time is important because, in Bergson's terms, we see with memory. And memory is important because that is how we navigate. The idea that we navigate space makes no sense because space, that thing we can divide up repeatedly, can by its own definition, be frozen. And if that is the case, then as Robbins (2014) points out, you could reboot the universe every other day. Except you would not be there when it was time to log in again.

There is some logic to agreeing that what we think of as space, is simply the flow of time; one moment indiscernible from the next. Like Bergson's (1988) reference to sound, where the transition between one note is indistinguishable from the next. It is the analogy which is important to this study. Thus, it seems that we are all constantly changing—including inanimate things like buildings because they too decay and eventually disappear. *Are we ever then simply 'objects in space'?* No, it seems we are events in time (Figure 4 on page 39). In what Robbins (2014) calls ***dynamic form. *How then do we interact with other events in time? What does the environment of interactions, that obey the laws of temporal metaphysics, look like? Where does use stop and how we feel about the use, begin? When is something an object and when is it an experience?*

My study of the Greenwich Park and Town Centre world heritage site (Figure 5 on page 41) has been a useful exercise in exploring these questions. Consider the grey area (top–left) as just part of the universal field, a vast interference pattern that Robbins (2014), in referencing Bergson, talks about, because as Bergson notes: "… is it not obvious that the photograph, if photograph there be, is already taken, already developed in the very heart of things and at all the points of space?" (1988, p.38). A few things are noticeable about the way people interact with their environment. The 'locals' appear to interact with, what I would like to describe as, memory–environment. The yellow

Figure 2. The paradox of Buridan's donkey: Architecture versus Heritage or, stated differently, Object versus Experience.

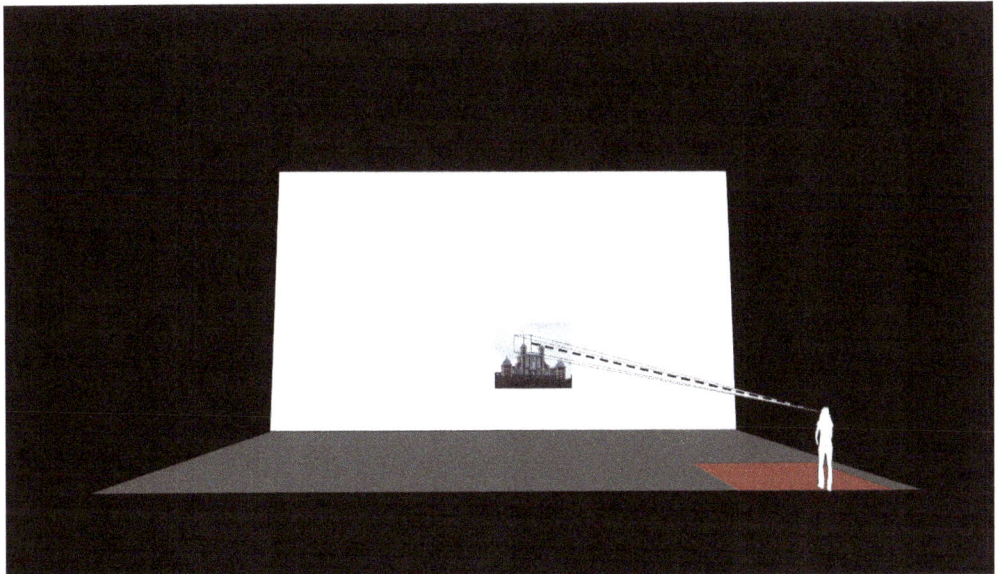

Figure 3. Perception as an event in time.

Figure 4. The event is part of our location, not of depth of space, but in space as depth of time.

CHAPTER 2 — THE IMPORTANCE OF VISUAL SUSTAINABILITY

circles (Figure 5 on page 41, top–right) represents a survey of local people's memory of events in time. Then, we see in the bottom–left diagram of Figure 5, what we can call the direct–environment, juxtaposed and loosely interpreted by way of the yellow blocks. Direct–environment interaction occurs with tourists because they have to use *memory from somewhere else* to interact with objects and events that are new to them. This is because they do not have local memory, so they must be interacting with what they see in front of them… from a different environment. The diagram (Figure 5, bottom–right) shows the effect of tourists and locals mingling indiscriminately and they all appear on the surface to see in the same way. But their application of memory is different: one fetches perception from out–with; the other (the local) from with–in. As observers in our environment, we expect to see the same thing: architecture that points us to heritage; and heritage that points us to architecture. But we are often steered away from such unifying thoughts by the objects themselves. In a way then WE are Buridan's donkey, in the sense that we are immobilized and alienated by an expectation that is not matched. Only, it is the opposite experience. Architecture and Heritage should be the same thing, but they are not. Because they are being spatialised, when in fact they exist as one entity. In other words, we are in a sense impoverished by this self–imposed duality and exist in the loop of ambiguity discussed on page 12.

To summarise (Figure 6 on page 41): *do tourists see architecture, while locals see heritage*? If so, *how then can they be seeing the same thing*? The answer is easy. Let us forget about the spatialisation of things—where everything is sub–divisible until it no longer makes sense—and observe things as if everything is in constant change. Then what the tourist is looking at is the architecture of heritage. And what the 'local' is looking at is the heritage of architecture. And each is a sequential dimension of one thing. Not of space, but of TIME.

PART 2
Object and experience

One example of what a flâneur may teach us lies in the experience of a complete stranger to a city. One such complete stranger was Person A, who visited Prague eight years ago in April 2015 (Figure 7 on page 41).

Most dear
When asked what their most memorable feature was—and still remains most dear to them—they wrote down the following: "Cobblestones, colourful building exteriors, narrow streets [and] local, not usual shops." Notwithstanding the rather unscientific adventures of Person A, a correlation

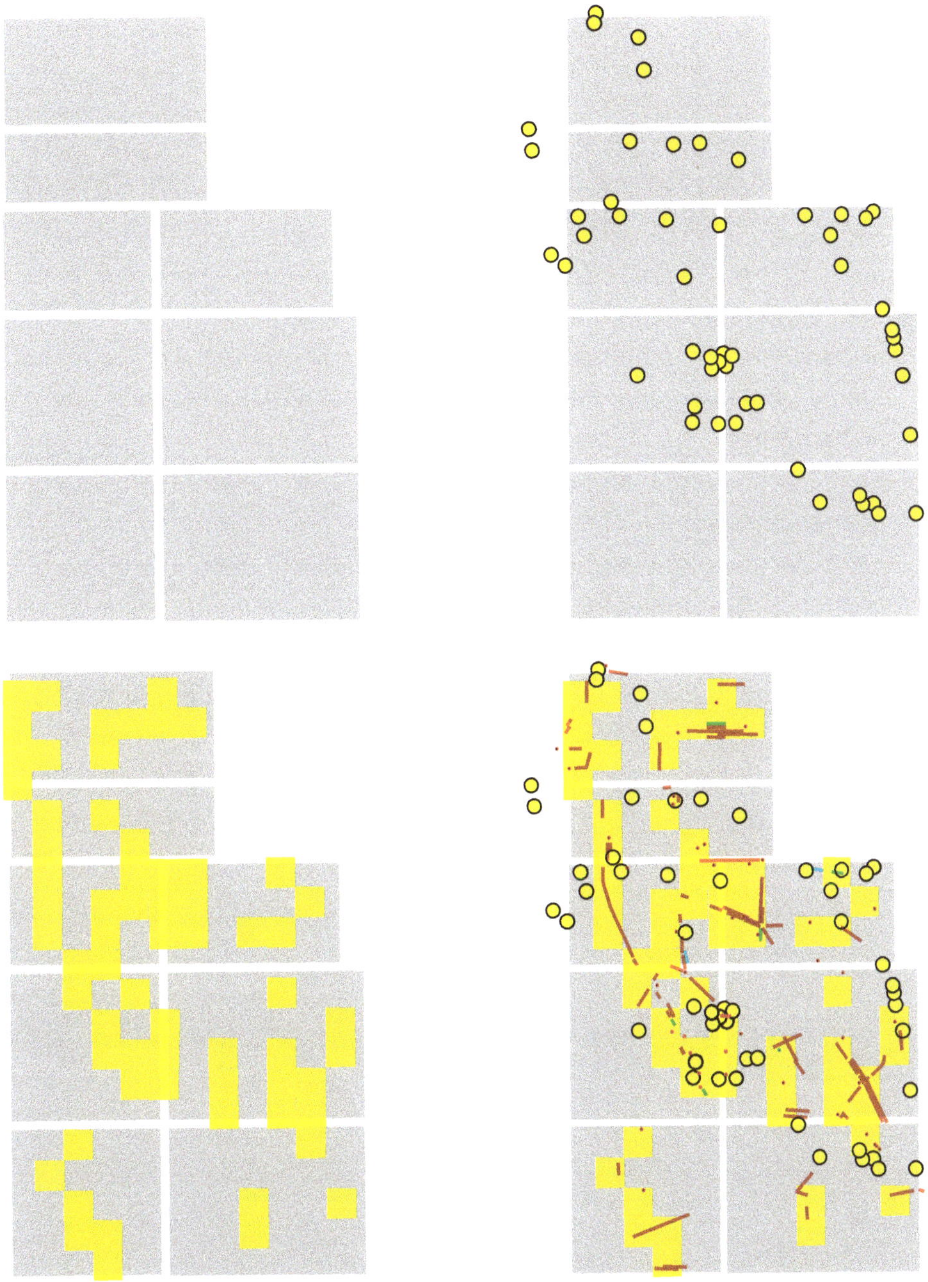

Figure 5. Tourists and locals mingle indiscriminately using different forms of perception: direct–environment versus memory–environment.

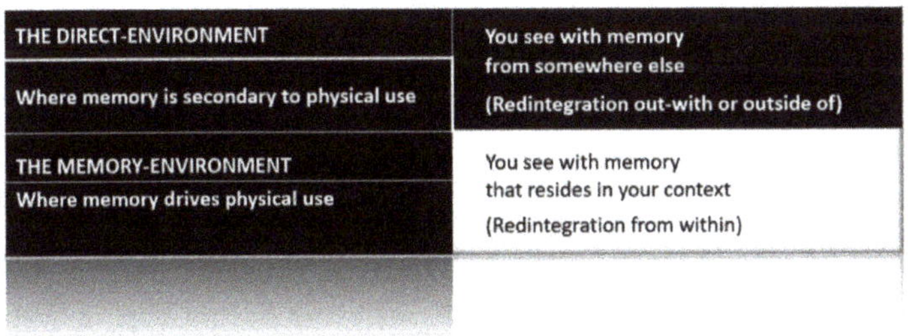

Figure 6. Direct–environment versus memory–environment.

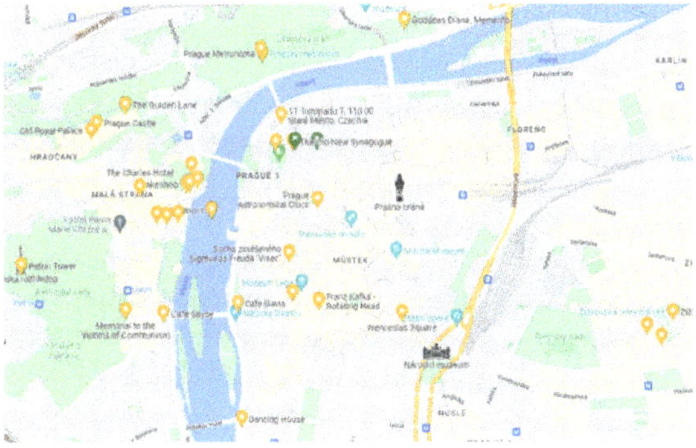

Figure 7. Person A's record of most meaningful locations visited in Prague (yellow accents).

CHAPTER 2 THE IMPORTANCE OF VISUAL SUSTAINABILITY

existed between what may be described as the use in what they saw (Physical Use), and how they felt about that use (Visual Use) (De Kock and Carta, 2020a; De Kock, 2020b; De Kock, Pieter, 2022a). In scientific terms we have here two variables which, when co–located, produce what in research terms (De Kock and Carta, 2020b) can be hypothesized as evidence of high visual sustainability, namely, that high values of each variable—existing in the same phenomenon—produce high levels of visual sustainability (Figure 8 on page 43).

The Experience

Person A was then asked to browse through the photographs they took on their trip. The photograph selected from the entire trip, as most dear to them, was a comparatively ordinary streetscape (Figure 9 on page 43: Bottom). It is a photograph that hints at the threat identified by Kádár (2013) of the impact of visitors on Prague's unique morphology and inherited infrastructural problems, in the form of pressure points that alienate locals from their own cultural attractions, so much so that we sometimes wonder whether 'people live upstairs.' The challenge we have in believing what we are seeing comes from the gradual hollowing out of society due to globalization, where the mystery we expect is now missing from what Havel calls visible usefulness (Havel, 2010). Instead, our experience and orientation in a city becomes a process of being steered from one globalist landmark to another, and culture and heritage are nothing more than sterile masks of simulacrum: worn for meaning that means nothing. The argument therefore is that meaning is found less in these environments and more in the ordinary inhabited by locals.

The Object

Straight after identifying the photo taken in 2015, Person A referred to another photograph for context (Figure 10 on page 43: Top). In their explanation for pointing out this second photograph, it became evident that the arched gateway structure provided the means by which OBJECT is unified with EXPERIENCE. The arched gateway was thus the object that, for Person A, introduced the (future) experience which (now) is held most dear in memory. The archway is simply the access point to the transformation, in that moment, for that moment. This then speaks somewhat to the idea of the currency we use when transacting with our environment. Which is our attention. We pay, let us say we pay a *LOCATION, to transact with our attention using the currency of time. The visual use is, in Bergson's terms, the entire melody, or the entire experience in Person A's memory. It is the transformation. It is what they felt. The premise is that

*The importance of location for commercial activity (see Table 7 on page 125 and "§. 21 Commercial application" on page 124).

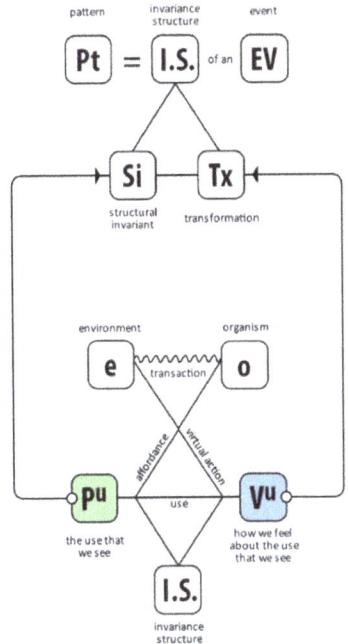 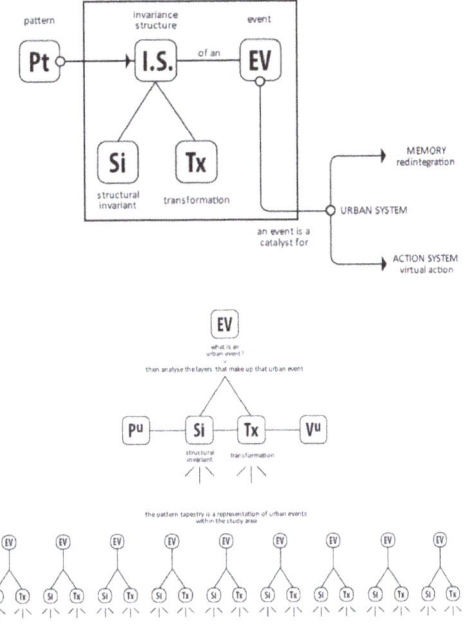

RHS (Top): Survey of an urban node: this diagram depicts the rationale behind the urban application of events. RHS (Bottom): Use pattern tapestry: a representation of urban events within the study area.

Figure 8. Use patterns premise, adapted using the concept by Robbins of patterns as invariance structures of events, to describe the environmental transaction between physical use and visual use (De Kock, Pieter, 2022, p.21).

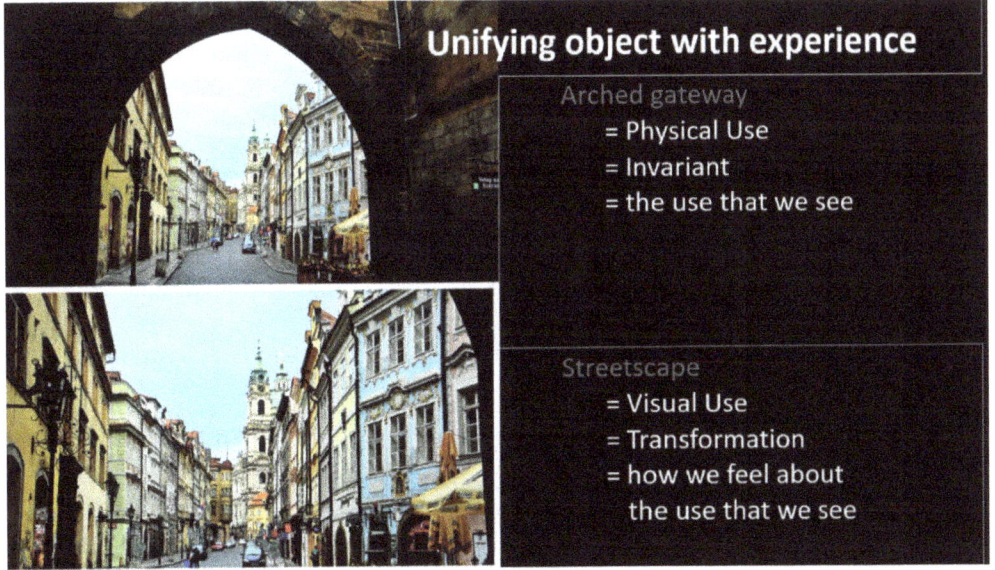

Figure 9. Unifying object with experience.

Figure 10. How data is represented in this person's experience.

together, these two variables represent what Robbins (2014) describes as an invariance structure of an event. Polanyi describes visual attention in terms of "the relation of a set of particulars to a comprehensive entity [or whole] ... We can be aware of... [particulars] uncomprehendingly, i.e. in themselves, or understandingly, in their participation in a comprehensive entity" (1969, p.128). In the context of the urban we thus focus on the meaning beyond the individual parts in any assemblage in what may also be described as emergent meaning. It can be argued of our urban that the 'whole' orients us, while the individual parts are (as described by Polanyi) subsidiary.

DISCUSSION

Let us use the two main themes from the Prague visit to make sense of OBJECT and EXPERIENCE, which are 1. Bergson's concept of qualitative multiplicity in terms of Person A's choice of what they recalled as 'most dear;' and 2. THE USE that this person saw and HOW THEY FELT ABOUT THE USE that they saw. Then we will use data from the semi–structured interview of one of the study area's respondents (see *Appendix B on page 193*) to consider the following: 1. The two uses, 2. Object and experience, and 3. Qualitative multiplicity in relation to what is most dear.

1 Bergson and qualitative multiplicity

The theory of Bergson (1988) is focused on temporal metaphysics and declares that we see—not in space, or spatially—but in time. We do not observe in the sense described by classic metaphysics, that is, in a regression of infinite divisibility and alienation of parts. Qualitative multiplicity is our perception of an entire event as a whole where:

> ...our urban can be said to be made up of indivisible experiences that blend past with present—in the same way we experience music. We can never tell, says Bergson, where one note stops and the other starts. It can be said therefore of our urban experience, that we see—with memory—the music being played right in front of us (De Kock, Pieter, 2022a).

In this case then the event in Person A's memory is their experience of that entire street. And it is to a certain extent irrelevant whether Person A saw it eight years ago or eight seconds ago, in the sense that the present is instantaneously the past. That is exactly how we see and what we see: we see, according to Bergson, with memory. The inevitable conclusion then is that Person A's perception is the entire indivisible journey, from arched gateway to the Church. It is not divisible. It is measured as a passage of time, not as a number of, for example, separate spaces or doorways or textures. It is not able to be spatialised into parts and components without losing its indivisibility and therefore its emergent properties. It is non-linear in the sense that the parts add up to more than the whole and therefore can be said to belong to the domain of *complexity theory. We therefore have what appears to be something similar to transparency in meaning suggested by Varela et al. (2016) where there is no duality but as one comes to the fore, the other recedes. An ecological complementarity of sorts. The transparency is the arched gateway as the OBJECT; followed by the EXPERIENCE of the streetscape stretching up to the next OBJECT: the Church. Their perception then is the entire indivisible journey from arched gateway to the Church. In one sense then it is a journey made from a point of PHYSICAL USE (where an object needs to be defined) TO VISUAL USE (being defined by an event consisting of a series of objects), and back again to an object that needs to be defined in terms of its purpose along the journey. This brings us to the second theme, namely physical use and visual use.

2 Physical use and visual use

For Robbins "Form is a quality" (Robbins, 2013, p.155) or dynamic form. It is time–extended; there are no static objects as they all have *qualia (2004). The

Figure 11. Interaction dominance: the stronger the shade, the more dominant the interaction type in that location.

Figure 12. Greenwich Town Centre and Greenwich Park observation data: interactions per minute (video) https://doi.org/10.6084/m9.figshare.24996215.v1.

*Complexity theory: environmental or human systems and/or behaviour which do not behave in a linear way, but which is non–linear i.e., dynamic, and unpredictable. A well–known example is behaviour in flocks of birds, but can equally be applied to scaling effects, bottom–up processes, and associated phenomena in cities (See, for example, Batty, 2007, 2012).

*Qualia is here meant as described by Robbins, for example in the redness of an apple (2004, 2013) and in more detail by Ramachandran and Hirstein in their three laws of qualia where: "First, they are irrevocable: I cannot simply decide to start seeing the sunset as green, or feel pain as if it were an itch; second, qualia do not always produce the same behaviour: given a set of qualia, we can choose from a potentially infinite set of possible behaviours to execute; and third, qualia endure in short-term memory, as opposed to non-conscious brain states involved in the on-line guidance of behaviour in real time." (Ramachandran and Hirstein 1997, p.1).

CHAPTER 2 THE IMPORTANCE OF VISUAL SUSTAINABILITY

suggestion I am making is that our intangible cultural heritage is linked to temporal metaphysics. In other words, we do not fully understand heritage without accounting for the nature of dynamic form, as data. These data exist as two variables—two forks of data—that represent the union of OBJECT and EXPERIENCE. This study holds that the two variables discussed previously in Chapter One, PHYSICAL USE and VISUAL USE, are expressions of an event (these data)—composed of STRUCTURAL INVARIANTS and TRANSFORMATIONS—that reflect Robbins' DYNAMIC FORM (Figure 8 on page 43). The physical use, therefore, that Person A sees is the arched gateway. It allows them to pass through what is otherwise an impenetrable wall. That, in terms of this event, is the invariant. The visual use is the entire song, or the entire experience of the street in Person A's memory that was captured in time. That is the transformation. Together these two variables can be argued to represent an invariance structure of an event. Thus, for Person A the following is true about the description from memory of what was most dear to them (Figure 9 on page 43 and Figure 10 on page 43):

- Arched gateway = Physical Use = Invariant = the use that we see.
- Streetscape = Visual Use = Transformation = how we feel about the use we see.

Together, these two variables represent what is, in Robbins' terms, an invariance structure of an event. Visual sustainability may be described in this scenario as elevated levels of both the use we see and how we feel about the use that we see.

Object and experience as a map

Let us now look at 1. The two uses, 2. Object and experience, and 3. Qualitative multiplicity in relation to what is most dear. In the semi-structured interview (see *Appendix B on page 193*) we see the constant swapping out of information as the interviewee, PM, seamlessly navigates through his memory, inspecting past events, and often using redintegration to establish new memories. At the end of the interview he interrupts anecdotal thought with the lingering memory which speaks to the high levels of visual sustainability active in him:

But those three spaces... [emphasis added]

Four words describe both object and experience in a time-extended event (which Robbins describes differently but with the same meaning). It is the same for Larry and Janet (in "Youtube: Larry And Janet Move Out" on page 206). Both are visually sustained in memory. For PM, if there was "structure" to an event, even a noisy event, it was "peaceful and tranquil" because "you were part of that." When he is asked to invoke dormant levels of qualitative multiplicity, 'the music' (meaning, the time-extended event) is right at his fingertips (page 204). In describing what he sees with memory, PM is clear about what he sees, for example, in correcting me about where he is. What he holds dear "gives him time to breathe," which resonates with the contradiction of life as we seek to "gain a little more breathing space…" (Something Rich and Strange: The Life and Music of Iannis Xenakis, 2022, 00:48:30). What we hold dear then may be thought of in terms of the need to think…deeply. So in terms of a process by which we are sustained and enriched in daily life through the visual relationship *we hold dear* to our surroundings, it may be argued that the longer interaction types are maps with directions about what we hold dear (and I have used these maps in my methodology). As for Larry and Janet ("Youtube: Larry And Janet Move Out" on page 206), I was struck by the influence of architectural materialism on both physical use and visual use—and by architectural materialism is meant the effect of non–human form, shape, and/or material on an observer (Voyatzaki, 2018).

Janet
We moved to The Heygate in 1973
Oh! it was lovely.

Larry
Lovely

Just like the archway in Prague which is physical use, acting as an invariant and something which Person A in that moment had defined but not been defined by, as well as playing a role as visual use from a different perspective, so too 'The Heygate.' The Heygate is, in one sense, a structural invariant (PHYSICAL USE). *Why*? Because it never changes in the minds of Janet and Larry. It has been defined but it has, in that moment, not defined them. It is simply 'The Heygate,' an affirmation of their location, and any feelings generated (TRANSFORMATION/VISUAL USE) are in the storytelling and not in the physical object or architecture or in any of its parts. The use is physical because, as a building complex, it is a background object that is defined by the couple *for its use to them*, in the way they are able to transform in their story-telling. The housing complex and its architecture are invariant because they are never described with feeling or in any detail i.e., in any sense of a transforming experience or interaction. But the use is also visual, in the sense that 'The Heygate,' as an ontological object, has transformed *them*. It has defined them. The reality produced by an invariant sets up moments of multiplicity which produces emergence in their interview through feelings (transformation). And even while still there, waiting to be moved out, in its neglected abandoned state, it is still a memory which they reference as being *lovely* and therefore dear to them both. The physical environment *has* therefore affected them but *implicitly*, which may be surprising to some given its infamous reputation as

CHAPTER 2 THE IMPORTANCE OF VISUAL SUSTAINABILITY

'a council estate.' Architecture and urban design seem to have this role to play, whereby their presence is implied but never articulated explicitly, vacillating between invariant and transformation depending on the exact moment of reflection. They are invariant and never change under certain psychic states, while transformative in other conditions.

PART 3
The map of what we have seen

Finally, in Part 3 I would like to look at how our experience is represented as data. *What does this mean in practical terms*? Data can be analysed in different ways (Figure 11 on page 45 and Figure 12 on page 45). It might not be essential to know the meaning or even the object being engaged but the most important data may simply be revealed by observing how we are interacting with our environment, and the measure of the quality of this interaction, through its duration. In other words: *how much attention is paid and in which location? This points us to an understanding of how it might be possible for temporal metaphysics to shift the way we think about our built environment, particularly in the sense that we should unify OBJECT with EXPERIENCE. The map of what 'we' have seen (in the study area), which when viewed as data and ordered in terms of interactions per minute, is demonstrated in the following video: https://youtu.be/y3am7wxlluo.

*The commercial relevance of how much we pay attention and in which location (see Table 7 on page 125 and "§. 21 Commercial application" on page 124).

CONCLUSION

If interaction is an act, then object and experience can be said to be a map which helps us find out more about how we see. Where globalization tends to rewrite that map, reducing the extraordinary until our senses are dulled and our attention directed to those few exemplars of iconic urban design, the point I am making here is that visual sustainability has the opposite effect. It transforms the ordinary into the extraordinary. *How does it do this*? It does so by way of qualitative multiplicity, by acknowledging the role of Bergson's duration: that we are immersed in a world of time, not space. Because HERITAGE is an experience existing in the domain of temporal metaphysics; one that serves to link us directly with the intangible. Through this transformation, then, because we 'take part,' we are truly 'part of' one domain of being: the architecture of heritage and the heritage of architecture. The suggestion is not that exemplars defined by the likes of UNESCOs world heritage sites have no value. They hold enormous value. But it is that our preoccupation with comparatively few iconic exemplars of heritage, limits our participation in preservation efforts on a much more important scale. Instead, the suggestion is that we continue to find new ways of understanding our surroundings.

Because there is a certain irony caught up in the relationship between direct–environment and memory–environment. As any stranger may point out to those who have stopped seeing, the music is in the ordinary. And we should remind ourselves that we are extraordinary for seeing the ordinary.

Finally, my argument from the reasoning between the four main philosophies discussed in the previous chapter, is that it is important to distinguish between several things. Firstly, there is physical use (the use that we see i.e., where we define something) and visual use (how we feel about the use that we see i.e., where that something defines us). Secondly, there is the link between interactions, object, and experience to consider. Lastly, there are structural invariants and transformations as part of invariance structures of events in patterns, which function as catalysts for memory and action in urban systems (as seen in Figure 8 on page 43). The interconnectedness can be argued as follows:

- Structural invariance is physical use—because we define something—so it changes (in our eyes) but we do not. And once defined it becomes invariant. It does not change from how you have defined it for that duration. It is a rock, not a stone; or a location (for example, the Heygate), not a building; it may be a sound, not a shape; or access point to the meaning beyond, but not an arch (the Prague example), etc.
- Transformation is visual use—because something defines us—so we change but it does not change. This is when the 'something' has become an invariant, unchanging—but we are changed through an associated emotion.
- None of these things are things that can be seen. I cannot see your building and you can not see mine. We will agree to have looked at the same thing but we cannot agree to have seen the same thing.
- At an individual level, what I define is not the same as what you define *even if* we both call it the same thing. If we both look at the same building, it is not the same building we see. I might see a face half way up the facade, while you may see a pattern of deep recesses as the over–riding feature of that 'something' known as a building.

So, what this argument shows is the impossibility of understanding the meaning of what people look at. Which is why the link between interaction, objects, and experiences must be carefully considered and one way to do that is by understanding object and experience as a map that links interaction i.e., our action in the invisible city, as described in the next chapter.

THE IMPORTANCE OF VISUAL SUSTAINABILITY

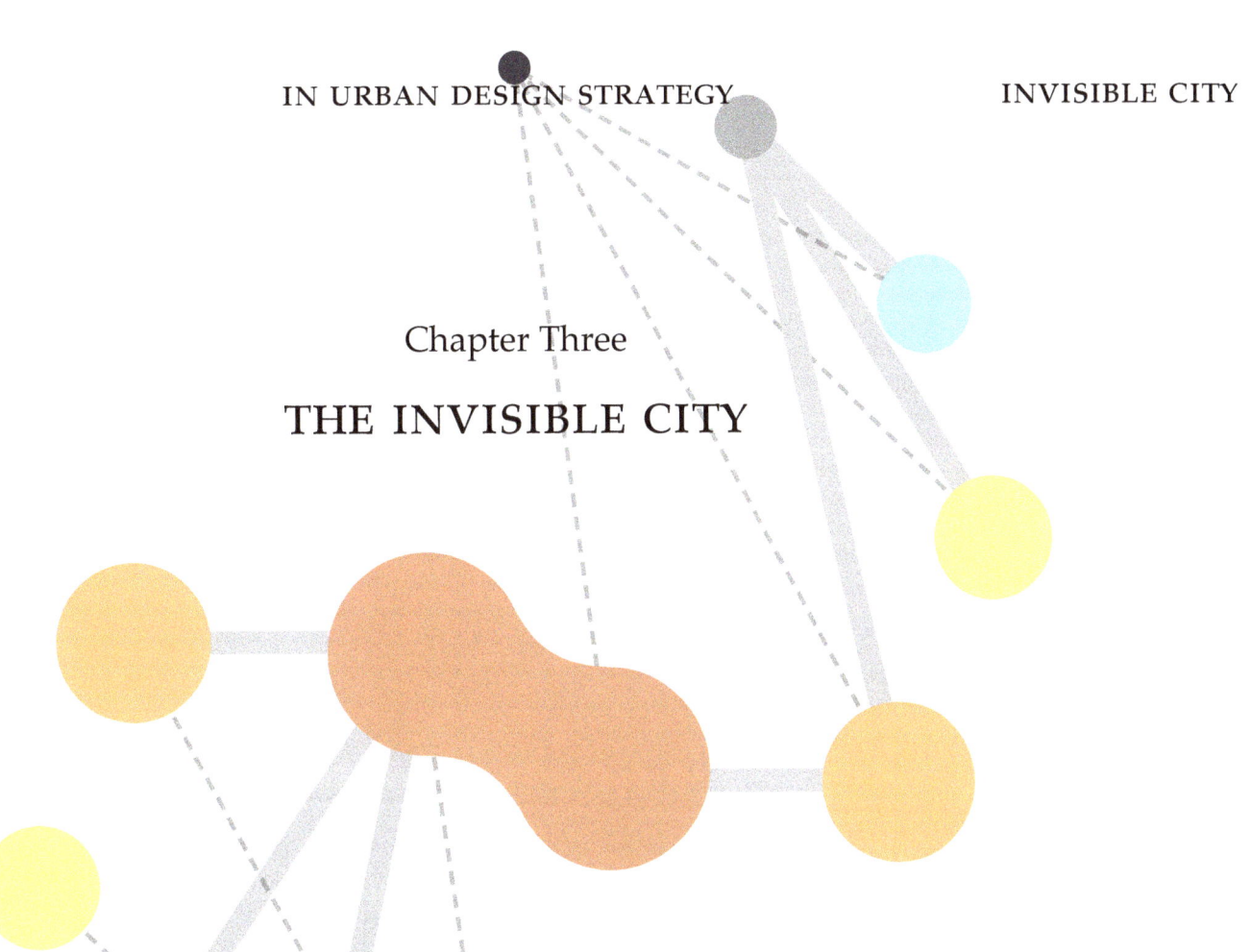

§. 10 *Invisible City versus Visible City*

Chapter Three
THE INVISIBLE CITY

The paradigm shift in this chapter is the idea that the relationship between INTERACTION, OBJECT, and EXPERIENCE can produce a *condition state change resulting in the emergence of what can be described as an INVISIBLE CITY. In this study I am looking at how we are visually sustained, and my argument is that both the INVISIBLE CITY and the VISIBLE CITY are the product of INTERACTION. And interaction is validated through OBJECT and EXPERIENCE. In the next chapter I will introduce the six INTERACTION–TYPES, their use as a device to measure with (Figure 18 on page 69 and Figure 19 on page 69), and in the chapter following that (Chapter Five: Findings) we will assess their potential as markers of meaning when combined visually and in harmony.

*Condition state change: for example, when water turns into steam or ice.

51

CHAPTER 3   THE IMPORTANCE OF VISUAL SUSTAINABILITY

INTRODUCTION

In the previous chapter the suggestion was that we should find new ways of understanding our surroundings because meaning was too nuanced in the way that we looked at things and their influence over us. And because good research tries to look beyond the visible and uncover what is hidden from view, we must account for this ongoing dialogue between intuition (Polanyi, 1966, 1969) on the one hand and our physical environment (Gibson, 2015) in describing how we *interact with our built environment. To discover more about the nature of this relationship I will now turn my attention towards developing an understanding about where common ground might exist between the four distinctly different ontologies discussed in Chapter One. The first addresses the act of seeing with intuition (Polanyi & Grene, 1969); the second, with direct perception (Gibson, 2015); and the third mediates between the two through 'seeing by acting', or as a form of action (Varela et al., 2016). And while there is some overlap in these different realities, they do not appear to be sufficient on their own. It is not until the fourth ontology that things start to make more sense for me: where I was are introduced into a world governed by temporal metaphysics (Bergson, 1988; Robbins, 2014). The missing clue is caught up in the concept of duration and qualitative multiplicity. Once one accepts the idea of temporal heterogeneity and that time, not space, is the missing ingredient, there is finally a sense of clarity about what sustains us in the act of seeing. And by act of seeing, I mean: the result of interactions we have with our surroundings (as described in Chapter One).

Let us consider the built environment more closely. We tend to think of a city in terms of its buildings. Buildings are, after all, the most visible elements, or components of any city. *But what if there is another built environment which is enacted by us through our location*? Let us call that instance the invisible city. This invisible city is, as an idea, responsive to what Bergson calls qualitative multiplicity and what Polanyi calls tacit knowing. Its experienced in time and is something that can't be expressed in words. The idea of something intangible like an invisible city to express the intangible meaning around us seems appropriate. *So how can it be expressed*? The answer is to be found in how the invisible city contrasts with the visible city because, while the visible can quickly become irrelevant, since space exists outside of us, the invisible remains within us, as a function of time. *What then exists within us and how can we measure it*? The answer to that is in what we give away through our engagement with the things that surround us: our interaction location, how many times we interact, and for how long. These provide the metric

---

*By interact I mean visual interaction, which consists in my argument, of both physical use and visual use. Both physical use and visual use make use of embodied interaction, and both make use of the kind of interaction afforded through sight. Therefore, visual interaction refers to what our body does when we look at something *as well as* what our eyes tell us about what we are seeing. In my argument, therefore, the act of seeing embraces several layers of what I would describe as the indivisible experience of 'seeing.' This premise is established through my analysis of the theories of Bergson, Polanyi, Varela, and Gibson.

that explains the invisible city. *What then are the signs **in people** that direct us towards the invisible city?* The answer appears to lie in the ***types*** of visual interactions people have with their surroundings. These ***types*** help describe visual sustainability as a *process and it is that process which we need to follow to point us towards the invisible city. Therefore, the visual relationship that we hold dear to our surroundings can be found in an environmental process. A parallel can be drawn between the relevance of visual sustainability and the relevance to us, of this 'other' reality, the invisible city—due to their **reciprocity, as each points to the other.

*Process: identifies the 'objects' at work, in other words, it "gives rise to an object" (Complexity Explorer Lecture: David Krakauer. What is Complexity? 2023, 00:17:19).

**Reciprocity: is a condition which enables the completion of a transaction (see "Dualism vs. reciprocity: the transactional dilemma" on page 20).

The premise then is that a city is comprised of two coincidental layers, where, as posited by Varela et al. (2016), one comes to the fore as the other recedes; acting as part of a constantly oscillating phenomenon. We interact with a physical city as well as with a visual city. The physical city has been defined by us through the location of its objects in space, whereas the visual city is defined by *our* location—in time. So, as seen on page 47, the physical city in this scenario is a proxy for the invisible city and 'The Heygate' was simply an affirmation of the interviewees' location as they described what they saw with memory.

PHILOSOPHICAL INSPIRATION

The suggestion by Robbins (2016, 2021) is that what is 'hidden from view' lies in a vast interference pattern and is accessible only with memory. Memory, because that is where the objects of our existence are captured, stored, restored, reused, and stored again; in an infinitely repeating loop (Robbins, 2021). These data are invisible to the eye and indecipherable from conventional perception. Conventional perception is here meant in the sense described by classical metaphysics, where everything is supposedly endlessly divisible through their inherent spatial properties.

There are two extremes at each end of this philosophical spectrum. At one end we encounter tacit feeling (Polanyi, 1966). Tacit knowledge is invisible but additionally lacking the logic which we find appealing in what lies at the other end of the spectrum, which is Gibson's theory of direct perception (2015). Intuition and tacit knowledge speak to a theory steeped in qualia: that which nourishes our senses. But for Gibson, what feeds our senses are real objects that exist in real time. Hence the location of these two philosophies at opposite ends of the spectrum. For Gibson, objects are activated by our movement as well as by light. Gibson thus describes the visible city plainly. His 'real objects' are confirmed by his explanation of movement around them.

CHAPTER 3   THE IMPORTANCE OF VISUAL SUSTAINABILITY

This, by way of alignment, then introduces Varela et al.'s (2016) notion of action: that we act in order to create our future. This action too is realised through movement i.e., by doing or by the movement in virtual action, of intending to do something. 'Being,' for Varela, is not a passive relationship we enjoy with our environment. This process of enaction (Varela et al., 2016) of our surroundings therefore begins to speak to the relationship between what we see and what we do not see—and is relevant to my study because of the parallels that can be drawn between the two ontologies. We have what appears to be one form of relevance investigating the other. One reflects my search for an invisible city from our location in a visible city, the other is the reality of the invisible city itself, waving its arms around furiously in an attempt to be recognised because its relevance is an invisible record of how we interact with our surroundings. It is the dark matter in the analogy presented at the start of this study in "§. 1 Introductory statement" on page 1.

If, as Varela holds, we see because we act (2016), then it rings true for what Bergson describes as virtual action, or what Gibson later calls affordance. For Bergson both real action and virtual action are enveloped in memory. And memory is a form of duration, which is best described in terms of an interpenetration of moments such that it is impossible to tell one moment apart from another (Bergson, 1988). The analogy with sound, melody, or harmony is apt because that is how Bergson explains qualitative multiplicity i.e., as a time–extended event. The analogy also serves the same rationale for Polanyi because there are no words to describe certain things. Which is what music does in us through the flow of time. It removes the need for words. And we intuitively latch on to the effects of a phenomenon, using song to describe and explain what can't be explained with words, which is the experience of, what Bergson calls, DURATION. Each event is inseparable from the next or preceding. As 'moments' they exist as one entity together in an assemblage where the whole is greater than the sum of its parts. And where the whole is greater than the sum of it parts, we stand on the threshold of emergence found in non–linear complex systems. But for Gibson at the opposite end of the comparison, these events are simply separate objects in space. And for Varela we only activate these events when we ourselves 'do something.' So, for the common ground between these philosophies, we have the following: Gibson's theory of direct perception represents the visible city (Figure 13 on page 57: Top). Polanyi represents the notion of an invisible city (Figure 13 on page 57: Bottom). And in between we have Varela with his suggestion that there is a kind of transparent layering effect going on (Figure 15 on page 59). It may therefore be said that it is through our selection (Gibson) from memory (Bergson) that defines what comes forward into view and what recedes from view (Varela) out of this vast universal interference pattern (Robbins).

As for the key differences, if I were to summarise these as simply as possible it would be as follows: for Gibson there is, so to speak, no music playing. What you see is what you get. For Polanyi, relevance is in the way we *feel* the music. For Varela, we have to play the music to see relevance. And finally for Bergson, music *is* relevance. What you see is what you hear. And what you hear is governed by time. The concept that the mystery of DURATION can be analysed using sounds is an idea that this study carries forward in the analysis of the types of visual interaction we have with our surroundings "Figure 19. Differentiating interaction type through time values in sound, where markers of time–extended events are used to signify durational qualities (video). See video at https://doi.org/10.6084/m9.figshare.25391044.v1." on page 69.

VISUAL INTERACTION TYPES

The visual interaction types that make up our invisible city are WHOLE (4 seconds duration/dark orange); HALF (2 seconds duration/orange); QUARTER (1 second duration/yellow); EIGHTH (half a second/blue); SIXTEENTH (a quarter of a second/grey); and SIM (no interaction/black). Chapter Four has more about these interaction types and how they have been produced from these data collected in the study area: Greenwich Town Centre and Greenwich Park, London. And the findings are presented in Chapter Five. But for now, it is enough to say that there is a certain irony in analysing data from what is essentially the home of classical metaphysics, where time is measured by a clock from the Prime Meridian Line. The point being argued in this chapter is that interaction type produces the invisible city and belongs in the domain of temporal metaphysics (Figure 13 on page 57: Bottom). It is the view we have of our city as we move in time from location to location. It is also data that does not appear to be collected or recognised in urban design strategy or policy–making, possibly because no one has really figured out a way of accurately representing this level of subjectivity before.

GRANULARITY

To avoid data collected becoming too broad and biased I needed to increase the levels of granularity and this is achieved through observation. The advantage of observing interaction behaviour is that data collected are stripped of the ambiguity which normally accompanies traditional survey methods, where respondents are asked for information about what it is they looked at. The

CHAPTER 3   THE IMPORTANCE OF VISUAL SUSTAINABILITY

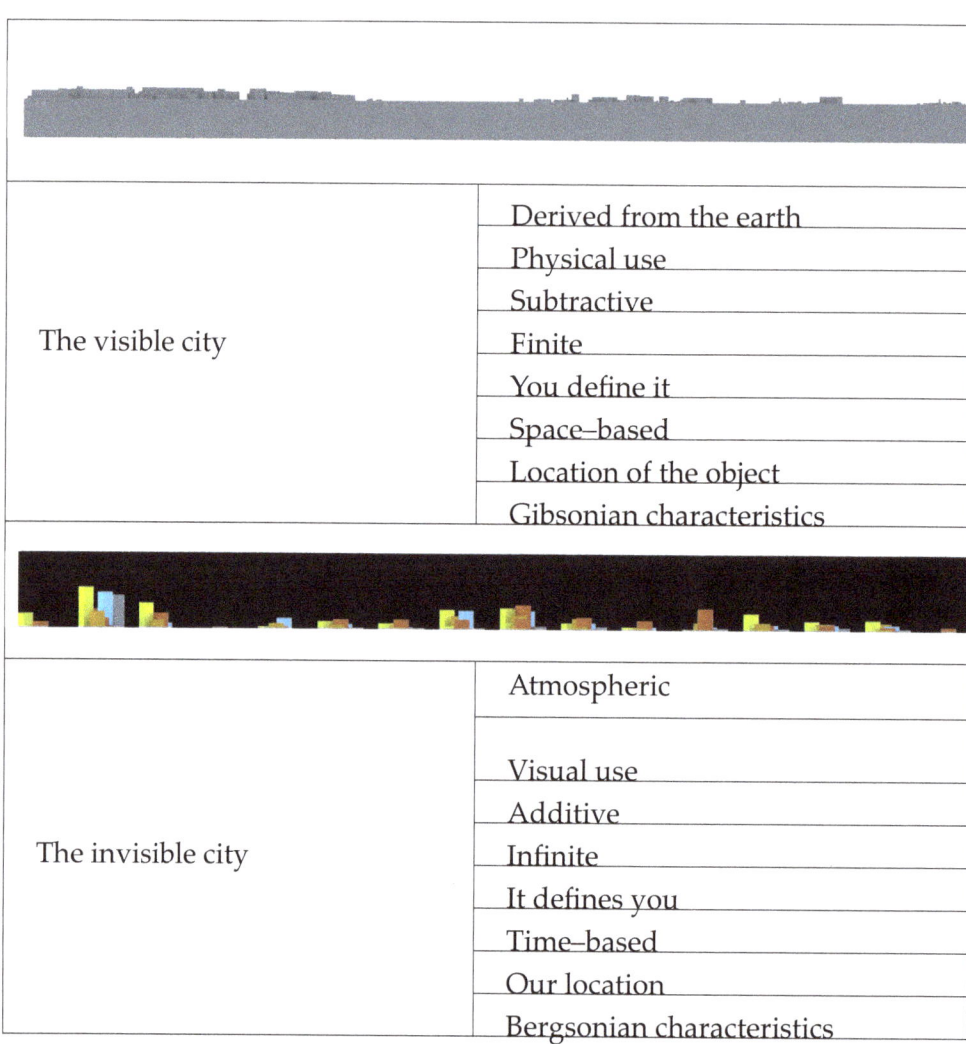

Table 3. The physical city is a proxy for memory; the invisible city is that memory.

*Redintegration: the law of redintegration in Gibsonian terms would be: A current event, E' redintegrates a previous event, E, when E' and E share the same invariance structure. Derived from "a term coined already in 1732 by Wolff, a disciple of Leibniz, in his Psychologia Empirica. It is defined roughly as "a part of a current event retrieves the whole of a past event," or as Klein (1971) puts it, a pattern in a current event retrieves a past event with a similar pattern" (Robbins, S. E., 2021, p.21).

"amount of visual information observers can perceive and remember is extremely limited" (Haun et al., 2017), for example, if respondents do not really know what they looked at, then these data becomes almost meaningless by the time a researcher has tried to properly interpret what has been written or said. People often simply do not know or cannot articulate properly exactly what they see. And often what they see is not an object but, for example, a flash of colour, a texture, or negative space between several objects. They have also most likely seen a hundred things which they are unable to process or account for, before settling on something meaningless, broad, or general enough to write down. Ellard relates to this problem of perception through his experience of what has been described by Robbins as *redintegration (2014):

> My mind was leaping effortlessly from place to place and from time to time, as my feet were making this path along the beach... combining what we see with what we think about, what we see with those mental

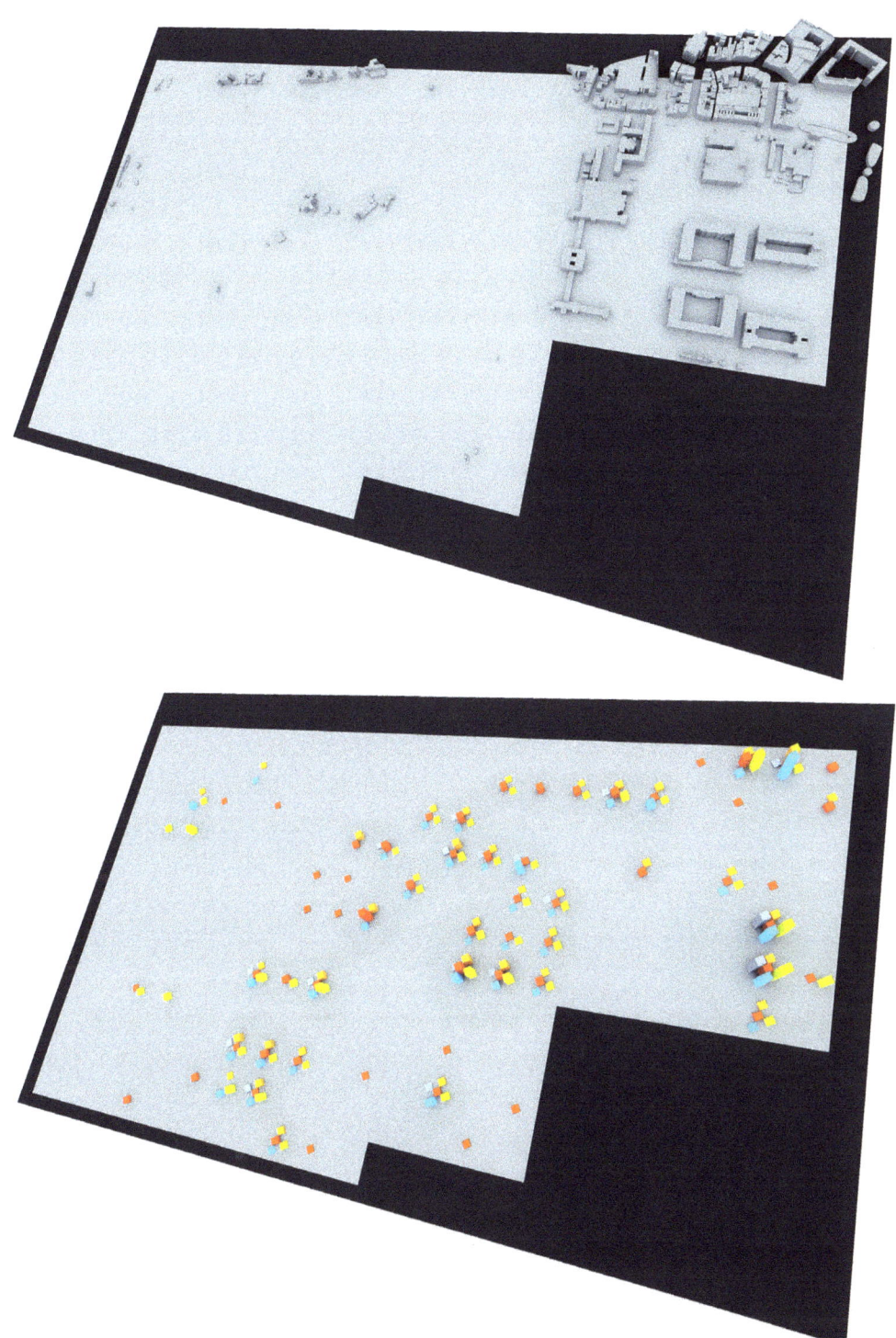

Figure 13. Top: The visible city: what we see is what we get. Buildings represent the most visible elements of a city, where location is an expression of 'space.' Bottom: The invisible city: contextual strength is evidenced by visual interaction type; where location as an experience and expression of 'time.'

leaps through space (TEDxWaterloo - Colin Ellard - Getting Lost, 2011, 00:01:40; 00:05:00).

There is simply no way these data can be conveyed in written form without being lost in translation. So, to achieve a finer level of granularity in these data, the solution was simple: The meaning or even what people looked at was disregarded. All that is needed is to concentrate on two things: 1. Counting the number of interactions, and 2. Recording the duration of each interaction. This is all I needed to understand the number, type, intensity, and mix of interactions that make up the invisible data. And best of all, in this approach, was that we can account for many more interactions than any respondent in a survey would have been able to provide. So then, for the purposes of uncovering levels of visual sustainability, the interactions that we observe can produce the most useful data to work with and can reveal more about the two realities that exist in our urban: visible versus invisible city (Table 3 on page 56 summarises the key differences between these two realities).

VISIBLE VERSUS INVISIBLE CITY

It is not so much that the visible city is completely irrelevant, but simply that an overriding weakness exists by way of its isolation from (what is being proposed as) the more meaningful city, namely, the invisible city. And it will remain isolated until we look beyond the visible and uncover these data which are hidden from view.

Interaction type, as summarised in Chapter Five, describes how the physical city and the visual city are different from one another (Figure 13 on page 57). And in Bergson's terms, the physical city is a proxy for memory while the invisible city *is* that memory. The levels of interest signified by these interaction types can be argued to be visual sustainability indicators of the quality of architecture and urban design of the physical city (Figure 13 on page 57: Top) because they indicate what is being looked at and in what way. What is different however is that the harmony (or lack of) that is presupposed by these interactions is produced by that which is invisible to us—and can be said to produce an effect that draws inspiration from Bergson's theory of qualitative multiplicity. The effect is not a reductive process in the sense described by classical metaphysics. The invisible, in this context, is a product

Figure 14. Urban design relevance.

Figure 15. Urban transect: the invisible city when combined with the visible city.

CHAPTER 3   THE IMPORTANCE OF VISUAL SUSTAINABILITY

*For data as sound, see "§. 23 Measuring our temporal urban" on page 147 and "Appendix C" on page 221.

**see also Figure 42 on page 119, Figure 43 on page 119 and Figure 45 on page 123.

of temporal metaphysics and, as in the example of *sound, is a phenomenon which behaves in a cumulative way. This is because it represents data collected about an experience. The 'real city' is not the physical city, it is the city of experiences and can be said to be more accurately represented in Figure 13 on page 57: Bottom. The importance and value of these experiences lies in the **mix of interactions, where, for example, the orange colours are indicative of elevated levels of visual sustainability.

DISCUSSION

There are several thought–provoking themes produced by this chapter, as follows. First of all, the mix of interaction types help better describe the quality of the built environment. They provide us with 'a device' for measuring and understanding levels of visual sustainability. We are able to better understand the process occurring between invariant structures and transformation, physical use and visual use, and the link between interaction, objects, and experience. For example, areas with predominantly blue and grey colours would serve as a warning of the presence of high levels of alienation. By contrast the warm colours (oranges) appear to signify higher levels of visual sustainability. The reasoning behind this is that the longer we look at something, the more meaningful it must be to us. Alienation, on the other hand, may be said to be consistent with of high levels of erratic, fleeting glances which appear to lose any sense of focus (De Kock, 2023).

Secondly, the idea that location is an expression of time is strengthened as a concept. This is because the visual interaction types are data which can only be activated as a function of time. While the visible city is a set of static objects, the invisible city exists because people have walked through the study area and have interacted with their environment for varying amounts of time. And the visible city has been part of the subject matter and part of these exchanges.

Thirdly, the invisible city's 'buildings' (interaction types) are more relevant than real buildings because they represent our attention span and all the transactions we have completed/invested in with our time (Figure 15 on page 59). That is to say, these transactions reflect where we have expressed an interest in our surroundings; regardless of whether the objects were near or far, and whether the exchanges were positive or negative.

Fourthly, for the visible city it is difficult to measure 'value', by which is meant: the value to people of a physical building. But 'buildings' consisting of interaction types in an invisible city are enormously valuable data, not only because they are markers of levels of visual sustainability but also because their value can be calculated in relative terms as a function of location.

Lastly, the space, in a Euclidean sense, between the two types of 'buildings' for each of the two 'cities' (Figure 14 on page 59) provides valuable data which can be used in urban design strategy and urban planning because the spread of the invisible city is an indication of *contextual strength. By this is meant that the physical city, when 'read' in conjunction with its invisible counterpart, exerts a level of influence over the surrounding landscape, which can now be 'seen.' In addition, the in–between spaces might reveal a disconnect between the **investment made in the physical city and its visual use (see an adaptation of urban segregation in De Kock and Carta, 2020b, p.12–13 which explores economic segregation in urban areas). This is because a poor return on investment is most likely evidenced by the lack of associated interaction type. If people are not looking at a building or attracted to urban design, then it means they are not visually sustained and, in all probability, alienated by what has been created. Which means that the designer or building owner may be alienating people without intending to do so.

*See "§. 21 Commercial application" on page 124 and Figure 51 on page 131

**The commercial reality associated with the invisible city (see Table 7 on page 125 and "§. 21 Commercial application" on page 124).

CONCLUSION

The argument in this chapter has been that the types of visual interactions we have with our surroundings, and how these impact on our experience of the built environment, are descriptors for the process which has been uncovered by this research and explained in the findings of Chapter Five. It is a process which better explains how the relationship that we have with our surroundings results in some form of visual sustainability, trending towards either an enriching experience or an alienating experience. These visual interaction types are important because they better describe the quality of our urban environment and help us to see the invisible city more clearly. My research into the importance of visual sustainability in urban design strategy is thus made relevant by the discovery of an invisible city. It is a 'city' which we subconsciously inhabit and which, when engaged, prevents us from participating, as authors, in an irrelevant conclusion. It is a city full of data and it is deserving of our attention.

THE IMPORTANCE OF VISUAL SUSTAINABILITY

IN URBAN DESIGN STRATEGY

PART TWO

Chapter Four

METHODOLOGY

§. 11 *Bergson and mixed methods*

In the last three chapters we have looked at interactions and their visual qualities—both visible and invisible, invariant and transformative, physical and visual. I have also tried to show how interaction links up with object and experience. I have made several references to the use of interaction type as a device for measuring the effect of the environment on us. In this Chapter the focus will be on interaction as a metric. The challenge has been to find a convincing strategy that will uncover enough of the invisible city in order to make more sense of it. My methodology embraces ten principles inspired by Bergson's theory (Table 4 on page 65 and Figure 16 on page 65) and while drawing on all principles, I will focus on the reciprocity between Principle 3:

CHAPTER 4 THE IMPORTANCE OF VISUAL SUSTAINABILITY

invariance structures, and Principle 7: dynamic form. Invariance structures, because they speak to the idea of our urban made up of patterns; and dynamic form because of its temporal relevance. In terms of the proposed methods some adjustments have been made because I was not sure which technique would produce the kind of data that would be most useful in the argument about the relevance of philosophy to urban design strategy, in other words, illuminating enough of the bridge between theory and practice. I initially planned for a range of methods, including surveys, interviews, observation, and quantitative analysis using statistical software. The overall order of events adopted initially was sequenced as follows (see also "Appendices" on page 175). I had decided from the outset that my methodology would be flexible enough to be able go where the research led but to start in a conventional manner and collect data using interviews and survey forms. There was thus a sense of grounded theory at work in that, at various stages, I was embedded in a process of establishing new theory from these data. But the approach varied from inductive analysis to abductive, because ultimately I was working back from what I had observed in these interactions. Later, in the qualitative analysis, the approach reverted to a deductive one.

1 I started by collecting secondary data from YouTube videos, which I analysed using NVivo and Adobe Premiere Pro software (see Figure 20 and Figure 21 on page 71 and "Youtube: Larry And Janet Move Out" on page 206). I wanted to understand the nature of human interaction directly from an event or series of real events that had occurred in the past, in the context of strategic urban design intervention such as social housing, and which formed part of people's memory since, according to Bergson, we see with memory. The Youtube videos were ideal in that they represent data which were unbiased from the standpoint of my research aim, including my own bias. The concept of duration is important in these Youtube videos because I was able to watch as an 'outsider' how reactions confirmed or rejected Bergson's idea that

> "it is impossible to distinguish between the duration, however short it may be, that separates two instants and a memory that connects them, because duration is essentially a continuation of what no longer exists into what does exist" (Bergson, 1965, p.49).

2 Primary data were then collected from a survey based on a randomised selection of postcodes surrounding the study area (see "Appendix A" on page 177). I had anticipated that this type of data would be most useful in the patterns found, using Nvivo software. As can be seen in Figure 17 on page 67 three main themes appeared to dominate, namely Memory, Perception, and Psychic States.

Principle 1	Our visual world is time bound; we see with memory (Bergson, 1988).
Principle 2	Perception is virtual action: it is to prepare action (Bergson, 1988).
Principle 3	Virtual action is discoverable in the urban through invariance structures; comprised of transformations and structural invariants (Robbins, 2004; 2013).
Principle 4	Our body in the urban behaves as the "centre of action" (Bergson, 1988, p.48).
Principle 5	Through orienting towards our centre of action we create *use* (Bergson, 1988).
Principle 6	We are the transaction between physical use and visual use.
Principle 7	Use is where our interest in urban design lies through the indivisible motion of dynamic form.
Principle 8	Urban dynamic form (Robbins, 2004; 2013) as a process of duration (Bergson, 1988) is our gateway to understanding urban qualitative multiplicity.
Principle 9	Visual sustainability is fully compatible with Bergson's concept of duration.
Principle 10	Within this framework of duration, visual sustainability is proposed to represent the *by-product* of emergence through the interaction between physical use and visual use.

Table 4. Theoretical principles (De Kock, 2022a, p.28–29).

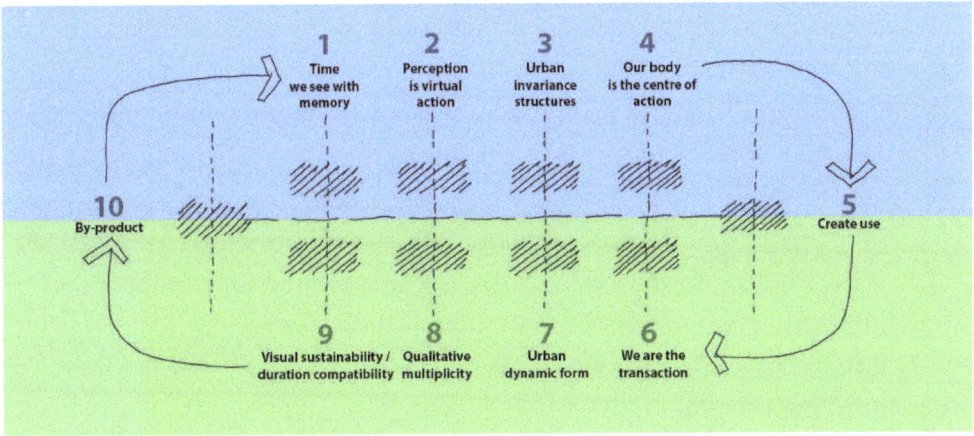

Figure 16. Theoretical principles. This diagram shows the ten key principles derived from the literature review, which will be used to more fully describe the application of physical use and visual use in urban design (De Kock, 2022a, p.18).

CHAPTER 4   THE IMPORTANCE OF VISUAL SUSTAINABILITY

3. This was followed by a semi–structured interview which was conducted with one of the respondents from the survey. It was then imported into NVivo and analysed along with the secondary data from item 1 above and primary data from 2 above (see "Appendix B" on page 193).

4. It was at this point that I decided to change strategy. I stopped the survey because I was not getting the right kind of data. I wanted more continuous data as I had enough categorical data and so opted instead for observation as my main method of enquiry—along with the analysis of the YouTube interviews. By 'right kind of data' I mean data which goes to the heart of my research question, where it is in *thinking* about the philosophy in a practical way, almost as an embodied research method. I could see the usefulness of the themes developed but I was not getting the sharpness I wanted to achieve in these data, about how visual sustainability had a role to play in urban design strategy. So, while the results of the survey were still useful in understanding people's experiences (see, for example, "Object and experience as a map" on page 46) especially of alienation, the highly iterative nature of my research was leading me to re–evaluate my chosen methods. The catalyst for this change in direction occurred as I found myself watching people's behaviour in the study area more closely during my day–to–day canvassing for participants, and it dawned on me that there was a considerable amount of excellent data available simply by observing the types of interactions people were having in real time. It did not have to be complicated, complex, yes, but not complicated. I therefore took a step back and re-evaluated exactly what it was I was trying to achieve. I reread my research question and decided that a better course of action was to use observation as my main method in understanding how it may be possible for visual sustainability to, in some way, play a role in urban design strategy. What I needed to do however was to find an unbiased way of collecting these data. I then decided on a metric to measure the types of interaction I saw, which could be used in an unbiased way. But there was one more thing to think about and that was to incorporate the practical application of Bergson's philosophy into the metric. Why? Because my entire study is centred on the usefulness of philosophy to understand the urban environment, as outlined in Objective 3 on page 6: To demonstrate how the practical application of Bergson's philosophy can be reconciled with urban design at a strategic level. The key philosophical argument in Bergson's theory is duration and it is in this context that the time value from the analogy of a melody (see NOTE in "§. 4 Key expressions" on page 6) is used because in Bergson's theory we see in a condition described by qualitative multiplicity (see

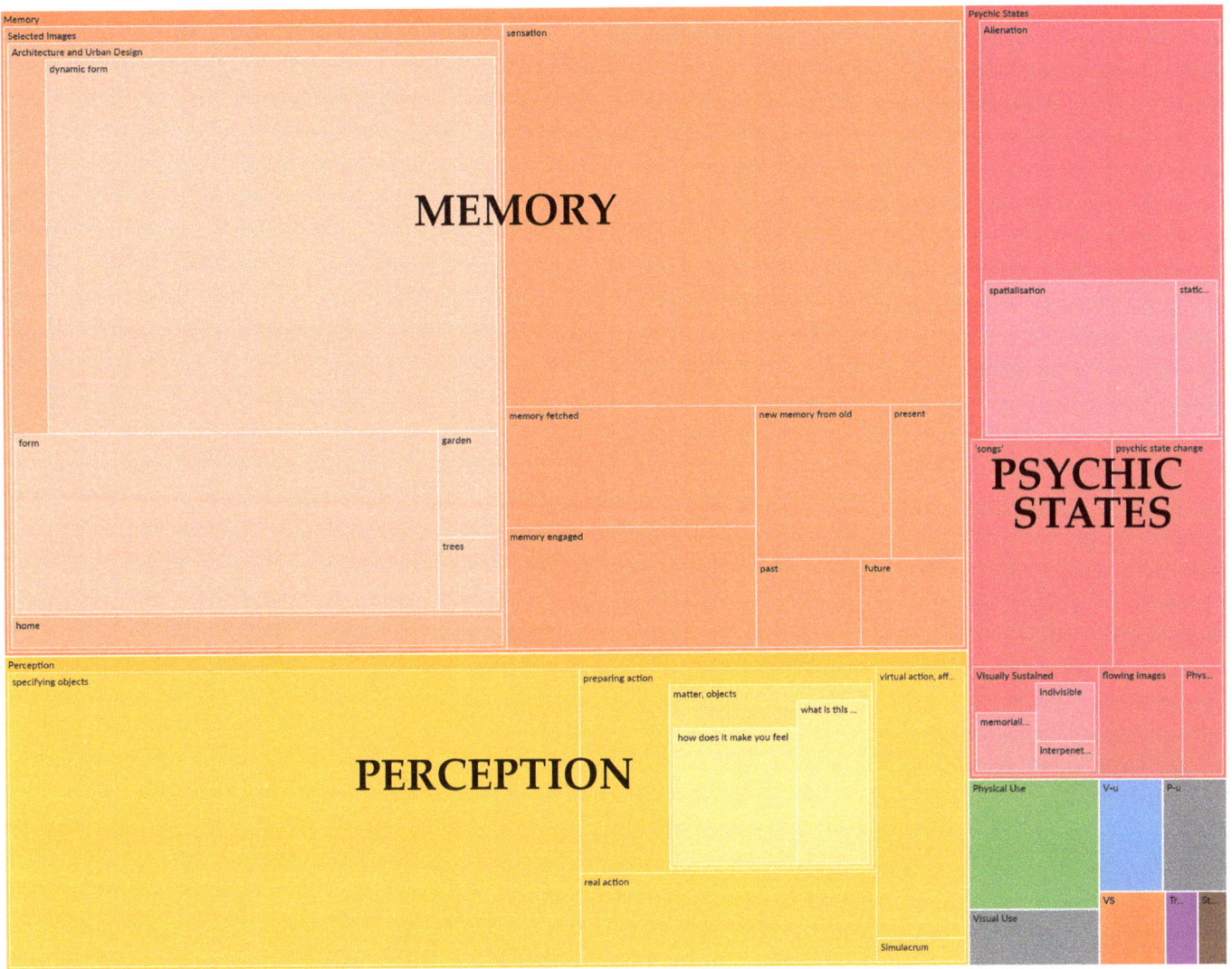

Figure 17. Nvivo coding references comparison highlights the dominance of the following three themes: Memory, Perception, and Psychic States.

CHAPTER 4   THE IMPORTANCE OF VISUAL SUSTAINABILITY

DURATION in "§. 4 Key expressions" on page 6). The five time values chosen therefore provided me with a means to anticipate the manner in which it might be possible for Bergson's philosophy of duration to inform data coming out of my observations. I was particularly interested in emergence in the context of our urban as a non–linear phenomenon with bottom–up characteristics as described in complexity theory. It is, I concede, a novel approach but well within the scope of what I had set out to accomplish in terms of my aim, objectives, and research question. And the role of these time values was intended to help spontaneously trigger the philosophical side of understanding in research. It is in understanding interaction in relation to surroundings from a temporal perspective using Bergson's notion of duration that I consider Objective 3 (on page 6) to have been addressed in a methodological sense.

5   The main method used in this study is therefore observation using a device to measure with (see Figure 18 on page 69 and Figure 19 on page 69) because, this way, I was able to understand more about what can be directly *observed* from people's interactions with their environment. And to re–emphasise the point, in "Granularity" on page 55, I have outlined the importance, in this study, of focusing in on the right type of data. My concern has been that, while useful for other studies, a survey would not yield enough of the kind of data I am interested in, which is interaction type, especially data that point to the invariance structures and dynamic form derived from Bergson (Table 4 on page 65 and Figure 16 on page 65) which I consider to be highly relevant to the thought that needs to take place behind urban design strategy, by all built environment professionals.

There is a sense of duality to mixed methods research which is united by data. On the one hand, there is empirical evidence and on the other, analysis of qualia and other indescribable phenomena (Robbins, 2013). Duality existed in Bergson's reality but was unified through the concept of qualitative multiplicity (Lawlor and Moulard–Leonard, 2021). And for Varela et al., who gravitated towards a singular existence called groundlessness, duality ceased to be problematic. So, for my study, Bergson's qualitative multiplicity is reflected in the method chosen, of using a device linked to rhythm of time values which communicate meaning in sounds, to measure both qualitative and quantitative data as meaning in time–extended events. The next section will demonstrate the salient aspects that influence the research methodology, from philosophy to the approach, design, and strategy of collecting data.

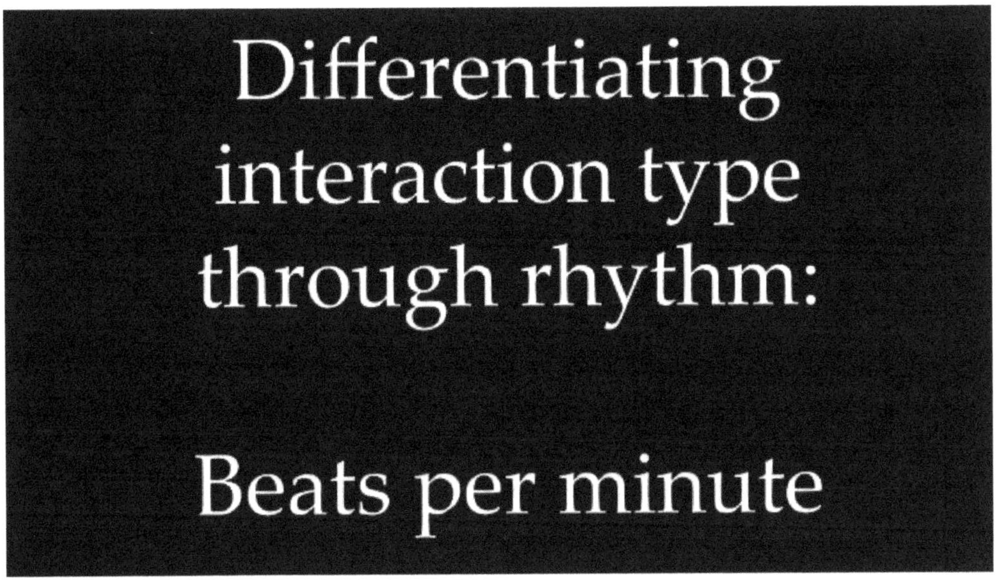

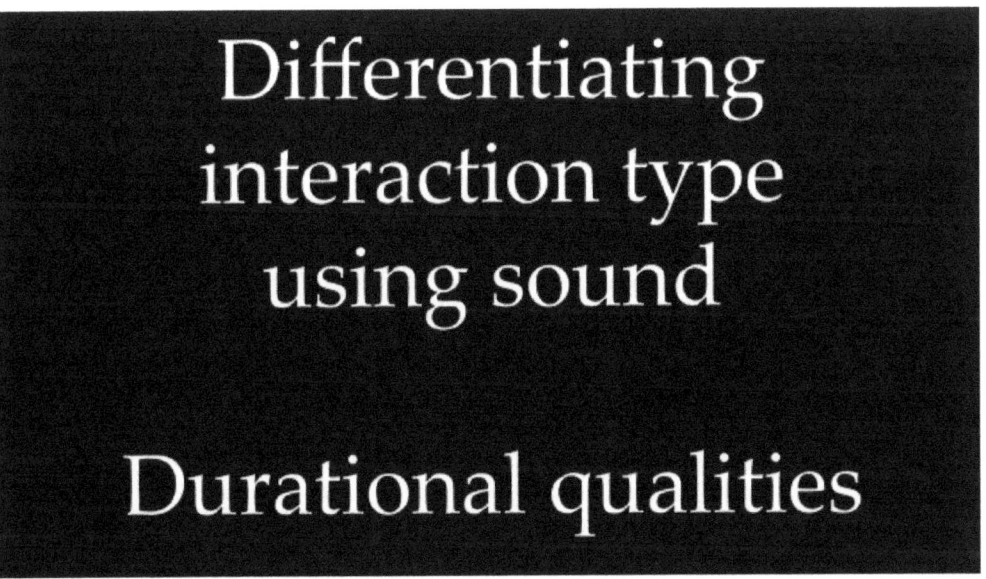

Figure 18. Differentiating interaction type through rhythm: beats per minute (video). See video at https://doi.org/10.6084/m9.figshare.25391047.v1.

Figure 19. Differentiating interaction type through time values in sound, where markers of time–extended events are used to signify durational qualities (video). See video at https://doi.org/10.6084/m9.figshare.25391044.v1.

CHAPTER 4 THE IMPORTANCE OF VISUAL SUSTAINABILITY

§. 12 *Research philosophy*

My research response seeks to circumvent ambiguity so that we may MEASURE how we interact with our built environment at a level which transcends current theoretical discourse. By measure is meant a metric able to bridge the divide between theory and practice. It needs to measure diverse types of data in the same way so that we can quantify characteristics of what's essentially an invisible phenomenon—without disturbing the inherent qualities of the phenomenon itself. The answer, as we've seen in "Visual interaction types" on page 55, is to use interaction type to measure both types of data i.e., qualitative and quantitative, categorical and continuous.

Types of interaction

I have chosen to use time values from sounds to represent these data collected because it helps me describe the time–extended events which Robbins refers to and which I observed in the interaction types taking place in the study area. It is useful also that interaction count can be measured as continuous data, while duration is, in the first instance, categorical data (a notation representing duration of a time–extended event). Duration has, I argue, the potential to invoke temporal qualities which are important in this study because they underpin Bergson's philosophy in Matter and Memory. However, for the statistical analysis, duration can also be converted into continuous data through its inherent properties as a measure of time in seconds, which is useful in regression methods where both independent and dependent values have to be continuous variables. Counts can be thought of as timestamps of events, while duration is timestamped with sounds, which I have called NOTES and these are used based on their lengths, as an ordering device in my data analysis. That is the beauty of the time value of a sound: it is a marker of a time–extended event, denoting a particular value. It is also *feeling* or transformation, existing individually as a form of measurement, but when combined together, has the potential to produce emergence (as described by Bergson's qualitative multiplicity) because together the sounds become a time–extended event able to define the quality of an urban environment in yet another dimension.

My working hypothesis is drawn from "The seeds sown by interaction" on page 27. In this study, visual sustainability is argued to be the result of emergent conditions. It is the by–product (Frankl, 2003) of the interaction we have with our surroundings. This is the argument of my study and is the basis for adopting a metric (as outlined in Figure 18 on page 69) which is

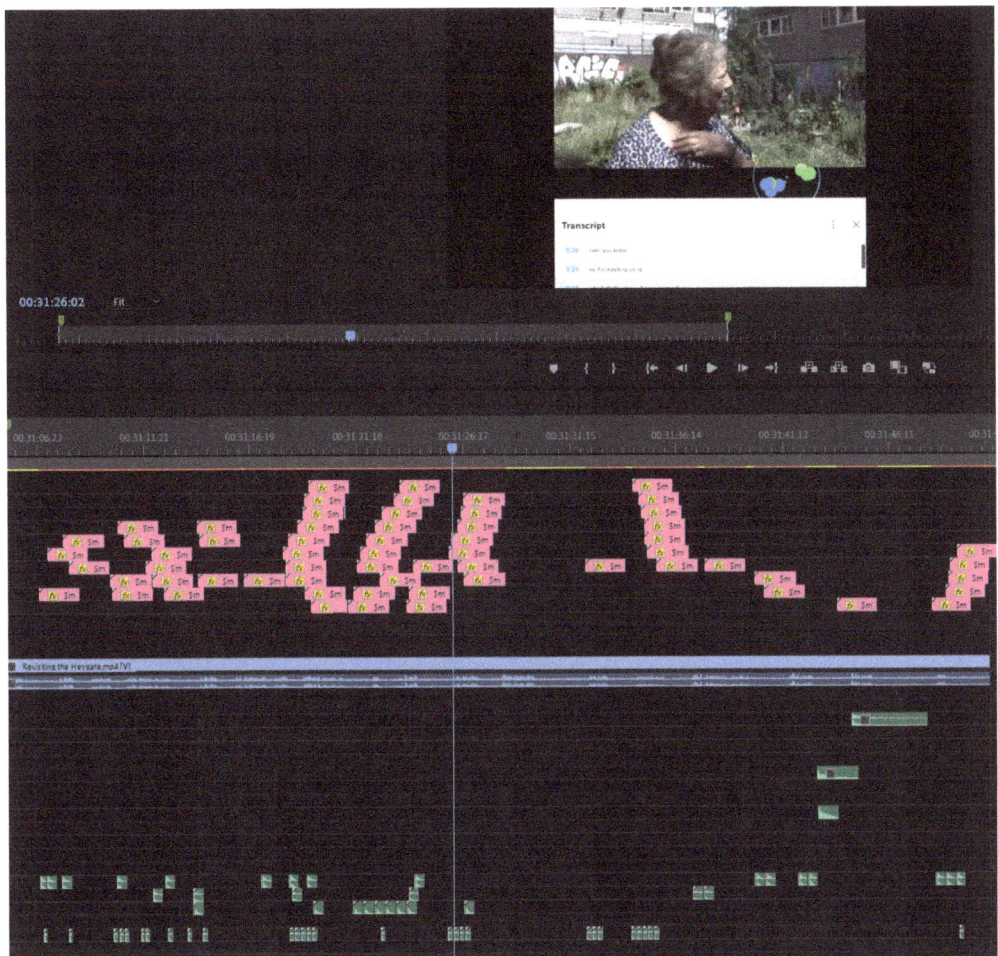

Figure 20. Interaction type analysis from YouTube video 'Revisiting the Heygate' showing timestamps as markers of a time–extended event (pink blocks).

Figure 21. Interaction type analysis from YouTube video 'Larry And Janet Move Out' with timestamps as markers of interaction types with time values as a metric (see *Appendix B* "Youtube: Larry And Janet Move Out" on page 206).

extended in its use by the influence of Bergson's theory (1988) of "temporal heterogeneity [where]... qualitative multiplicity defines the duration" (Lawlor and Moulard-Leonard, 2021, pp.8, 9) in Figure 19 on page 69. The device to measure interaction with, allows me to quantify emergent properties without needing to unpack the visual richness and meaning, which form an integral part of that emergence and, as De Landa reminds us, are dependent on interaction occurring (2012, 00:22:00). Or as Krakauer points out, for emergent phenomenon "there's no need to look under the hood" (Complexity Explorer Lecture: David Krakauer. What is Complexity? 2023, 00:17:55). Because as soon as I try to unpack and isolate visual richness and meaning "the emergent properties would disappear" (2012, 00:22:00).

The metric

My measurement therefore is to categorise type of interaction, not only by count but also by type, through its duration. This method remains true to Bergson's reasoning of temporal metaphysics in relation to matter and memory, in that the interaction types which reveals more about visual sustainability, is time. And, conversely, time is the measurement which reveals interaction, or at least, more about each interaction.

The videos (Figure 18 on page 69 and Figure 19 on page 69) show how I categorised interaction types as sound and rhythm (or beat). Both these methods describe the metric for recording interactions. This method was inspired by Bergson's theory of qualitative multiplicity and Robbins theory concerning invariance structures. There are six types of interaction which are categorised as NOTES. The six interaction types categorised as sounds being proposed in this study are:

- WHOLE (4 seconds long)
- HALF (2 seconds long)
- QUARTER (1 seconds long)
- EIGHTH (Half a second long)
- SIXTEENTH (Quarter of a second long)
- SIM (Zero seconds long)

These are also referred to in the following ways:
WH, HA, QUAR, EIGHTH, SIXT and SIM; or: WH, HA, QU, EI, SI, and SIM.

Each of these interaction types represents the time value inherent in a sound (called a NOTE) and which points to a time–extended event. Sound notes themselves are simply expressions of a language full of characters and symbols used to comprehend/measure sound, and communicate meaning. Here, in this study, they act in the same way: to comprehend/measure what we see when we experience time–extended events. By using time values, in terms of Bergson's concept of duration, to measure interaction, I was also able to differentiate more easily between two things:

- Discrete data i.e., number of interactions (count), and
- Continuous data i.e., duration of interaction (how long the engagement lasted, typically in seconds and fraction of seconds).

The types of interaction recorded are a result of observations made about people's engagement with their surroundings, evidenced in discernible head movement as proof of some form of engagement. The premise being that head movement is a strong indicator of attention levels or levels of engagement. The underlying rationale behind this premise is that engagement with the environment is almost always evidenced by the movement of a person's head, for example, in studies citing "numerous instances of gaze shifts to known targets where head movements precede eye movements in an anticipatory manner" (Daemi and Crawford, 2015; Kothari et al., 2020, p.15). And from an artist's perspective it appears to be about head movement as well, for example, Hockney remarks how Picasso's paintings, were about the observer's movement: "it's about your movement, just moving the head and so on" (David Hockney - The Art of Seeing, 2018, 00:15:40). The implication therefore is that it is an action where, as Varela et al. argue, we create the world. The act, in this case, is moving our head. I am not certain there is another method that is quite as suitable without biasing the results by making people aware of what it is you are observing, or otherwise, in ethical matters relating to a right to privacy such as interfering or making them uncomfortable. The use of technology such as visual biometrics was not considered suitable for use in this study, the shortcomings of which are outlined in "The problem with AI" on page 74 below.

The sixth interaction type named SIM (for simulacrum) is in fact a form of non–engagement and exists at both extremes of our engagement with our surroundings i.e., in the shortest and longest looks. As the name suggests, SIM (for simulated) is an indication that there has been no meaningful engagement made, no interaction has taken place in the environment, or an unknown interaction has taken place within a simulated environment, such as being engaged with a phone or tablet, or simply not engaged and daydreaming. This type of interaction is referenced as a zero value in the statistical analysis. These two extremes have also been *bracketed because our "... visual system

*Bracket: to eliminate from consideration (Merriam Webster Dictionary, 2023).

CHAPTER 4   THE IMPORTANCE OF VISUAL SUSTAINABILITY

has a built-in paradox—we must fix our gaze to inspect the minute details of our world, but if we were to fixate perfectly, the entire world would fade from view" (Martinez-Conde et al., 2004). Conversely, long stares also indicate that we're seeing with (or we're going into) such a state because there's no new information or we're swapping out memories for what's in front of us, as Ellard suggests (TEDxWaterloo - Colin Ellard - Getting Lost, 2011, 00:01:40; 00:05:00). It is one example of when an object fades from view or disappears, and we start to no longer see in Gibson's terms of direct perception. In a sense we are recollecting, or daydreaming, or fantasizing an alternate reality into existence. The same can be said of inattentional blindness (the invisible gorilla: Simons and Chabris' 1999, "Gorillas in our midst" experiment). Concentrating on the affordance of a subset of objects means that we do not see other objects that have no use to us in a particular action being performed, either virtually or as real action (as described by Bergson as well as Robbins). We always ever only see what we have 'specified' (to use Gibson's terms). In a relaxed state, it is fair to assume saccadic eye movement is accompanied by head and/or body movement. We generally do not walk around moving only our eyes. We turn our head or body (or both), even if only slightly, when we are attending to something visually i.e., when there is physical use (PU) or visual use (VU). When orienting our gaze, we generally, in a relaxed normal state, functioning routinely, look at what we want. We want something for its physical use, as an affordance or virtual action i.e., the use that we see; or we want something for its emotional value i.e., its visual use; how we feel about the use. If there is neither physical use nor visual use then we are seeing nothing in a real sense, because "objects presented during a saccade are actually invisible" (Robbins, 2006). That is arguably fertile ground to experience phenomenon such as simulacrum: something that's not real and not true. One example is seeing someone talking on a phone while walking. They are employing memory from somewhere else or are collapsed in a state of simulacrum. They are looking at something invisible, and not what's there in view. In this study therefore these observations have a zero value because there is no engagement with surrounding objects.

The problem with AI

The methods of observation should also be favoured over AI methods of visual surveillance and biometrics because observation of people's interactions with the environment requires the soft skills that are absent in machine dependent observation. By soft skills is meant the tacit knowledge which Polanyi refers to: that we understand something intuitively even if we can't prove its presence (1966; 1969). This is important, not only for interpretation and understanding

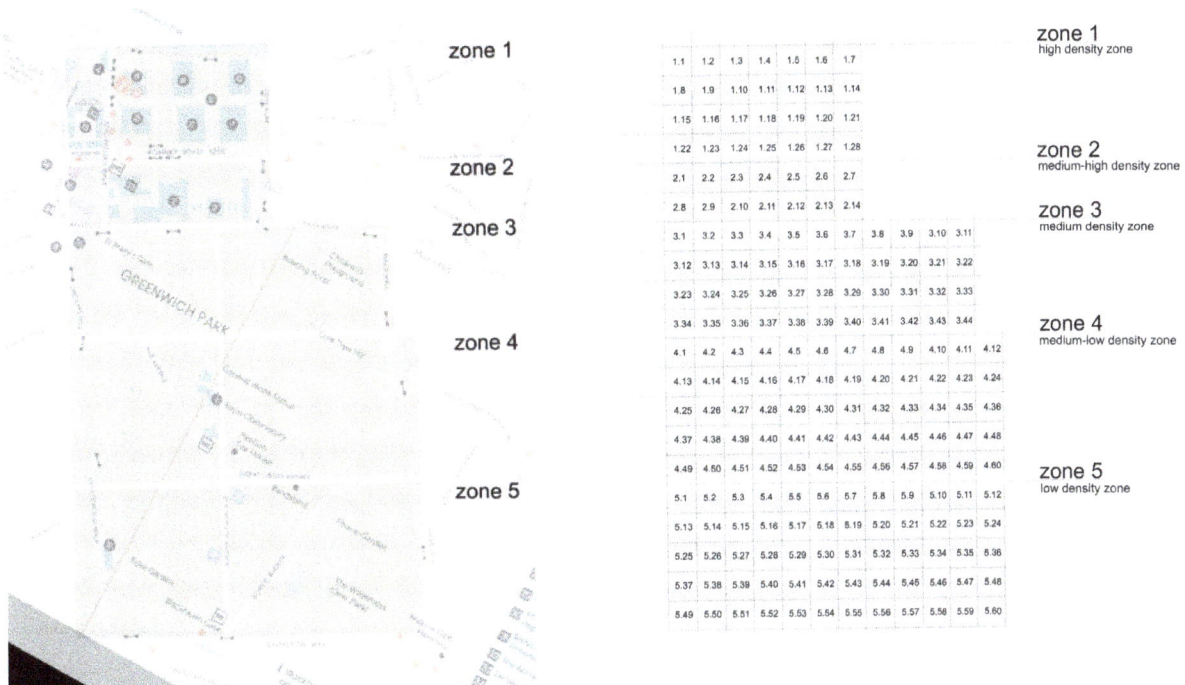

Figure 22. The study area: Greenwich Town Centre and Greenwich Park, divided into Zones and Blocks.

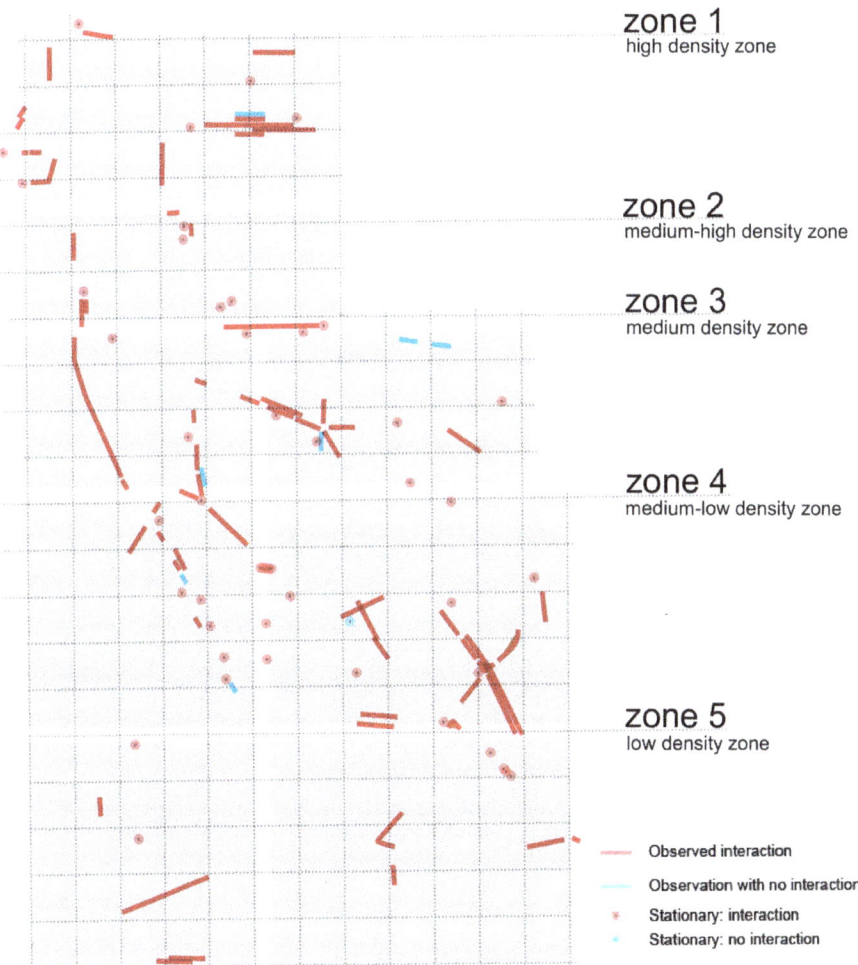

Figure 23. Study Area with observed visual interactions.

CHAPTER 4 THE IMPORTANCE OF VISUAL SUSTAINABILITY

of context out in the field while observing, but also for recall, in triangulating and analysing the footage later. Eye tracking technology and biometrics claim to provide excellent data on user engagement and emotion, and this may be useful in many types of research but are also hindered by their limitations, not least of which are ethical concerns (Kröger, Lutz and Müller, 2020). Other drawbacks include configuration and fitting, for example, having to wear headgear produces biased results due to the intrusive nature i.e., of all the tech attached to a person's body; and security concerns where for a large study area, trying to fit these to a large number of random strangers would be difficult and risky. This technology is not well suited to fast head movements and it is not able to analyse subjects whose heads are turned away. It appears to be best suited as a stationary device in front of a computer (Tam, 2019; Tobii, 2023). Most importantly, there is the weakness that, while this technology is able to produce vast amounts of data, it is lacking in, what can be described as, contextual human understanding.

Avoiding problems in data

Then there is the problem of the amount of data. I really just want to collect enough data, and too much will have been paralysing and distracting. Another important point is that I was not interested in what people looked at or the meaning of the objects or events. The fact that they were engaged with something around them for a certain amount of time is all the data I needed to understand a little more about the concept of visual sustainability (see also "Granularity" on page 55). This is based on the premise that "there are two variables (V): V1: you change the object (by defining it) P–u [Physical Use]; and V2: the object changes you (the feeling in response to your defining the object) V–u [Visual Use]" (De Kock, Pieter, 2022a).

Avoiding problems of perception

The observation carried out relies on the concept discussed, of PHYSICAL USE and VISUAL USE. If a person's head moves to look at something they do so in order to define it (PHYSICAL USE). The length of engagement after locking on to something, can be said to be a direct result, usually, of their interest in what they see; and their interest is usually governed by, or a consequence of, how they feel about what they see. This last point relates to my research philosophy — in terms of understanding interaction types in a *transect such as exists in the study area and observing head movement. The premise is that we're observing how mixing occurs between action and memory or virtual action. It appears from what has been discussed so far that action is PHYSICAL USE and memory is VISUAL USE. The logic is that any action straight after being

Transect: is a cut or path through a given environment, which essentially provides a snapshot of a range of different habitats (Deal, 2017, p.4).

alerted to something usually denotes the presence of PHYSICAL USE because we must first define it and only then are we defined by it through some form of transformation (*feeling*). This study is aligned with the idea by Bergson that our brain is simply matter: a decoder, like a telephone exchange (Robbins, 2021). It's not an encoder or homunculus. We're decoding, from the vast interference pattern that is our universe, bits from memory, redintegration, virtual action, and real action—all of which immediately become memory again. Our experience of the environment is constantly oscillating between past and present (Bergson, 1988; Robbins, 2014). Theoretical speculation about where these memories are stored, is for another day, but the argument that they are stored in our brain makes, as Robbins points out, no sense.

§. 13 *Research approach*

The research approach is informed by my research philosophy in Section 12 above. As discussed previously, a commonly used method of research involves surveys, most often in the form of a questionnaire, which, when combined with participant interviews, offers a researcher an interesting array of data to work with. It soon became evident however in my research, that I needed to focus in on another level of enquiry, one that offered an analysis into the *essence* of the problem of the act of seeing. By 'the essence of the problem,' I mean I wanted—in a way similar to adjusting a camera lens—to get the right subject matter into sharp focus. And for my research into interaction type, this meant moving away from studying people through, for example, surveys and interviews. In other words, my strategy was to observe, not people, but interaction type. In so doing I was able to take control of both qualitative and quantitative data to quickly establish a working hypothesis. This mixed methods approach enabled iterative research to take place between theoretical and statistical data. The population, therefore, being studied is interactions (not people).

§. 14 *Research design*

QUANTITATIVE DESIGN

In order to gather data about interaction type, I decided to undertake a naturalistic, covert, non–participant form of observation in the study area, Greenwich Town Centre and Greenwich Park, London. These data to be collected were the number and duration of interaction types observed, which

CHAPTER 4 THE IMPORTANCE OF VISUAL SUSTAINABILITY

would point my research towards an understanding of how it may be possible for people's engagement with their surroundings (how they were visually sustained or alienated in some way by what they saw) to inform urban design strategy. The site was divided up into five zones and 206 blocks. The zones were identified according to the density of the built environment ranging from highest density (the town centre) to lowest density (the quietest area of the park). The blocks were used to identify movement patterns in relation to location. Unobserved recordings of a people's levels of attentiveness while they are out walking in public were made from a distance. No attempt was made to identify what people looked at; or the meaning to them of what they looked at. People were not approached and remained anonymous. The people are of no interest, only the type of interaction was of interest. Subjects were adults and no distinction was made between sexes. Notes about weather conditions were made and observation took place in varying weather, during various times of the day, and following random routes through the study area. These data from the observation of people's interactions with the environment were counted and categorised using a combination of software, including the Adobe Suite, Excel, and R statistical software. The time spent in each zone was roughly equal and calculated on the following basis. In Zones 3 to 5 an average of 90 seconds was spent in most blocks every day for seven days. This equates to approximately ten minutes per block. In Zones 1 and 2, I only spent one day but here an average of ten minutes was spent in most blocks. Because my survey was focused on recording interaction type (and ultimately the mix of these types) and not necessarily count, I was not too concerned with an overly strict allocation of my time in each block/zone. But for all intents and purposes, the time spent can be said to be equal over all zones and for most blocks. I say I covered most blocks because I was reliant on interactions between people and the environment to occur from within the bounds of each block. Where there were no people, a zero interaction was recorded. Similarly, where there were people but no interaction, a zero count was entered. There was no bias in the time spent in tourist hotspots as each block received the same kind of attention.

QUALITATIVE DESIGN

These data to be collected were similar to the quantitative section, in that I wanted to collect data about the number and duration of interaction types observed in what the interviewee's *spoke* about, which would point my research towards an understanding of how it may be possible for people's engagement with their surroundings (how they were visually sustained or alienated in some way by what they spoke about) to inform urban design strategy. The emphasis in my qualitative design was on alienation because alienation is highly subjective in the sense that it belongs in Polanyi's reality i.e., as a reality internal to us which is substantiated by intuition and *feeling*. Which, as we know from sensations like pain, can be argued to be no less real than the direct perception we have of 'real' objects around us, as described by Gibson. Indeed, alienation may be argued to be a form of pain. Therefore, understanding more about visual sustainability meant that I needed to look at the subject of urban alienation where we are repulsed by our surroundings (Bhugra et al., 2019). It was impractical to attempt to discern levels of alienation in the quantitative approach because my observation method was conducted from behind the subjects and at a distance. But with the YouTube videos and interviews I was able to look for signs of alienation by not only listening to what was said, but also by watching how it was said, along with the associated body language. In order to get a better understanding of alienation, I chose a case study from an article called 'Trojans of ambiguity vs resilient regeneration: visual meaning in cities' (De Kock and Carta, 2020b) which was written jointly with Dr Silvio Carta's section 3.2 Sidewalk Labs' Quayside, Toronto. Alienation has been defined as: the discomfort we feel by the objects and events (or lack of) by which we are repelled. A process of alienation "identifies a distinct kind of psychological or social ill; namely, one involving a problematic separation between a self and other that belong together" (Leopold, 2022). Or, a simpler definition might be that alienation is *the absence of the things that we hold dear*. There can be no better account given of the effects of alienation than from the testimony of people who have experienced it first–hand. In 'Revisiting the Heygate' (2013), a video published by the 35% Campaign on YouTube, the opening and final scene are of the same person being interviewed. I used these data to measure interaction types using the same criteria as in the quantitative section, that is, using time values (NOTES) as a device to record duration of visual interaction. These data were used along with several other YouTube videos (Sheena, 2010; 35% Campaign, 2012; 35% Campaign, 2013; LSBUA, 2013; Larry And Janet Move Out, 2016) to develop themes in NVivo software. One key point is that there is a difference in the quality of data between analysing a video and analysing interaction through head movement in the study area. In the videos I was able to look at eye movement as well as head movement. As for observing people from a distance in the study area I was only able to rely on head movement (in conjunction sometimes with attitude) to record the level of people's engagement with their surroundings. So, while the videos provide me with a higher quality dataset, this equates simply to developing a more robust definition of urban alienation. My contention is that the observation carried out in the study area are as useful and, in any event, both sets of data are evaluated using the same 'durational' device: the time values (NOTES).

Summary of research approach and design

My argument for the strategy chosen to collect and analyse data is the following:
- Each block represents a certain tempo or energy (COUNT), as well as an intensity or effect (VALUE). For further explanation of my argument around these two considerations, see "Tempo or Energy" on page 83 and "Intensity or Effect" on page 83.
- When evaluating these blocks and zones, it is important to remember that they represent values 'from where we fetch our objects.' In other words, an interaction type may relate to somewhere within a block or zone, or outside of it. But the interaction, in terms of the theoretical analysis charted in Chapter Two and Three (see also Figure 3 on page 39 and Figure 4 on page 39), is satisfied in the location where the 'transaction' occurs.
- My suggestion is that, in speculating about the emergent conditions produced by visual sustainability, it appears to be produced by interaction mix, tempo (energy), and intensity (effect) as outlined below in "Supplementary Terminology and Rationale" on page 82.
- My methodology, overall, is based on the thought of people as magnets, moving around through our urban environment, able to attract data that has value 'baked in', or specific contextual properties, the idea of which aligns with Gibson's characterisation of "perception as an act of picking up information" (Ben-Zeev, 1981, p.119, citing Gibson).

§. 15 *Data collection*

QUANTITATIVE DATA

The study area summary

I divided the Study Area, Greenwich Town Centre and Greenwich Park (Figure 22 on page 75), into five zones and 206 blocks. Each zone in this urban transect represents a distinct urban environment. Each block is 68m x 68m and represents what many in urban design circles consider to be an ideal sized urban block. The different zones can be characterised as follows:

Zone 1 represents the busiest and most built–up area around the town centre. This zone includes the main commercial strip, Greenwich Market, the Cutty Sark, and the Old Royal Naval College, within which part of the University of Greenwich campus is located. The A206, a busy road, separates zone 1 from zone 2.

Zone 2 consists of more sedate historical activity such as the National Maritime Museum and Queen's House; but also includes a modern building housing the University of Greenwich on the western boundary of the study area. There is little commercial activity.

Zone 3 represents the lower part of Greenwich Park. It is also lower in topographical terms. This zone includes St. Mary's Gate, the Boating Pond, and the Children's Playground. This zone serves, in a sense, as a forecourt to the Royal Observatory complex overlooking it.

Zone 4 is distinct because of its higher elevation with views not only over Zones 1, 2, and 3 but also across the city over Canary Wharf and beyond. It is on higher ground and, except for the Royal Observatory, is much quieter than Zone 3. One Tree Hill is situated along the eastern flank overlooking Zone 3.

Zone 5 is naturally separated from Zone 4 by The Great Cross Avenue and represents the quietest area of the park, with notable features such as the Bandstand, the Flower Garden, and the Rose Garden.

Figure 23 on page 75 shows the areas where interaction was observed.

Sample size
Based on an estimated 5–million visitors to the park (Statista Research Department, 2024), my calculation is that this equates to 13,698 per day or one person per minute in every block at any one time during opening hours. I used the park figures for the entire site. I calculated that, for the duration of my observation (equating to 10 minutes per block), the entire population present was:
Zones 1 and 2: 6,787.
Zones 3 to 5: 21, 848.
Total: 28,635.

But because, I am interested in a population of interactions, not of people, the number of interactions possible per second is incalculable because there is no basis with which to determine how many times interactions occur every second of the day in humans. Therefore, for interactions, which represent an infinite population (Singh, 2023) the minimum sample size is calculated at 385 (95% confidence interval/ margin of error of 5%). In this study, however, the actual sample taken—of interaction types observed during the 8 days I was out collecting data—was 1,272.

SUPPLEMENTARY TERMINOLOGY AND RATIONALE

For the remaining analysis I will be using several expressions that describe how I reconcile my findings with Bergson's theory. These expressions include the following.

Interactions–per–minute and percentages
(see "Data Summary" on page 86).
Interactions per minute is introduced to provide a means of equal comparison between types of interaction and their location. This comparison is further enabled when data are converted to percentages. This means that in any location in the study area I can compare 'apples–with–apples.' The main elements (applied to Blocks and Zones) are:

- Interaction–minutes. This is the total video time for all interactions (which is different from the total footage).
- Interactions–per–minute. This describes and distinguishes between individual types of interaction so that I can see where certain types may be more dominant. It represents rate of interaction for all types. For example, in every minute of observed time in zone 1 (23.28 minutes) there were 19.24 interactions. *But how sustained were they?* To find that out we need to identify the type of interaction and their mix.
- Numbers and percentages for each type of interaction. For zones: interactions–per–minute–percentages are averaged as follows: 80 WHOLE's / 23.28 (interaction–minutes) = 3.43 WHOLE's per minute; then 3.43 / 19.24 (total interactions per minute) = 17%; 56 HALF's / 23.28 (interaction–minutes) = 2.40 HALF's per minute; then 2.40 / 19.24 (total interactions per minute) = 12.5%. This is the method of calculation and is repeated for each interaction type in each zone.
- The calculations are carried out to represent un–weighted data (tempo/ energy); but are also applied to weighted data (intensity/ effect) for my analysis of commercial value in "§. 21 Commercial

application" on page 124.
- For SIM (simulacrum) only the count of each occurrence is noted as the duration of these events is not a consideration in this section.

Tempo or Energy

See Figure 46 on page 123.

The premise in this study around tempo or energy refers to what the totals of each duration type (WH to SI) do to influence the rhythm of interactions which have been measured in each location. Whether, for example, a location reflects a high energy or low energy. It may also be thought of as the beat. The beat reflects the mix of interaction types: how fast or slow; and whether harmonious or discordant patterns may be distinguishable from the data. Tempo or energy may be said to generally describe physical use. We define what we see and get a 'buzz' from the use that we see. Tempo or energy may thus be considered in terms of opportunity through affordance. We are in an active state of defining things around us in terms of use and the blocks with more interaction thus reflect higher levels of tempo or energy than the blocks with less regular interactions observed.

Intensity or Effect

(applies to the commercial analysis on page 124).

The premise I am arguing for in the use of the term intensity refers to the influence or effect of a proposed spectrum of value when applied to the original data; and is also referred to as the weighted values or the weighting effect. It refers to what may be considered to be the push–pull factors that exist in any selected location. Whether, for example, a location is in *compression or tension (*see "Effect of compression and tension" on page 132).

*Compression and tension in the forces of urbanisation, see also Brenner, 2018.

The **push–pull effect lies in understanding the difference between a long look and a rapid glance. There is more value in a long look because something is demanding our attention which means that it is significant. A rapid glance appears to mean that we are not closely inspecting something. It is an interaction which can be likened to way finding, where we are simply processing information to be put to use through virtual action or real action. Intensity or effect can thus be said to describe visual use. We are defined by a *feeling*. It is how we feel about the use that see. We are energised dynamically because we are being defined and so in some locations, we feel an intensity of meaning while in others less so. The weighting of each interaction type is allocated to reflect the 'effect' we experience, of intensity of place. It is thus proposed as a more realistic reflection of what the real impact of these values

**The push–pull effect refers to the forces of urbanisation at work in cities (Brenner, 2018).

are, according to the principles of duration of engagement. The longer the engagement, the more value that recorded interaction holds for us; and the more we start experiencing meaning as opposed to use. A spectrum ranging from 0.01 to 0.99 and divided equally between the six notes is used to achieve this effect. The higher the value, the more visual sustainability may be said to exist. The spectrum employed is:

- P1: 0.99 maximum level of engagement
- P2: 0.80 high level of engagement
- P3: 0.60 medium–high level of engagement
- P4: 0.40 medium–low level of engagement
- P5: 0.20 low level of engagement
- p6: 0.01 min. level of engagement. Assumed to be always zero since it is 0.01 of a negligible amount.

These points will be explained in the context of the argument presented in "§. 21 Commercial application" on page 124.

Chapter Five
FINDINGS

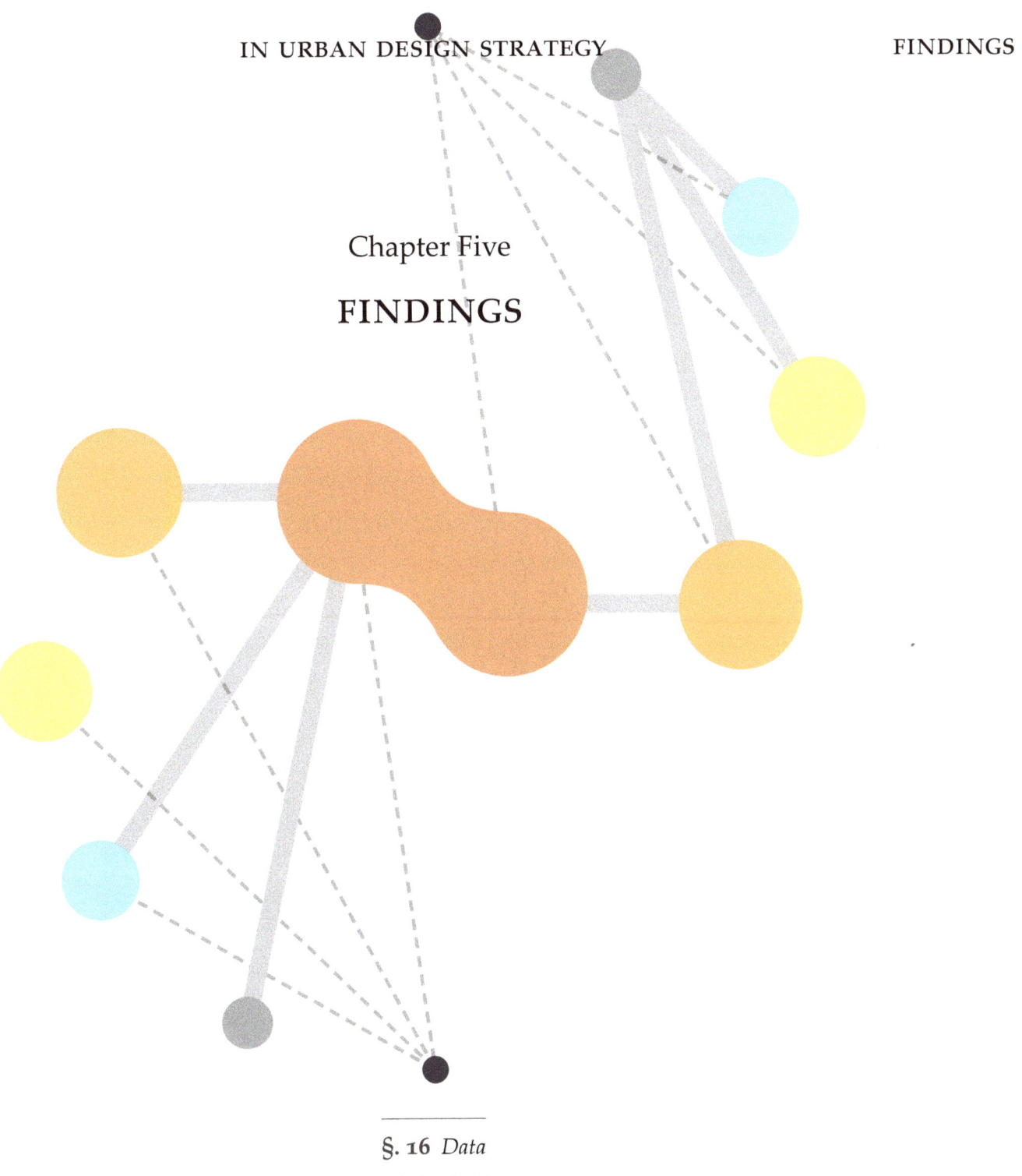

§. 16 *Data*

There are *several inferences that can be drawn from the strategy of using INTERACTION TYPE as a device to measure the relationship between urban heterogeneity and how we are visually sustained through engagement with our surroundings. My aim in this chapter is to provide evidence to support my argument that Bergson's philosophy of duration is unique in the way it reveals to us how, in practical terms, visual sustainability plays a role in urban design strategy. To understand more about how the mix of interaction type is relevant to urban design strategy I will start this chapter with an overview and summary of these data collected and will then go on to look at two themes, from the previous chapter, namely **interaction count and interaction mix.

*See "§. 22 Findings summary" on page 135.

** (see page 77, page 80, and page 83).

CHAPTER 5   THE IMPORTANCE OF VISUAL SUSTAINABILITY

DATA SUMMARY

Square pie charts

A

Over a period of eight days, 1,272 interactions were counted and categorised.

Interaction types					
WHOLE	HALF	QUAR	EIGHTH	SIXT	SIM
344	194	333	263	92	46

A. *Total number of interactions for each interaction type.*

The total number of interaction–minutes was 65.54 minutes.

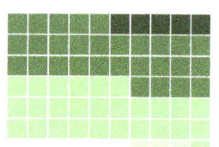

B

Interaction–minutes				
Zone 1	Zone 2	Zone 3	Zone 4	Zone 5
23.28	1.79	17.51	18.85	4.11

B. *Total interaction–minutes for each zone.*

The total interaction–minutes *per block* was quite different from 3.2 above.

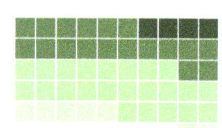

C

Interaction minutes per block				
Zone 1	Zone 2	Zone 3	Zone 4	Zone 5
0. 83	0.13	0.40	0.31	0.07

C. *Total interaction minutes per block.*

The total number of interactions per minute per zone ranged between 32.96 and 12.65 minutes. The figure for Zone 2 is inflated due to a low interaction minutes count (see 3.3 above).

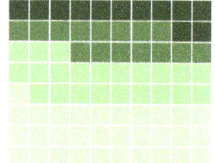

D

Interactions per minute				
Zone 1	Zone 2	Zone 3	Zone 4	Zone 5
19.24	32.96	22.10	14.85	12.65

D. *Total interactions per minute for each zone.*

Total *duration of interaction types per zone (top: seconds; bottom: minutes).

The *duration in seconds for all interaction types in each zone.				
Zone 1	Zone 2	Zone 3	Zone 4	Zone 5
635.75 (10.56)	122.25 (2.03)	814 (13.56)	595 (9.91)	84.5 (1.40)

E. *Interaction type *duration: per zone.*

E

Total *duration per interaction type (top: seconds; bottom: minutes).

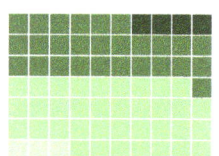

F

The *duration in seconds for all interaction types.				
WHOLE	HALF	QUAR	EIGHTH	SIXT
1376 (22.93)	388 (6.46)	333 (5.55)	132 (2.2)	23 (0.38)

F. *Interaction type *duration for the entire study area.*

Table 5. Data summary: square pie charts (LHS); tabulated data (RHS).

An equal amount of time was spent in each of the five zones. This equated to approximately 10 minutes per block (where observable interaction was practically possible). Some areas were much quieter than others (Table 5 on page 86). In Zone 2, for instance, with 14 blocks, there were 1.79 interaction–minutes recorded (SEE B); which is half that of Zone 5. But, if accounted for by block (SEE C), Zone 2 is higher in interaction–minutes than Zone 5 with 60 blocks. Zone 1 (the town centre) is the busiest at 0.83 interaction–minutes per block. Zone 2 is an anomaly and in a normal urban transect, should be in the range between 0.83 and 0.40 interaction minutes. This reflects its distinctive historical character. Generally, people were engaged with their surroundings in a meaningful way (SEE F) with WHOLE, HALF, and QUARTER interaction types dominating the landscape, in a metaphorical sense. And this is true for each zone calculated on duration percent (Table 6 on page 87) with the minor exception in Zones 1 and 5, where QUARTER interaction type beats out the HALF interaction type. What this suggests is that the busiest and quietest zones rely, for some reason, more on the QUARTER interaction type. The reason for this may be that people scan their environment for different information when in busy (Zone 1) and empty spaces (Zone 5) using the QUARTER interaction i.e., a 1–second glance.

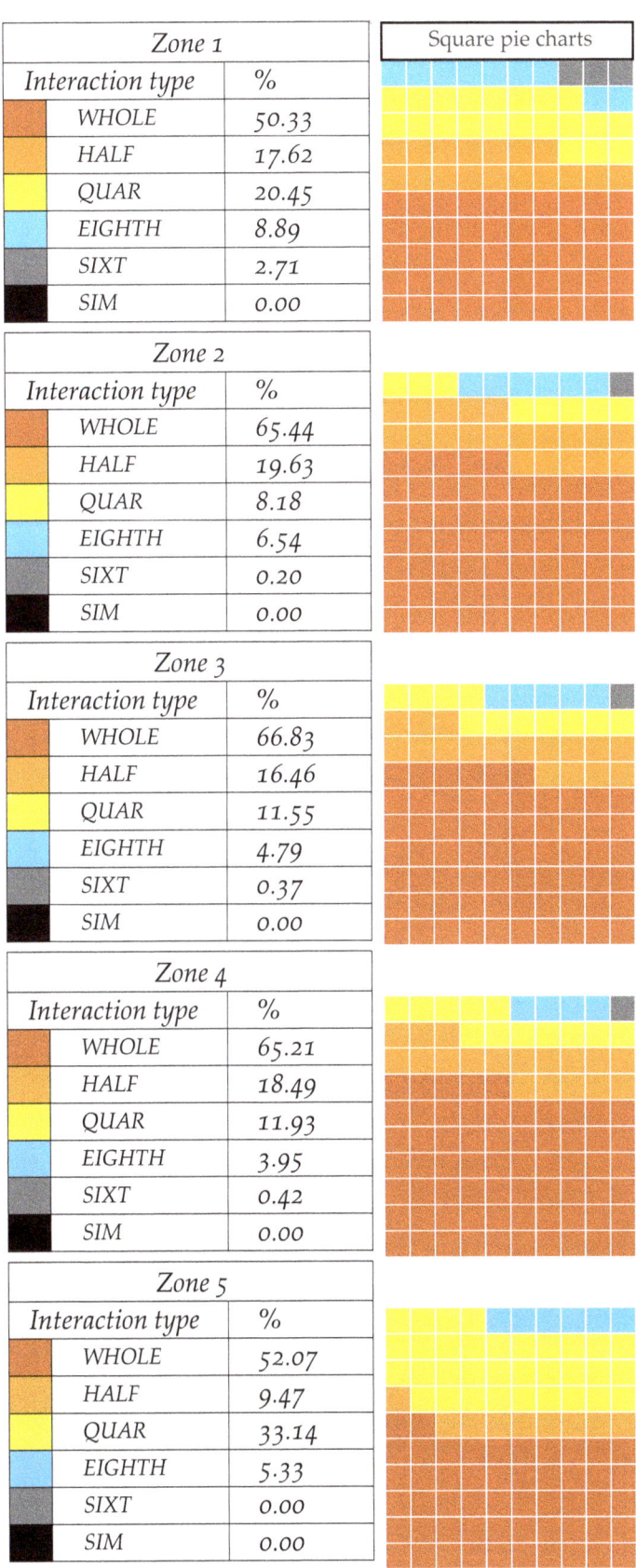

Zone 1	
Interaction type	%
WHOLE	50.33
HALF	17.62
QUAR	20.45
EIGHTH	8.89
SIXT	2.71
SIM	0.00

Zone 2	
Interaction type	%
WHOLE	65.44
HALF	19.63
QUAR	8.18
EIGHTH	6.54
SIXT	0.20
SIM	0.00

Zone 3	
Interaction type	%
WHOLE	66.83
HALF	16.46
QUAR	11.55
EIGHTH	4.79
SIXT	0.37
SIM	0.00

Zone 4	
Interaction type	%
WHOLE	65.21
HALF	18.49
QUAR	11.93
EIGHTH	3.95
SIXT	0.42
SIM	0.00

Zone 5	
Interaction type	%
WHOLE	52.07
HALF	9.47
QUAR	33.14
EIGHTH	5.33
SIXT	0.00
SIM	0.00

Table 6. Percentage duration of interaction type, per zone.

CHAPTER 5 — THE IMPORTANCE OF VISUAL SUSTAINABILITY

In my overall analysis I have adopted a two–pronged approach. The first approach analyses the dataset in its entirety, focusing on data COUNT. The second approach excludes the SIM variable and purges the dataset of all blocks where the sum of an entire row is zero. Here the goal is to better understand the MIX of interaction types. There will be some overlap when discussing each approach. Pie chart A (Table 5 on page 86) is helpful in describing the relationship between the observed interaction types across the entire site. The transect is dominated by the WHOLE and QUARTER types (4–second and 1–second interactions). The half–second glance is next (type EIGHTH) followed by the 2–second look (HALF). But in terms of the time spent engaged, pie chart F reveals how the site is dominated by the 4–second look (WHOLE) which makes sense since it is a lasting engagement, for example, lasting twice as long as HALF. What is interesting is that the 1–second glance is strongly represented when seen in the context of WHOLE and HALF types. As a site–wide *time–extended event, WHOLE and HALF provide us with a sense of the 'personality' of the study area because it has what may be described as good energy ("Tempo or Energy" on page 83). We can infer from this that people are generally actively engaged with their surroundings by way of the interaction *count*.

*Time–extended event: refer to Robbins (2014, 2021).

In Table 6 on page 87) I have noted (in the data summary page above) how the QUARTER type appears to be over–represented in zone 1 (in relation to HALF) and that this imbalance (in what I expected as an even gradation of interactions from end to the other) is more acute in zone 5. What this signifies is that people in zones 1 and 5 rely more on a 1–second glance for some reason — in the site's busiest and quietest urban areas. The question is, *if QUARTER is a pattern of statistical significance (or even if it is not), could this responsiveness indicate the possibility that virtual action (Bergson) plays a role in people when occupying most and least active (and presumably stimulated) urban areas?* By virtual action I mean in the sense described by Bergson, where people prepare for action in their mind, let it go, then prepare again — in experiencing a sort of 'fight or flight' impulse as they process objects and events around them: over–stimulated in the busy area (fight) and under–stimulated in the quiet area (flight). The QUARTER type thus appears to broker some effect and represents what can be thought of as an early warning, because, while both scenarios are acceptable in their current state, the warning is that if either case is taken to an extreme, alienating conditions are more likely to occur in these two zones, leading to alienation in people (see "§. 12 Research philosophy" on page 70 which describes the effect of 'zoning out' through too short or too long a duration of interaction).

Pie charts B, C, D, and E relate to the urban qualities of each zone. I have accepted the anomaly of Zone 2. It exists as a mild form of simulacrum because it represents history on a pedestal, so to speak. In other words, the history of this area is not seamlessly integrated into the rest of the urban. This is because it is divided by the main road and is fenced off in a significant way, such that it exists as a 'little island full of monuments'. This is not a criticism, only an explanation about why I consider Zone 2 to be more different than it should be in relation to its location in the *transect. If we discount Zone 2, the remaining zones appear to be normally distributed for a transect, that is, there is, as intuitively expected, a fairly even gradation (in a hierarchical sense) of the types of interaction (duration and count) from one end to the other.

Transect: is a cut or path through a given environment, which essentially provides a snapshot of a range of different habitats (Deal, 2017, p.4).

§. 17 *Hypothesis test*

Null hypothesis: WHOLE = HALF = QUAR = EIGHTH = SIXT

UNDERSTANDING THESE DATA
Overview of direction taken

The type of quantitative data is discrete (interaction count); while the level of measurement is ratio (Stevens, 1946) and not interval because it has an absolute zero point. Interaction count is organised into one of six categories of INTERACTION TYPE. These TYPES are also referred to as NOTES because they represent duration in a time–extended event and are referenced as follows: WHOLE (WH), HALF (HA), QUARTER (QUAR/QU), EIGHTH (EI), SIXTEENTH (SIXT/SI), and SIM. When referring to duration these data are continuous since they can be measured in seconds and parts of seconds.

This count data has a low (zero) mean and distribution which is not normal. In Figure 24 on page 91, I compare the histograms of these data collected in three ways. The first way (LHS) is to take a look at the distribution of *all* these data and how skew these data are. Secondly (Middle), with zero rows omitted, the overall shape of the histogram is similar to the first. The number of times there were zero interactions is therefore still a factor in the non–normal distribution of data but less so. Thirdly (RHS), with the zero rows omitted and a log transform carried out, these data take on a more normal distribution. This is important because, when considered along with the requirement only for the residuals to be normally distributed, it allows me to analyse relationships between variables later on, using linear regression. It became clear early on that my data were best analysed using a

CHAPTER 5   THE IMPORTANCE OF VISUAL SUSTAINABILITY

non–parametric method called the Kruskall–Wallis test. I then realised that to account for the overwhelming number of zero values I should look to Poisson regression to produce a more balanced outcome. This then led me to some final testing using the zero–inflated Poisson (ZIP) and then finally, the zero–inflated negative binomial (ZINB) regression methods to account for the excessive zeros.

Mix of interaction types

The focus is generally on establishing how the mix of interaction type at various scales of analysis (individual, blocks, and zones) is influential in our experience of our surroundings and what that might mean in relation to the *non–linear characteristics of complexity theory. For the analysis of MIX of interaction types (see also page 102), the strategy adopted was to omit all the blocks where no interactions were observed. This does not mean no data exist in these areas but simply that, in my random walks with camera in hand, I did not come across any people interacting with the environment in any of those locations. While the zero values are important data (especially in, for example, comparing and projecting count between zones), the reason for discounting all the zero rows is because I am interested in the relationship between the categories i.e., the mix of data, not in the relationship between different areas, for example, between different zones. This avoids, for the time being, having to deal with highly dispersed data which requires a method known as zero–inflated negative binomial regression analysis to deal with the highly skewed data that many zeros produce. I initially compared the median values of each variable as it is more reliable than comparing the means because the means would be influenced by the extreme values produced by outliers. The box plots in Figure 25 on page 91, describes these data in terms of their median values. On the left–hand side, the entire dataset is displayed. To get a better picture of these data I excluded, in the box plot on the right–hand side, zero rows and the SIM variable. The result is a much clearer view of the relationship between median values of the remaining five variables. The implications for the null hypothesis stated at the start of this section are discussed below. However, it is reasonable to suggest at this point that the variables do not appear to be the same.

Descriptive analysis

In my initial analysis I checked the following general assumptions before proceeding with the tests:

- These data are not normally distributed, although the residuals appear to be normal enough.

*Complexity theory, non–linearity, and emergence versus top–down organised complexity, see also (Batty, 2007; Batty and Marshall, 2012; Reading Ancient Minds: Metaphor, Culture, and Complexity, 2012; Ortman, Lobo and Smith, 2020). See also: (Batty, 2007; Batty and Marshall, 2012; Reading Ancient Minds: Metaphor, Culture, and Complexity, 2012; Ortman, Lobo and Smith, 2020).

```
> shapiro.test(Observation_KEEP_0_AdjCols_3.long$INT)

        Shapiro-Wilk normality test

data:  Observation_KEEP_0_AdjCols_3.long$INT
W = 0.292, p-value <2e-16
```

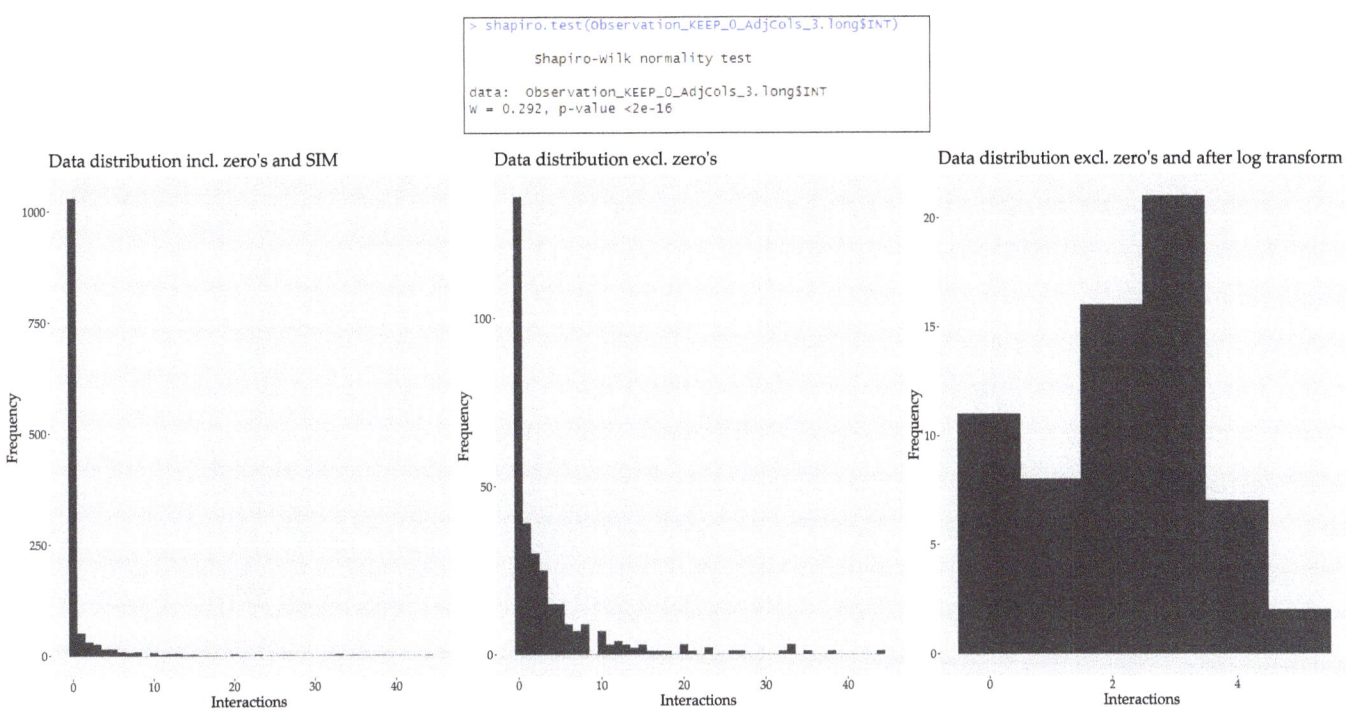

Figure 24. Histograms: LHS: incl. zeros, SIM; Middle: excluding zero rows; RHS: excl. zero rows after log transform.

```
> data_summary_VAR
  NOTES NOTES_Total NOTES_Mean NOTES_StDev
1  WHOLE         344    1.66990      4.0083
2   HALF         194    0.94175      2.7473
3   QUAR         333    1.61650      5.2743
4 EIGHTH         263    1.27670      4.8636
5   SIXT          92    0.44660      3.3195
6    Sim          46    0.22330      1.3210
> |
```

```
>         data_summary_VAR
  NOTES NOTES_Total NOTES_Mean NOTES_StDev
1  WHOLE         344     5.2923      5.6561
2   HALF         194     2.9846      4.2408
3   QUAR         333     5.1231      8.4178
4 EIGHTH         263     4.0462      8.0242
5   SIXT          92     1.4154      5.8226
> |
```

```
>        print(kwTest)

        Kruskal-Wallis rank sum test

data:  Observation_OMIT_0_AdjCols_3.long
Kruskal-Wallis chi-squared = 43.6, df = 1, p-value = 3.9e-11

> |
```

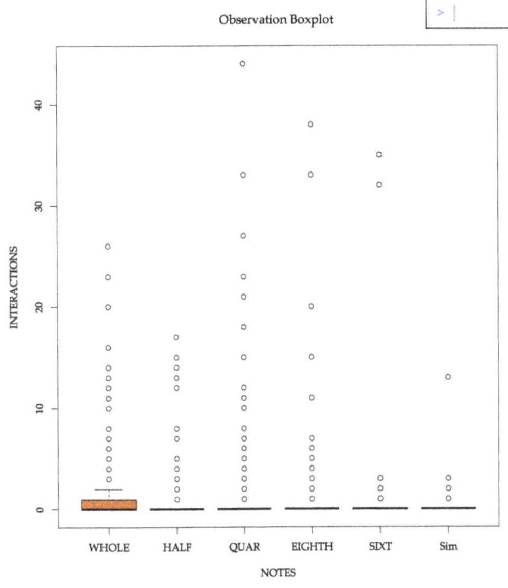

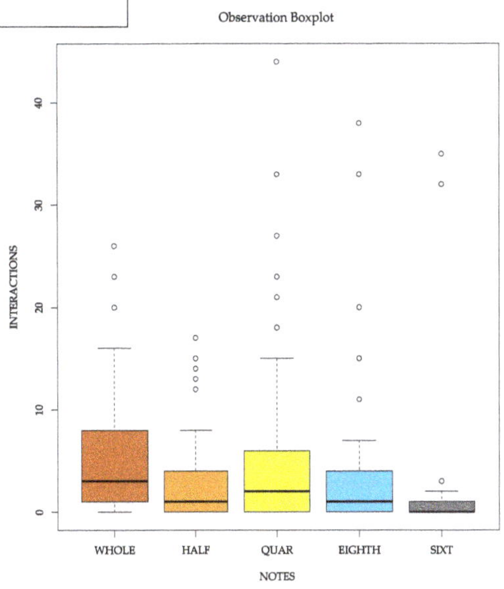

Figure 25. Boxplots. LHS: including zero rows; RHS: excluding zero rows and SIM.

- The interactions are chosen at random and independent of each other (their values are not related to one another).
- The population (interaction) variances are not the same for all groups.

I also tested for normality of residuals and the residuals reflect a normal–enough distribution. Unless otherwise noted, the following descriptive tests were done on data where blocks of rows with zero values were omitted, and a log transform operation had been completed.

Shapiro test and standard deviation

The Shapiro–Wilk test (a non–parametric test to check for normal distribution of data) was statistically significant (p = 0.004538) which means that these data do not fit a normal distribution. The implication of this result is that it affects the types of tests which are most appropriate to use as the analysis proceeds (for example, for the variables comparison and regression tests) because, for example, normal parametric tests require a normally distributed sample population.

As for the variability in these data, Figure 25 on page 91 (the top right table) shows the Standard Deviation (SD) for the interaction types. This test looks at how spread out these data are in relation to the mean. As can be seen, there is greater variability in the QUAR and EIGHTH interaction types which suggests that these data are more random. There is also similarity between WHOLE and SIXT types. The HALF type appears to be most compact of all. The mean values indicate a difference from the rest in at least three types: HALF, EIGHTH, and SIXT. Because the spread of data is an indicator of how sure I should be of the estimates i.e., there is less certainty in the accuracy of more wide–spread data, the QUARTER and EIGHTH interaction types (in the comparison excluding zero rows) appear to be less convincing than the others.

95% Confidence Interval (CI) for the average interaction

To try to understand the statistical significance of these data I then proceeded to establish the confidence interval to see how representative the sample I had taken was of the entire population of interaction types. With a mean of 5.9515 (data excluding SIM) and standard error of the mean of 0.49419, the confidence levels were: lower 4.9819 and upper, 6.9210 (two tails because either trending towards visual sustainability or towards alienation). The confidence interval does not include zero, therefore the null hypothesis should be rejected because there appears to be an effect between interaction types. The precision of my results based on the sample size of 1,226 interactions (excluding SIM) over an area of 206 blocks, can thus, within the lower and upper range stated above, be stated with 95% certainty and, within these parameters, is therefore statistically significant.

Inferential analysis

Based on the results of the Shapiro test, I chose the Kruskal–Wallis non-parametric analysis (also known as a one–way ANOVA on Ranks) because with these data I had, it was the most appropriate test to perform *to avoid results being significantly impacted by outliers*. It is also the test used when the distribution of data is not normal. My decision was based on the following conditions:

- There is one variable with one or more groups.
- Continuous data (Interval/Ratio).
- Three or more groups.
- Skewed data (these data were skew even if the residuals appeared normal enough).
- The presence of outliers.

The result is that the probability of an observed result assuming the null hypothesis is true, is less than 0.05% (see Figure 25 on page 91 where the p–value is less than 0.05). This means I can reject the null hypothesis and conclude that, from this test, there *is* a difference between the mean ranks of all the groups in this test. I then decided to perform a parametric test, using a one–way ANOVA as these are considered very robust tests to compare multiple group means simultaneously. A one–way ANOVA is appropriate for the analysis of a continuous quantitative discrete variable (interaction count) at the ratio level of measurement. In this test I had to be aware, however, that the results can be significantly impacted by outliers (which I had in my data). Nevertheless, I was interested to see whether the results were similar to the Kruskal–Wallis test in terms of the p–value significance. The resulting f–statistic was also <0.05 (0.00452). This, like the Kruskal–Wallis test, confirms, therefore, that there is sufficient evidence to reject the null hypothesis at the 5% level.

HYPOTHESIS SUMMARY
Null hypothesis: WHOLE = HALF = QUAR = EIGHTH = SIXT

The following describes the null hypothesis:
- Interactions are evenly distributed and thus have no effect on visual sustainability or of being visually sustained in the act of seeing.
- The mean of the interaction is the same for the five types of observed

interactions.
- There is no difference in the way we interact with the environment, for these five types of interaction.
- Visual sustainability consists of an even spread in the type of interaction we experience when engaged with the environment.

Alternative hypothesis: WHOLE ≠ HALF ≠ QUAR ≠ EIGHTH ≠ SIXT
The following describes the alternative hypothesis:
- Interactions are *not* evenly distributed and thus *have an effect* on visual sustainability or of being visually sustained in the act of seeing.
- The median and mean of the interaction is not the same for the five types of observed interactions.
- There is a difference in the way we interact with the environment, for these five types of interaction.
- Visual sustainability consists of an uneven spread in the type of interaction we experience when engaged with the environment.

Decision
- At least three of the medians are not equal. They represent something else; thus, there is a difference.
- While generally, the inter quartile variability is similar, there are differences in the means between the five types of interaction.
- The f statistic for both parametric and non–parametric statistical tests is < 0.05.
- The null hypothesis is therefore rejected. The statistical evidence, based on these data collected, is that the types of visual interaction we have with our surroundings is significant in the act of seeing and has an impact on our experience of the built environment.

SECTION DISCUSSION

The study of Bergson suggests that we see with memory, but it is inconclusive about how we might be interacting with our environment in one respect: *do we interact equally, or in other words, is the attention we pay to the things around us, indiscriminate; and thus, discriminated only afterwards, in our memory of it?* It is by understanding more about the number of interactions and length of these interactions that we may be able to understand more about what visual sustainability might be and how visual sustainability plays a role in urban design strategy. Based on my rejection of the null hypothesis, we do not appear to look at things around us in the same way. WHOLE and QUAR interaction types are approximately similar to one another. The same is true for HALF and EIGHTH. But these two sets of data are quite different from each other. And SIXT appears to be different from them all and infrequent. Confounding perhaps is that it is more difficult in the observations carried out, to differentiate interactions that only last one sixteenth of a NOTE long i.e., 0.25 seconds. However, one might argue that quick, jerky movements of one–sixteenth of a note, would be even more obvious and thus at least equally observable. I believe the latter to be more probable of the two explanations and therefore it should be as observable as any of the other interaction types, especially when reviewing the footage in Adobe Premiere Pro. Perhaps it is simply a case that—in this particular study area—SIXT interaction types occur less often in people's day–to–day interactions with their environment because they are more visually sustained.

SECTION CONCLUSION

We should reject the null hypothesis that visual sustainability consists of an even spread in the type of interaction we experience when engaged with the environment. The next step in my research is to look more closely at the differences in the variables and what significance to attach to these differences. To help me do this I will, in Part Three, look at the following:

1   Variability in these data collected.
2   Interaction mix.
3   A variables comparison.
4   Non–linear correlation.
5   A digital tapestry.
6   Commercial relevance.

PART THREE

§. 18 *The dataset in its entirety*

By rejecting the null hypothesis, I was able to continue and do a variables comparison. But first I needed to consolidate my understanding of these data. I started by looking at the spread of interaction type as follows.

1 Variability in data collected

Distribution

In Figure 26 on page 99 we can see from the histogram of the *entire* dataset (with x--axis for the number of interactions and the y–axis, how many there are of them) that there is not a normal distribution and that the number of zeros that are zero is disproportionately high. This is not unexpected since in many blocks there were either zero interactions observed; or there are always zero interactions in that block, for example, in visually inaccessible terrain. A summary of these data revealed a median of 0.0 and mean of 6.175 (including SIM). The variance was 335.00. The variance is therefore more than the mean which indicates over–dispersed data. Over–dispersed data were a factor when deciding between testing methods in the next stage of evaluation.

Linear characteristics

In seeking to determine whether a linear relationship exists, I am interested in the relationship between zone and interaction count because, in one sense, location influences the interactions we have with our environment; but there is also the notion that the number of interactions we have, influences the location which we are in; by which is meant the value of the location (see also Table 7 on page 125). In this section, however, what I am interested in, is how location (blocks, precincts, zones) influences the number of interactions we have with our surroundings. I am therefore interested in the predictors for the number of interactions observed. The predictive variables, as far as location is concerned, are blocks and zones, and these two variables will be tested. The count data were skewed by the large zero values which means that these data need to be analysed using a Poisson's regression model or if confirmed as over–dispersed, a zero–inflated negative binomial test (ZINB).

Interaction type characteristics

*Complexity theory, non–linearity, and emergence versus top–down organised complexity, see also (Batty, 2007; Batty and Marshall, 2012; Reading Ancient Minds: Metaphor, Culture, and Complexity, 2012; Ortman, Lobo and Smith, 2020). See also: (Batty, 2007; Batty and Marshall, 2012; Reading Ancient Minds: Metaphor, Culture, and Complexity, 2012; Ortman, Lobo and Smith, 2020).

Figure 27 on page 99 provides more information about this dataset in terms of the effect of interaction type on interaction count. There does appear to be a general trend downwards from WHOLE to SIM in the compact range (as indicated by my red line) which supports the integrity of the concept of a healthy urban transect where WHOLE is most dominant across the site and SIXTEENTH, the least. It is a pattern which may suggest a scaling relationship between interaction type and interaction count, possibly even of a statistically significant power law which is typically identified in non–linear events found in *complexity theory. In Figure 28 on page 99 we can get a better idea about how each of these interaction types are represented in each *zone*. QUARTER and EIGHTH appear to be most spread out in every zone (so it appears to be a less accurate description), while WHOLE appears to be fairly narrowly distributed in every zone (meaning I can have more confidence in the accuracy of these data). Types SIXT and SIM are compact but because of the low counts, it's hard to tell whether I can attach any importance or significance to their distribution. The green lines indicate how the zones differ in character. For example, WHOLE and

HALF behave as we would expect, with a gradual decreasing level of interaction as building density decreases in each zone. But QUAR (1 second) and EIGHTH (0.5 second) are unique, in the sense that, for the compact area (i.e., the more accurate data), these interaction types appear to *increase* as building density *decreases*. This is quite strange, but one explanation is that the more isolated we become the faster our type of interaction, generally speaking, becomes.

We could also generalise for Zones 1 to 5 in the QUARTER and 1 to 5 in the EIGHTH by including the *entire* range of values (the compact area as well as the spread out points) and in that case, the behaviour is similar to Zones 1 to 5 in the WHOLE and 1 to 5 in the HALF i.e., a decrease in interaction matches the decrease in building density. Compare this to Figure 29 on page 99 where we can observe the differences in count, by interaction types but this time by *Block* (1 to 206). The overall effect in the blocks (Figure 29) is similar to the spread of data for the zones (ignoring the different vertical and horizontal scales between that of Figure 28). We should expect this similarity as it is the same data, but the zones appear to provide a better read of what is going on (because the blocks are ordered from left to right in rows and so mask the true effect up and down between zones).

Interim summary 1

So far we have seen how:
- The QUARTER type (yellow) appears to act as an early–warning device for alienating conditions.
- The null hypothesis, that interactions are evenly distributed and thus have no effect on visual sustainability or of being visually sustained in the act of seeing, can be rejected.
- A pattern has emerged which is suggestive of a scaling relationship between interaction type and interaction count. Whether it is a non–linear phenomenon (as seen in complex systems) is inconclusive so far.
- Higher counts of WHOLE and HALF interaction type coincide with areas of higher urban density/activity, but for the compact range of data of QUARTER and EIGHTH the opposite is true.

Interaction types: Poisson model
Understanding these data in the context of the number of zeros

The underlying requirements for a Poisson regression model are that it is suitable for count distributions (such as these data I have collected) where there are many zero values and where my mean for all these data is close to zero. The interactions observed occurred randomly and independently of each other, and the integers are all non–zero. There is no requirement for

CHAPTER 5 THE IMPORTANCE OF VISUAL SUSTAINABILITY

the predictor variable, for example, there can be one or more predictors and they can also be continuous, discrete e.g., counts, or categorical data, but the most important area to look at is the coefficients. For this I will be using interaction count as my y–axis (dependent or response variable) and fitted along the x–axis (independent or predictor variables) will be the interaction types WHOLE to SIM. It was helpful for the following reasons (see Figure 30 on page 101).

- Firstly, we can see the effect of each of the independent variables and they were all significant because their p–values are less than 0.05 (red highlight).
- Secondly, the negative value (green highlight) for interaction type SIXT indicates that the more SIXTEENTH interaction types there are in a block, the less there is of the response variable (on the y–axis) i.e., the count (the number of interactions observed), which in this case means, the fewer interaction types are observed overall. For all the other interaction types, the values are positive and so the more there are of them, the more (count) interactions there are overall. In other words, where there are these short 0.25 second interactions active in a location, we can expect fewer number of overall interactions. The effect on the urban of the presence of the SIXTEENTH interaction type is a key point to think about when we later consider the effects of INTERACTION MIX, because the overall hypothesis is that interaction type mix is an indication of the existence of levels of sustainability. And so here we see evidence of the 'reflection pool' where we see ourselves reflected in the invisible city, because one type of interaction negatively influences the existence of all of the other types, in other words, we behave negatively in some areas and the report card for that behaviour is full of 0.25 second glances. It reflects the behaviour of people who are uncomfortable or repelled by what they are seeing and want to leave the area as quickly as possible. As a reminder, the premise is that the upper range of interaction types proposed in this study (WH, HA, QU) are indicative of conditions of higher levels of visual sustainability; while the lower range (EI, SI, SIM) are symptomatic of lower levels of visual sustainability, as shown in Figure 33 on page 103 as well as from the results of the qualitative analysis described in Chapter Four. But too recap, from our initial look at these data at the beginning of this chapter, we know that QUARTER doesn't seem to behave in the way we expect of the upper range, so the upper range really consists of the two types: WH and HA.

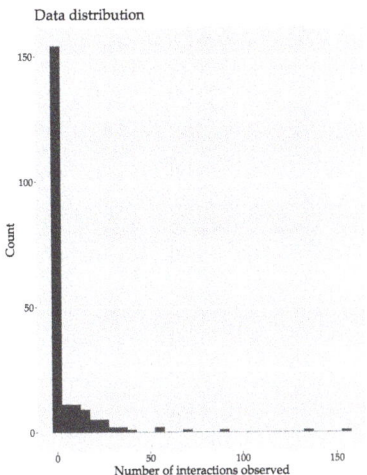

Figure 26. Distribution: histogram of interaction count.

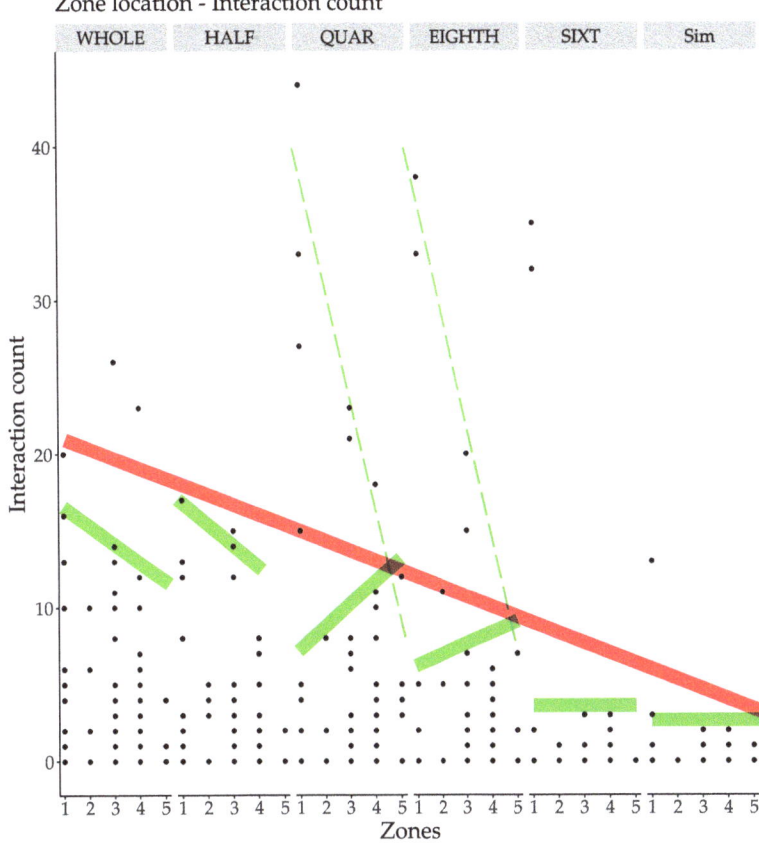

Figure 28. Interaction type characteristics: spread by zone.

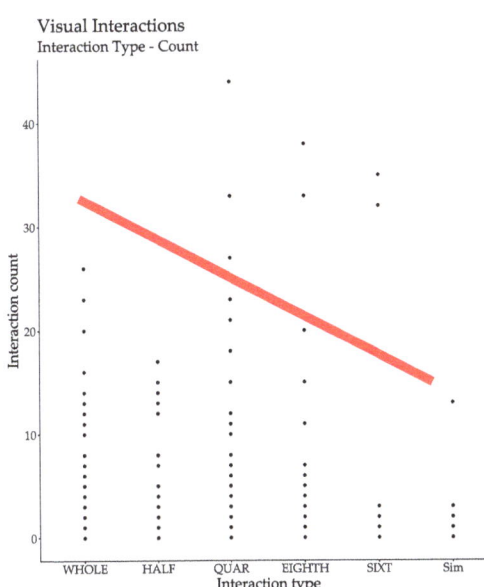

Figure 27. Interaction type characteristics: spread by count.

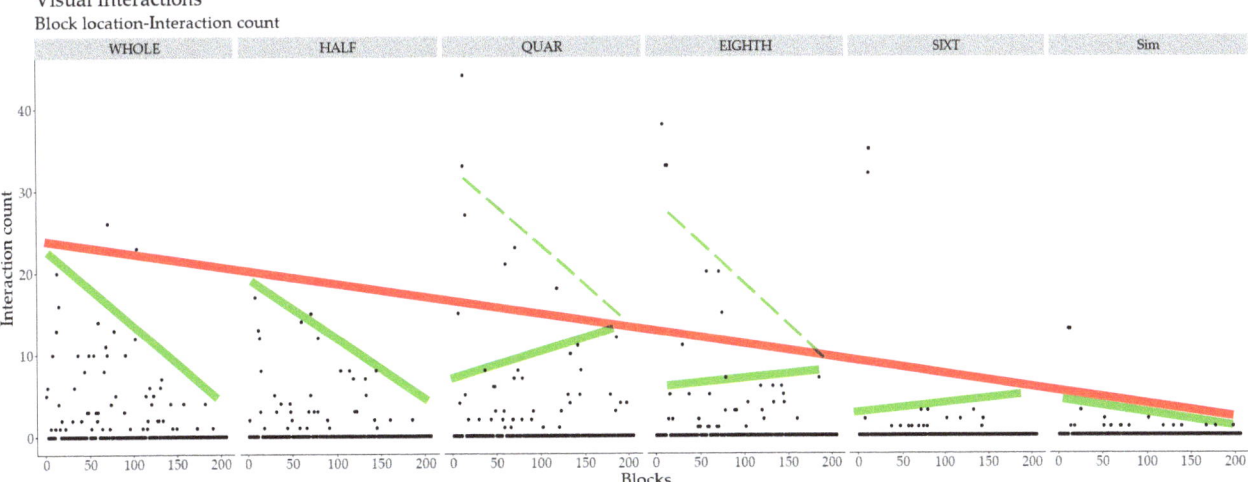

Figure 29. Interaction type characteristics: spread by block.

- And thirdly, the Poisson regression results also confirmed that these data are over dispersed by quite a large amount (the residual deviance divided by degrees of freedom is more than 1). What this means is not that it changes the estimate but that the standard error will be underestimated i.e., the p–values will be extremely small (which they are) and there is a likelihood a false positive. And because the mean is not equal to the variance (which is most likely caused by the excess number of zero values in these data i.e., zero–inflated) it was necessary to account for this difference in dispersion using the zero–inflated negative binomial (ZINB) regression method.

My attempts to run a zero–inflated Poisson (ZIP) regression, or the zero–inflated negative binomial (ZINB) regression, on the full set of interaction types was unsuccessful, using the R package 'pscl'. The error produced is known to R users (see for example: Stack Overflow, 2017) and might be due to outlier(s) or the lack of variation in variables i.e., too close to zero. However, by eliminating the lower spectrum of interaction types (EIGHTH, SIXTEENTH, and SIM) I was able to produce a regression without error. This proved less useful for comparison purposes. But when applying these two tests to the study area's ZONES (instead of the BLOCKS) the results were inclusive of all these data. So, the predictive variable used about the number of interactions observed, is *zones* and the test for this follows.

Interaction zones

Negative binomial (NB) versus zero–inflated negative binomial (ZINB)
In the negative binomial and zero–inflated negative binomial regression tests (which are suitable for the count data I have) I wanted to understand the significance of these data in terms of the study area's zones by taking into account the excess zeros. These tests break these data up into two parts. The blue vertical line in Figure 31 on page 101 is for the count, ignoring the excess zeros. The yellow vertical line in Figure 31 is the logistic model result for the zero inflation, where it changes the odds of a zero being an excess zero. The software then splits the zero values into two: between what it judges are the true zero interactions that took place during my walks, and the interactions that were always zero and therefore excess in my data. It then discards the excess zeros and returns the true zeros into the analysis. The conclusion reached is the following.

- The residuals appear to be approximately zero, meaning that the quality of fit is acceptable (see purple highlight Figure 31 on page 101).
- The predictor 'Zone' in the part of the negative binomial regression model predicting number of interactions (count) is a significant predictor

```
Call:
glm(formula = Interactions1 ~ WHOLE + HALF + QUAR + EIGHTH +
    SIXT + Sim, family = "poisson", data = Observation)

Coefficients:
             Estimate Std. Error z value Pr(>|z|)
(Intercept)  0.805530   0.045572  17.676  < 2e-16 ***
WHOLE        0.040073   0.007138   5.614 1.97e-08 ***
HALF         0.120209   0.013204   9.104  < 2e-16 ***
QUAR         0.048795   0.006567   7.430 1.09e-13 ***
EIGHTH       0.028478   0.006407   4.445 8.79e-06 ***
SIXT        -0.115723   0.028517  -4.058 4.95e-05 ***
Sim          0.235483   0.066319   3.551 0.000384 ***
---
Signif. codes:  0 '***' 0.001 '**' 0.01 '*' 0.05 '.' 0.1 ' ' 1

(Dispersion parameter for poisson family taken to be 1)

    Null deviance: 4562.8  on 205  degrees of freedom
Residual deviance: 1247.6  on 199  degrees of freedom
AIC: 1537.8

Number of Fisher Scoring iterations: 6
```

Figure 30. Poisson model: used to understand the data containing so many zero values.

```
R 4.1.3 . ~/

Call:
glm.nb(formula = ObservationBLOCKnos$Interactions1 ~ ObservationBLOCKnos$Zone,
    init.theta = 0.1181165144, link = log)

Deviance Residuals:
    Min      1Q  Median      3Q     Max
-1.1219 -0.8911 -0.8028 -0.1592  1.5389

Coefficients:
                         Estimate Std. Error z value Pr(>|z|)
(Intercept)                3.8533     0.5780   6.667 2.62e-11 ***
ObservationBLOCKnos$Zone  -0.6658     0.1540  -4.322 1.55e-05 ***
---
Signif. codes:  0 '***' 0.001 '**' 0.01 '*' 0.05 '.' 0.1 ' ' 1

(Dispersion parameter for Negative Binomial(0.1181) family taken to be 1)

    Null deviance: 155.47  on 205  degrees of freedom
Residual deviance: 140.23  on 204  degrees of freedom
AIC: 780.03

Number of Fisher Scoring iterations: 1


              Theta:  0.1181
          Std. Err.:  0.0171

 2 x log-likelihood:  -774.0330
> ObservationBLOCKnos.zinb1 <- ObservationBLOCKnos
>     ObservationBLOCKnos.zinb1 <- zeroinfl(ObservationBLOCKnos$Interactions1 ~ ObservationBLOCKnos$Zone, link = "logit",
dist = "negbin" )
>     summary(ObservationBLOCKnos.zinb1)

Call:
zeroinfl(formula = ObservationBLOCKnos$Interactions1 ~ ObservationBLOCKnos$Zone, dist = "negbin", link = "logit")

Pearson residuals:
    Min      1Q  Median      3Q     Max
-0.4556 -0.4015 -0.3480 -0.1547  5.2180

Count model coefficients (negbin with log link):
                         Estimate Std. Error z value Pr(>|z|)
(Intercept)                4.1248     0.5308   7.770 7.83e-15 ***
ObservationBLOCKnos$Zone  -0.5170     0.1547  -3.341 0.000834 ***
Log(theta)                -0.8565     0.3849  -2.225 0.026075 *

Zero-inflation model coefficients (binomial with logit link):
                         Estimate Std. Error z value Pr(>|z|)
(Intercept)               -0.5271     0.5729  -0.920    0.358
ObservationBLOCKnos$Zone   0.1985     0.1431   1.387    0.165
---
Signif. codes:  0 '***' 0.001 '**' 0.01 '*' 0.05 '.' 0.1 ' ' 1

Theta = 0.4247
Number of iterations in BFGS optimization: 10
Log-likelihood: -384.5 on 5 Df
>   AIC(ObservationBLOCKnos.nb3, ObservationBLOCKnos.zinb1)
                            df      AIC
ObservationBLOCKnos.nb3      3 780.0332
ObservationBLOCKnos.zinb1    5 779.0826
> 779.0826
```

Figure 31. Negative binomial (NB) model versus zero–inflated negative binomial (ZINB) model.

[0.000834 ***] (red highlight, Figure 31 on page 101), which means that 'Zone', as a predictor variable of the number of interactions observed, is therefore significant.

- The predictor 'Zone' in the part of the logit model predicting excessive zeros, is not statistically significant [0.165] (blue highlight, Figure 31 on page 101) which indicates that there is a 16.5% chance that zone is not meaningful as a predictor in the zero–inflation part of the model i.e., the odds it has generated about which zeros are true and which zeros can be discarded.
- For these data, the expected change in count for a one–unit increase in interaction is –0.5170 (green highlight, Figure 31 on page 101). I initially thought that this suggests an overall decline in the projected observations for each zone in terms of the actual dataset but this coefficient is only a description of the negative binomial part only, ignoring the zeros (i.e., the non–zero values). Therefore, in the negative binomial part ignoring the zeros, the zone count will increase by -0.5170 for every one unit increase in the response variable i.e., the interaction count, but that does not mean the counts in my *actual* dataset will change by that amount.

Interim summary 2

We can now also see how:

- The more SIXTEENTH interaction types there are in a block, the fewer other interaction types are observed overall. This appears to confirm that the role played by alienation is highly influential where the SIXTEENTH interaction type is dominant.

§. 19 *Reciprocity in data*

2 Interaction mix

Interaction mix stems from the idea of reciprocity (page 22) and discussed throughout the first couple of chapters. The *mix* of interaction types is important because it might be the key to understanding visual sustainability as an emergence and provide grounds for a practical application of principles in urban design strategy. In Figure 32 on page 103, we see the distribution in each zone of the five interaction types WH, HA, QU, EI, and SI. The colours to take notice of, in terms of whether urban design strategic intervention is required, are the blue and grey colours because where these are dominant the premise in this study is that levels of visual sustainability are low (see black dashed outline, Figure 33 on page 103). Conversely, the two orange colours indicate

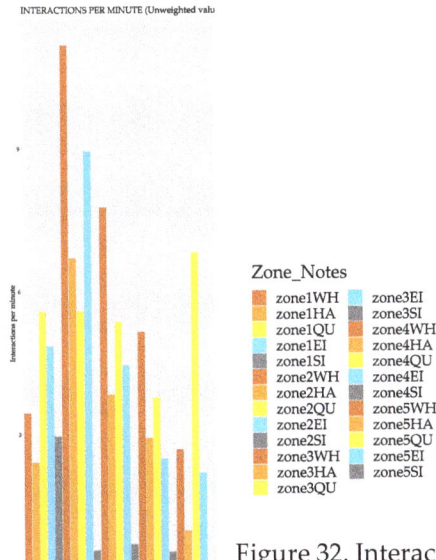

Figure 32. Interactions per minute in each zone. Zone 1 is high density; Zone 2 medium–high; Zone 3 medium; Zone 4 medium–low; Zone 5 is low density.

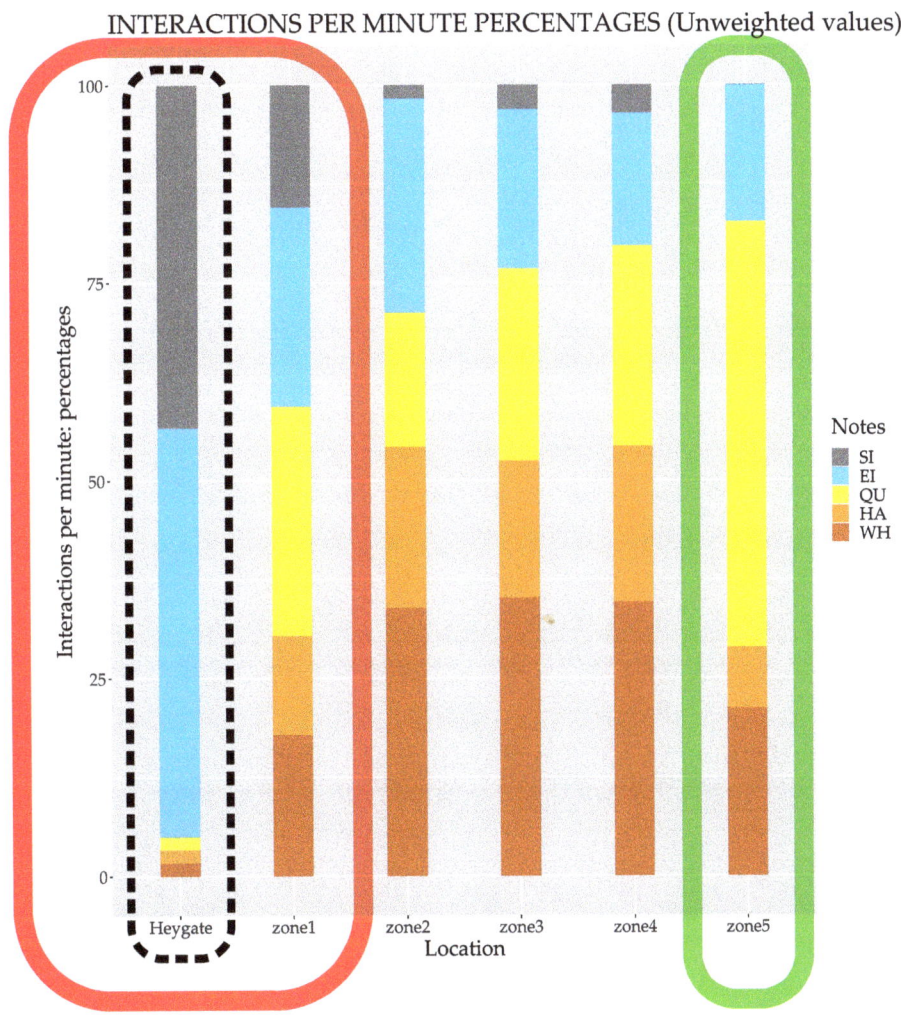

Figure 33. What is alienation? A depiction of conditions of alienation (far left dashed black outline) can be compared with each of the five zones in the study area.

CHAPTER 5 THE IMPORTANCE OF VISUAL SUSTAINABILITY

good levels of visual sustainability because they signify a more engaged relationship with the surroundings, while the yellow, as we have seen ("Interim summary 1" on page 97), appears to be a predictor of alienating conditions. The highlighted area in Figure 33 on page 103, provides us with a visual explanation of what alienation looks like in terms of interaction mix. This stacked chart summarises the findings from the qualitative study into alienated urban conditions (Figure 20 on page 71 and Figure 21 on page 71). If we compare this visually with zones 1 to 5 of Figure 33, visual sustainability appears to improve from the (comparatively speaking) high–density town centre (Zone 1) towards the lower–density areas of the study area (Zones 2 to 5). Zone 1 has the most representative spread of interaction types but Zones 3 and 4 have what is arguably the most balanced with a good upper range (dark and light orange) and less influential lower range (blue and grey); while in Zone 5—the quietest zone—we can see (as we did in Table 5 on page 86) how dominant the QUARTER (1–second long) interaction is in relation to the HALF interaction type. *What does this mean*? The suggestion from Figure 33 on page 103, is that zones 2, 3 and 4 reflect the most balanced mix of interactions with diversity thatpoints to good levels of urban heterogeneity. Whereas, in Zone 1, there is a good representation of the SIM interaction type, which means no discernible engagement at all. The implication for Zone 1 is that comfort levels are quite reduced and stress levels heightened—most likely due to the noise, overcrowded pavements, and traffic—as the trend towards alienation grows. There is also a disproportionately large representation of the QUARTER interaction type when compared to HALF (which I have covered in "§. 16 Data" on page 85). As for Zone 5, there appears according to my premise of a subtle trend towards alienation, to again be an over–representation of the QUARTER interaction type.

Figure 34 on page 105, shows the mix of interactions in terms of how they vary within each block, for every block of every zone. What appears to be evident is that every location varies from every other in terms of what I posit as levels of visual sustainability. It is important to note that these stacked charts in Figure 34 vary in scale along the y–axis for each zone and are intended to show only the relationship of interaction types *within* each block, and not between blocks. In this depiction the yellow and blue colours are of interest for the following reasons:

- The yellow quarter (1–second) interaction type appears to be able to influence a shift in either direction in informing us about the levels of visual sustainability.
- The blue EIGHTH (half–second note) shows us where our interactions

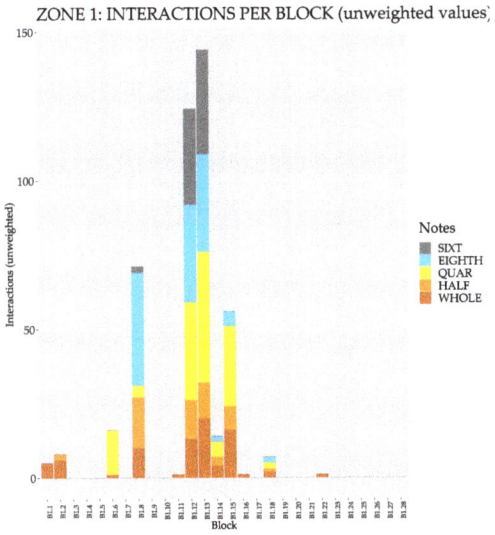
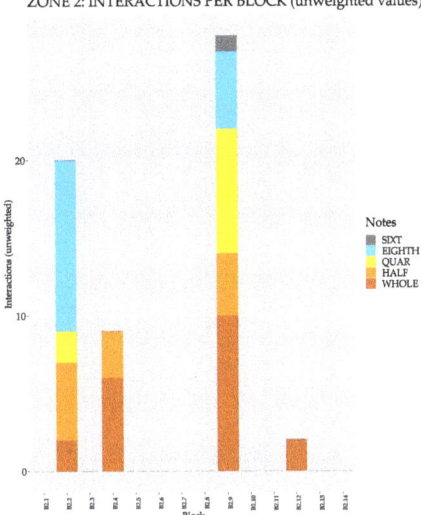

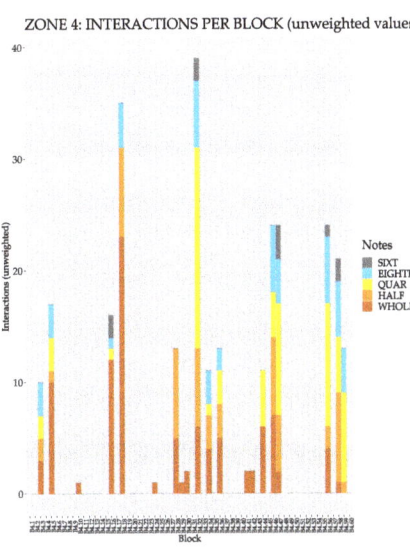
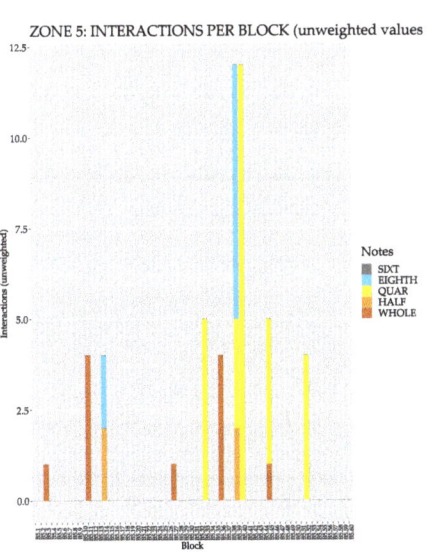

Zone 1 reflects counts of up to 60 EI and SI interactions (blue and grey). Compare this with the other zones 2 to 5, which range between 5 and 15. This indicates that higher density areas such as a town centre support alienating functions which we generally try to avoid engaging with. Un–weighted interactions in this study represent the tempo or energy of a location.

These stacked charts vary in scale along the y–axis for each zone and are intended to show only the relationship of interaction types *within* each block, and not between blocks.

Figure 34. A visual description of the relationship between interaction and location. This shows the distribution of interaction types at the block level, for each zone.

- become faster and by implication, less engaged.
- We can infer with a certain amount of confidence that on their own they (blue and yellow colours) are visual indicators of an urban of declining quality, as people become less and less engaged in a meaningful way. This is simply based on the premise that something cannot be meaningful if we do not pay attention to it for any length of time. It does not mean that we are not visually sustained in these areas but that there's an overall tendency of wariness in shorter glances.

In Figure 35 on page 107, we can see what appears to mostly represent a fairly healthy mix of interaction types in each block of each zone. Here the interaction types are presented as percentages of each other and therefore the relationship between variables (interaction types) are easier to interpret. But, again, there are some places with a conspicuous amount of yellow and blue. We can see also how, in most cases, the interaction types in the upper range of oranges (WH, HA) are dominant in what is posited, are conditions of high visual sustainability.

To summarise: dominant blue and grey colours are strong indicators of areas where interventions may be required in the urban fabric because these colours appear to be consistent with levels of alienation. In my study area, however, there do not appear to be any concentrated areas of alienation.

Pairs plot

The pairs plot (Figure 37 on page 109) shows the relationship between blocks and each interaction type (black dashed outline). In this illustration (as we have seen in Figure 27 on page 99 through to Figure 29 on page 99) WHOLE interactions appear to be most evenly distributed across the study area; with the other types showing a proportionately reduced influence over the blocks. See Figure 42 on page 119 for a spatially accurate representation of these areas of influence. This scaling dynamic or hierarchy between interaction types can help explain the existence of what I refer to as push–pull factors that exist in blocks as a result of the dynamics at play between these interaction types. In explanation of this we need only remember how we may have felt in certain parts of the city when compared to other parts. The differences are the dynamic I am referring to. This 'push–pull effect' that I refer to helps explain the possible existence of forces of compression and tension in the study area: between what we are willing to pay attention to (compression) and what we try to avoid and move away from (tension). This can be argued

IN URBAN DESIGN STRATEGY   FINDINGS

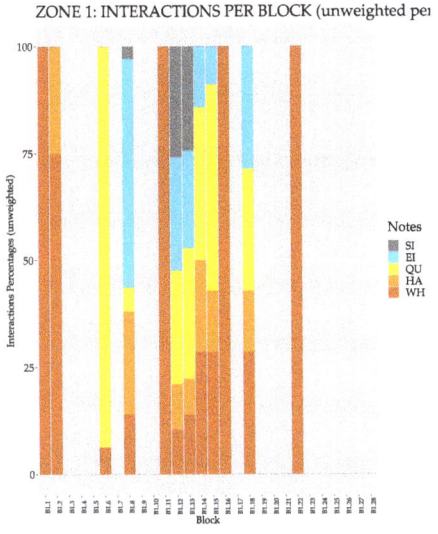
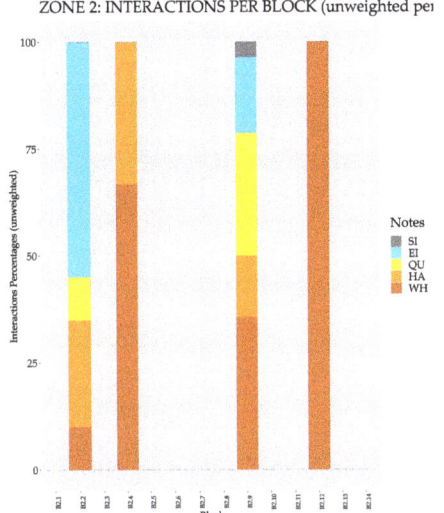

A percentage–style visualization provides a clearer picture of the relationship between upper and lower range interaction types. The predominance of oranges and yellow describe a study area full of visually sustainable engagement with the environment. With the exception of Zone 4, there is also a presence of alienating conditions – as suggested by the blue and grey of the lower range of interaction types.

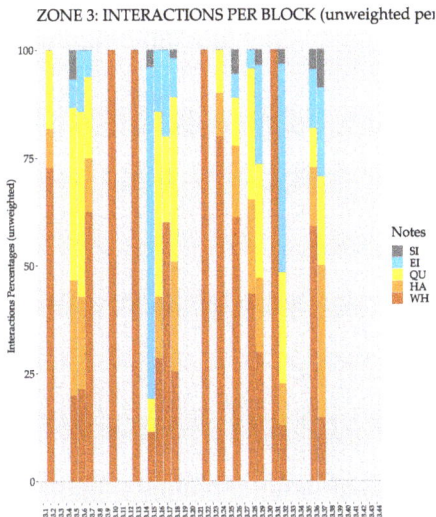
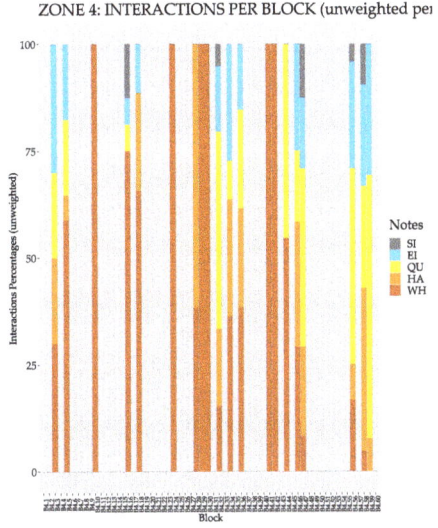

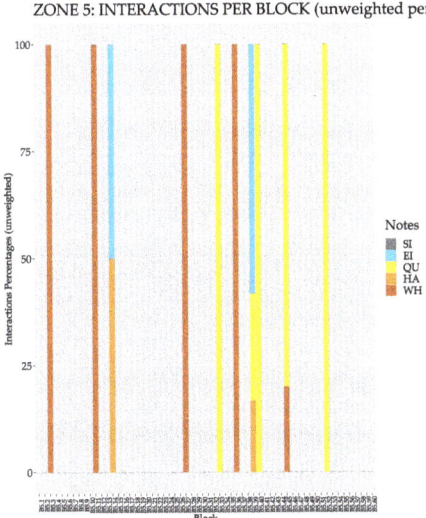

Figure 35. A visual description of the relationship between interaction and location. This shows the interaction percentages per block, for each zone.

to influence commercial value (see "§. 21 Commercial application" on page 124). The relationship between the interaction types themselves is also of interest in this pairs plot (red outline). The strongest connection appears to be between WHOLE and HALF; while HALF and QUARTER; and QUARTER and EIGHTH share a similar but reduced spread of data. These relationships are further discussed in the variables comparison below and in Figure 38 on page 111.

§. 20 *The building block*

3 Variables comparison

The second characteristic of interaction type I would like to look at in trying to better understand the relationship between interaction types and their potential (in the right mix) to produce an emergence which I am referring to as visual sustainability, is the variables comparison. I analysed the relationship between variables using the Wilcoxon Rank test which is compatible with the Kruskal–Wallis test used earlier ("Inferential analysis" on page 93). I am interested in the effect of six grouping variables (WH to SIM) on the number of interactions (interaction count). In a Wilcoxon Rank test, I have looked at interactions as the dependent variable (DV) in relation to the independent variables (IV) which are the six interaction types (WH to SIM). My reasoning for this is that interaction type (the length of engagement) appears to affect the interaction count, which I am interpreting as the level of interest associated with a location. Thus, for the 'R' analysis:

Interactions (count) = WHOLE + HALF + QUAR + EIGHTH + SIXT + SIM interaction types.

My contention is that the level of interest (by people in interacting with their surroundings) that is associated with a location, influences, not just the count but the mix of interaction types. In other words, strong interest in a collective sense, shown in a block or zone, is produced by a mix of a diverse range of interactions—mostly from the upper range of interaction types i.e., WH, HA. What I am looking for is whether the 'secret' to visual sustainability lies in the mix. This is because the upper range is a register of thoughtful engagement. And the reason for this is that, as a general rule, it is entirely logical to suggest that there can only be limited considered, meaningful thought in the most fleeting of engagement with one's surroundings. The results of the pairwise comparison (Figure 38 on page 111) shows that there is a significant difference in the following pairs i.e., $p = <0.05$:

WHOLE–HALF 0.017; WHOLE–EIGHTH 0.010; WHOLE–SIXT 3e–07; WHOLE–SIM 3e–07; HALF–SIXT 0.006; HALF–SIM 0.007;

QUAR–SIXT 0.001; QUAR–SIM 0.001;

EIGHTH–SIM 0.010; EIGHTH–SIM 0.010

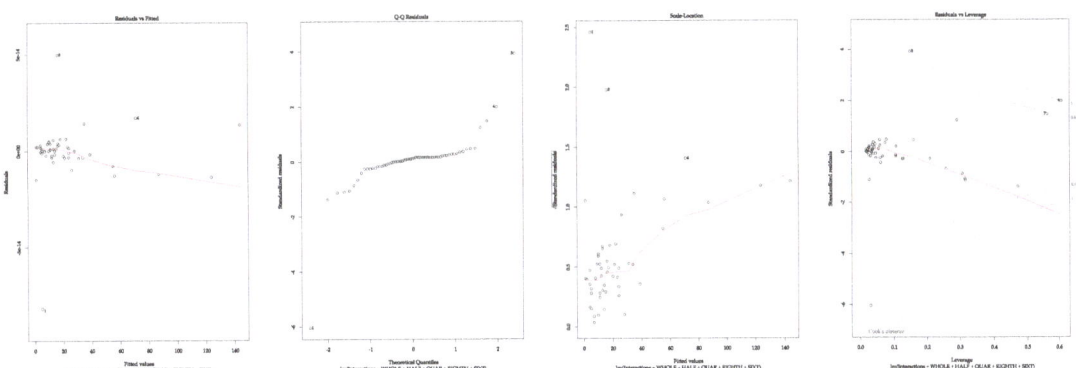

Figure 36. Linear model diagnostics plot to check for violations of the assumptions of linearity, homogeneity of variance and normality of residuals. The data appear to be conducive to further analysis using regression methods.

The fitted values in Figure 36 on page 109 (far left) appear to be a random pattern which indicates a linear relationship between interactions (count) and interaction types. In terms of leverage (far right) there do not appear to be any points outside Cooks, and thus no influential outliers that may be overly influential.

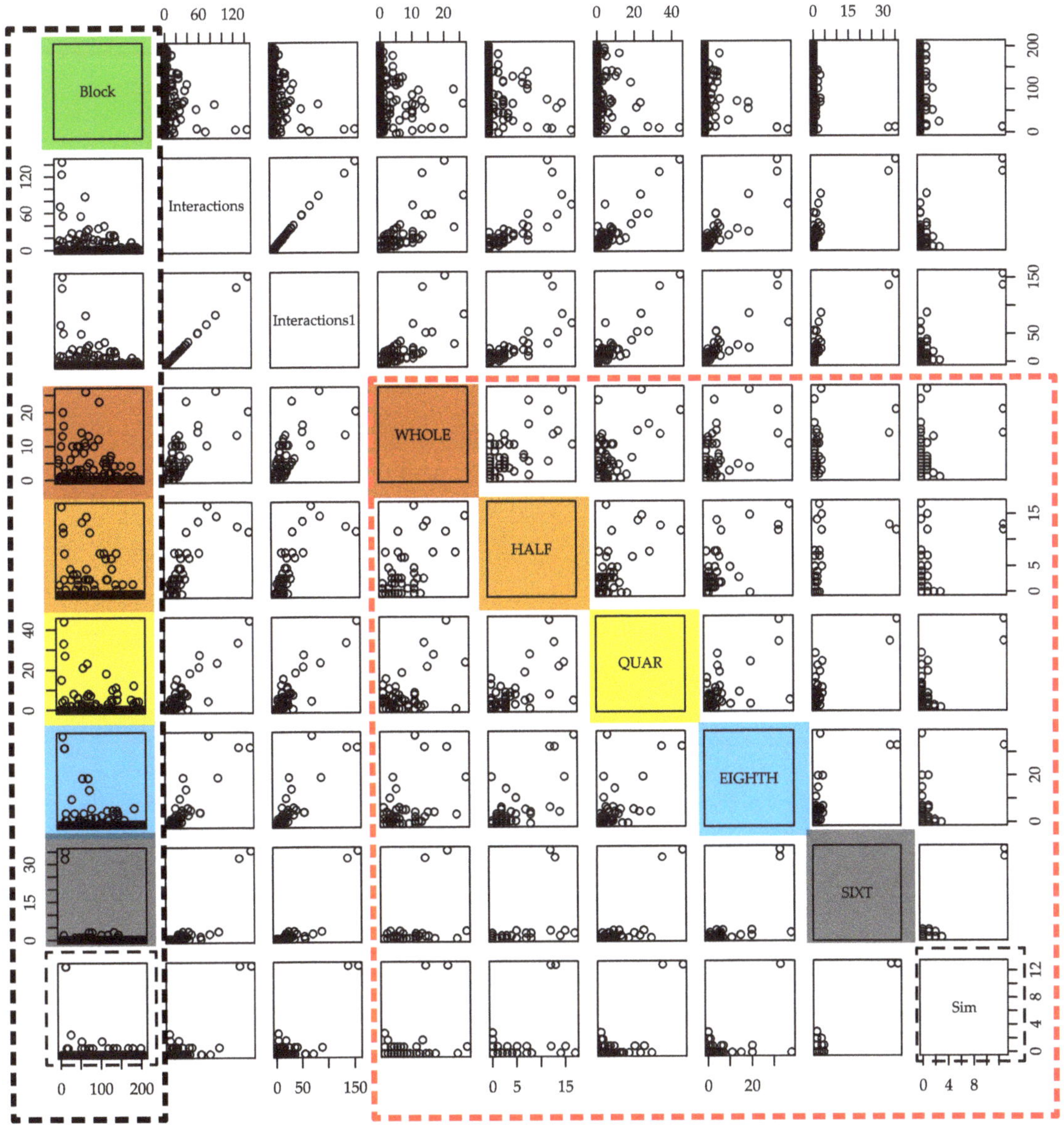

Figure 37. Pairs plot between blocks and each interaction type.

CHAPTER 5   THE IMPORTANCE OF VISUAL SUSTAINABILITY

What is telling about this result is that there is no significance in the relationship between WHOLE and QUARTER or HALF AND QUARTER. This then confirms my initial findings that QUARTER as an interaction type which goes against the trend, as shown in Zone 1 and Zone 5 (Table 6 on page 87 and Figure 33 on page 103). Instead, QUARTER appears to enjoy a significant relationship with SIXTEENTH and SIM (see Figure 38 on page 111). The 1–second glance thus appears to be a signifier or marker of lower levels of visual sustainability, which makes sense because it appears to be an interaction trending towards alienation. The implication is twofold: 1. That we look out more and more for objects and events that satisfy our demand for comfort/security in the quietest zone: Zone 5. So, if I am interacting with my surroundings in a way that seeks to be reassured that I am safe and oriented properly, then the trend is towards conditions of alienation. The sense is then that the QUARTER interaction type, by orienting me to check my surroundings more often, is a signification of a trend towards alienating conditions. That is the pointer in the direction of the one extreme. 2. The other extreme appears to be dormant in Zone 1 (the busiest zone) although it's conceivable that the trend towards alienation may also be triggered if the imbalance in the amount of the QUARTER interaction type in the mix becomes too great. The supposition in this case is that people, when overwhelmed by 'busyness,' start shutting themselves off from their surroundings. If we look at Figure 33 on page 103 again, it is entirely conceivable that the urban environment can deteriorate to such an extent that the stacked bar for Zone 1 collapses and begins to resemble the stacked bar for Heygate (see the red outline denoting this comparison). At the other end of the chart, in Zone 5 (see the green outline), *do we start to see signs of a collapse, signifying a trend towards alienation*? It appears conceivable because the yellow (QUARTER 1–second) variable is dominant and therefore serves as an early warning of alienation in people; not necessarily that alienating conditions exist but that they have the potential to, and will exist if the stacked bar (green outline) starts to resemble the Heygate (dotted black outline). On the other hand (back to Figure 38 on page 111), the WHOLE interaction type is significant in its relationship with *every other* interaction type (apart from QUARTER). The 4–second look is most dominant. There is a certain logic to this, and it comes as no surprise that the longest engagement we have with our surroundings before 'zoning out' (so top speak) at the one extreme, is the one which sustains us the most. We look for 4 seconds because we are absorbed by the meaning of what it is we are looking at. And as we have already discussed, this meaning may be physical, by defining an object (PHYSICAL USE), or visual/transformational, by being defined by the object (VISUAL USE).

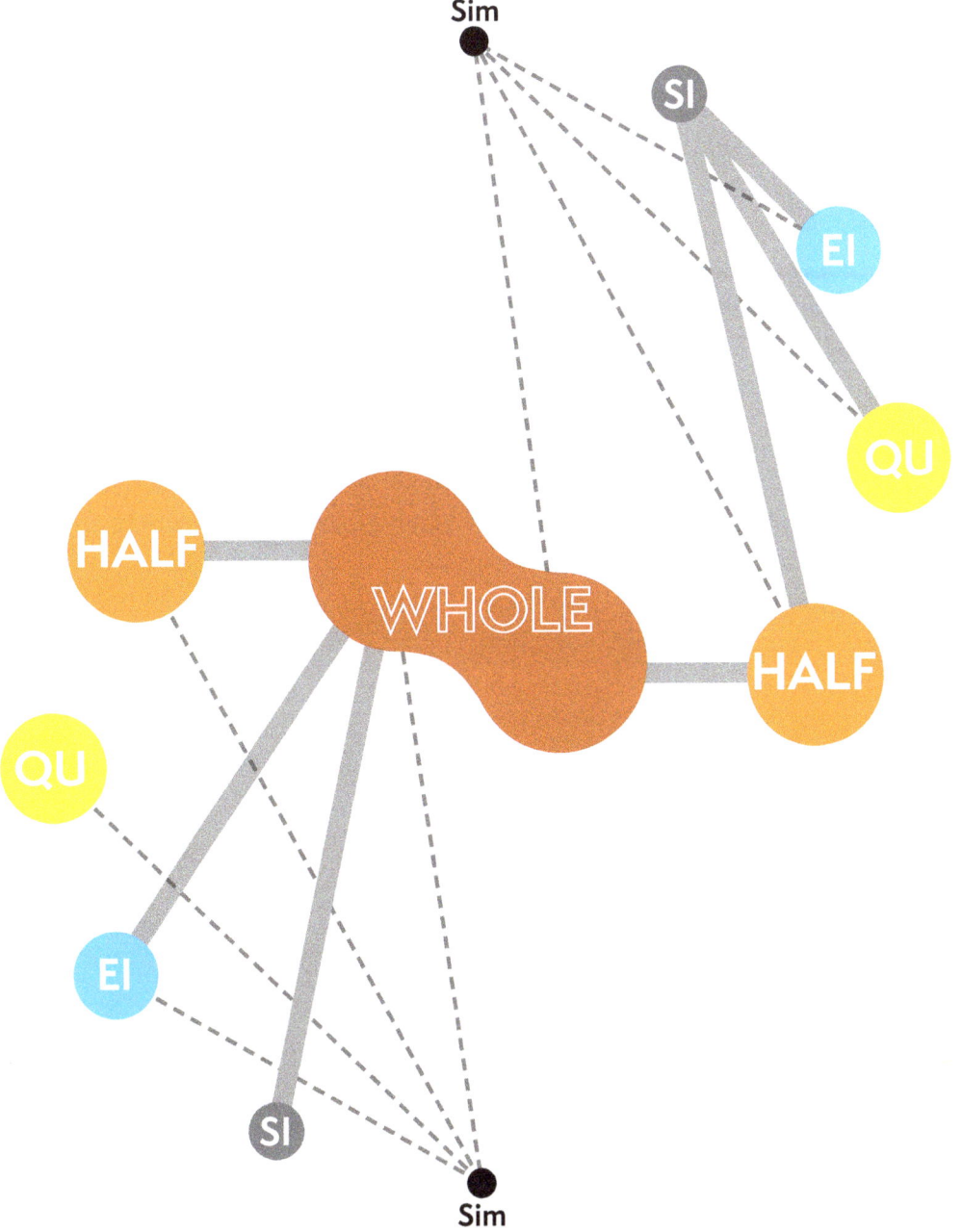

Figure 38. The building block: diagram showing interaction types with significantly different means: therefore, reject the null hypothesis at the 5% level of significance.

CHAPTER 5 THE IMPORTANCE OF VISUAL SUSTAINABILITY

4 Non–linear correlation
Interaction mix and non–linear characteristics

The non–linear nature of my data appear to be confirmed by three findings:

1 There is a difference between interaction types and the null hypothesis is rejected.
2 There appears, from the variables comparison, to be a non–linear relationship between variables.
3 There is also the 'problem' of the quarter type because the lack of significance of its relationship with whole and half especially (but also with eighth) is in itself significant.

Having, in this way, now understood more about the nature of the relationship between variables and which ones, from these data collected, are significant ($p=<0.05$) my next goal is to see whether emergent conditions can be identified from a MIX of interactions. By mix, I mean that there is more than meets the eye if I look from individual interaction types to a combined effect, for example, the effects of WHOLE and HALF in combination; or EIGHTH, SIXTEENTH and SIM combined together. By emergent I mean, stemming from a *non–linear world of complex systems and power law distributions. So, I am interested in what these combinations might reveal about the phenomenon of visual sustainability. The findings so far (see interim summaries on page 97 and on page 102) suggest that visual sustainability i.e., THE PROCESS OF CONNECTING TO WHAT WE HOLD DEAR, is strongest where WHOLE, and HALF notes are dominant (see orange blocks in the pairs plot Figure 37 on page 109).

To recap: I am interested in the idea that visual sustainability occurs when the 'right' mix of interaction types exist in a location. I do not know what that mix is or whether it can be applied consistently across the site, but at this stage I am reminded of two things:

1 I may, in dealing with cities, need to consider variables through the lens of complexity theory, as essentially non–linear events where the whole is *not* the sum of its parts, but more than because "we can't just understand a system by looking at its components, we *have to look at their interactions*, and it's more than the sum" (Complexity a Guided Tour - Melanie Mitchell, 2013, 00:06:40, emphasis added). For Bergson, Polanyi, and Varela the whole is *more than* the sum of the parts. In explanation, Bergson uses time, Polanyi uses intuition, and Varela uses enaction. All three principles influence this study. The idea is that **cities are regarded as bottom–up, emergent phenomena (as opposed to top–down organised complexity).
2 That the location in the study area takes precedence, even if what is

---

*Non–linearity and emergence versus top–down organised complexity, see also (Batty, 2007; Batty and Marshall, 2012; Reading Ancient Minds: Metaphor, Culture, and Complexity, 2012; Ortman, Lobo and Smith, 2020).

**Complexity theory: environmental or human systems and/or behaviour which do not behave in a linear way, but which is non–linear i.e., dynamic, and unpredictable. A well known example is behaviour in flocks of birds, but can equally be applied to scaling effects, bottom–up processes, and associated phenomenon in cities (See, for example, Batty, 2007, 2012).

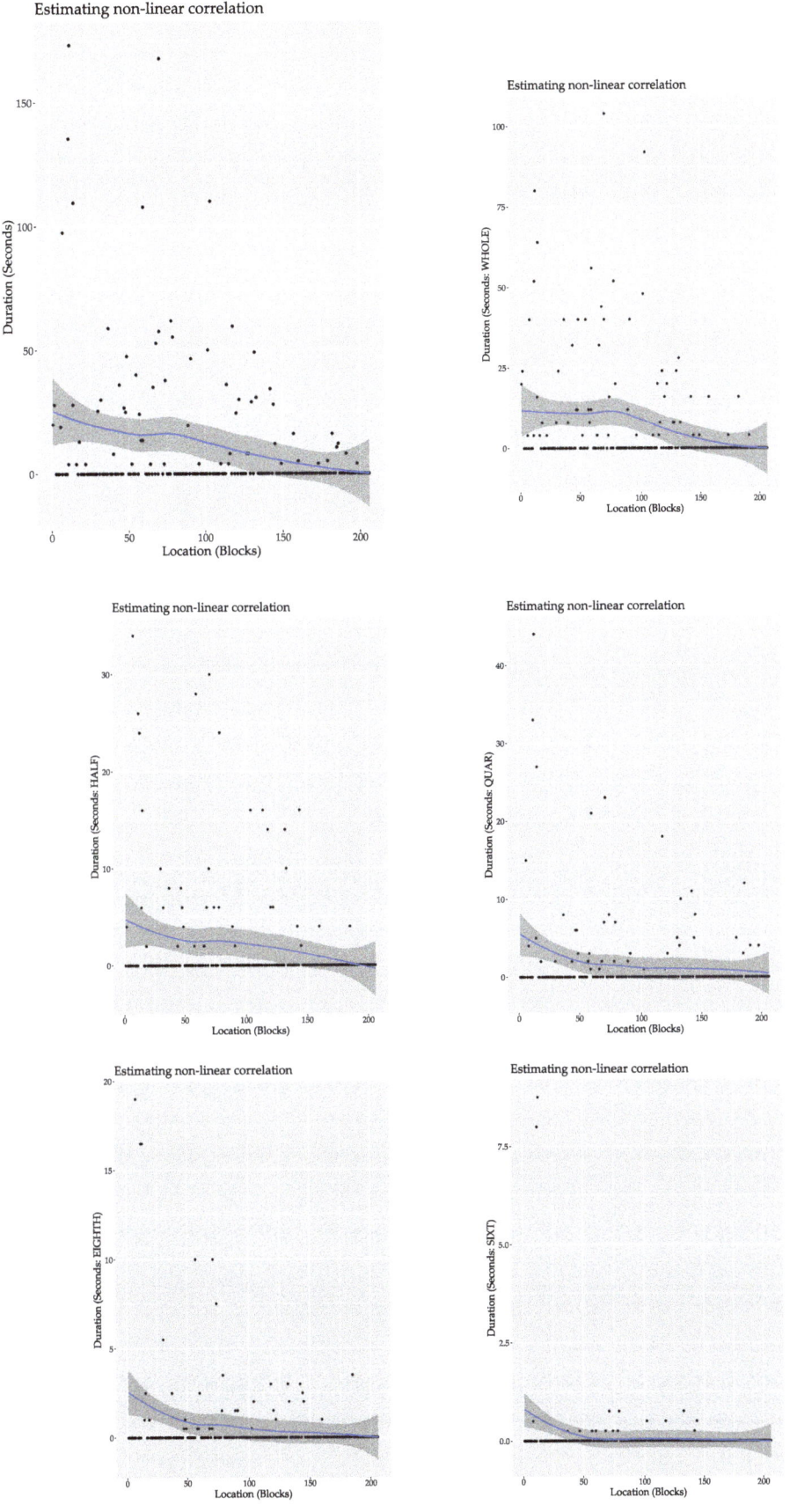

Figure 39. Estimating non–linear correlation: Location (Blocks) and Duration.

Using 'nlcor' in R: Correlation estimate should be between 0 and 1 and the higher the value, the greater the non–linear correlation. In Figure 38, the linear correlations are small but with some linearity present, while non–linear correlation of Zone 2 to Zone 5 are low.

ALL Top-left:
Linear correlation = -0.2588009.
Non–linear correlation estimate = 0.2588009.
Adjusted p–value 0.

WHOLE. Top-right:
Linear correlation = -0.09410546.
Non–linear correlation estimate = 0.09410546.
Adjusted p–value 0.47.

HALF. Middle-left:
Linear correlation = -0.04289046.
Correlation estimate = 0.2324577.
Adjusted p–value 0.29.

QUARTER. Middle-right:
Linear correlation = -0.1880352.
Non–linear correlation estimate = 0.1572375.
Adjusted p–value 0.23.

EIGHTH. Bottom-left:
Linear correlation = 0.02748747.
Non–linear correlation estimate = 0.2324577.
Adjusted p–value 0.29.

SIXTEENTH. Bottom-right:
Linear correlation = NA.
Non–linear correlation estimate = 0.2324577.
Adjusted p–value 0.28.

CHAPTER 5 THE IMPORTANCE OF VISUAL SUSTAINABILITY

being observed, or its meaning, resides outside that location i.e., in the distance somewhere. The scenario which describes this reality best is as follows: the object in the distance is a part of me here. It belongs to me... here. This is where I am transacting with the environment and paying for the transaction with my attention.

It is going to be useful therefore, in terms of my understanding of the mix of interactions, to know whether and in what way, the effect of one interaction type depends on the levels of any other interaction type, in the sense that these variables combine or interact to produce responsiveness which is location specific. The response I initially anticipated relates primarily to interaction between types WH, HA, and QU because I suspected a significant relationship between these interaction–types based on my premise that, due to length of engagement, they are the interaction types which are primarily responsible for conditions of high visual sustainability. However, what has emerged from the findings so far is that QUARTER (QU) appears to play a different role (as summarised in "Interim summary 1" on page 97 and "Interim summary 2" on page 102). So, the two main sources of visually sustainable conditions appear to originate in WH and HA. If, in the real–world, visual sustainability is a non–linear phenomenon, in a process governed by the principles of complexity theory, then I will need to somehow account for this. My data appears to indicate that the variables associated with each other, from WH to SIM, do not change in a constant ratio to each other. However, I found no evidence of non–linearity when using R's 'nlcor' to assess non–linearity between total interactions (independent variable) and each of the dependent variables (WH to SIM). This is the logical outcome since, in this state, the variables are parts of the whole and therefore linear, while emergence occurs when the whole is more than the sum of its parts. So, I looked for an object in my data related to the MIX of interaction types, which might reveal non–linearity using 'R". When I concentrated on mix rather than count, I found evidence (using R's 'nlcor') of non–linearity in the relationship between location at the block level, and duration (in seconds) of interaction type (see Figure 39 on page 113). The results, however, are less interesting than when I moved on and looked at the different *zones* (see Figure 40 on page 115) where there is stronger evidence of non–linearity in the relationship between location (at the zone level) and duration (in seconds) of interaction type. Zones 2, 3, and 5 appear to show stronger non–linear characteristics with estimates between 0.45 and 0.5. This means that the zones in my urban transect appear to offer the greatest potential for producing emergent conditions (such as described in complexity theory) from the visual interaction types (and, of course, revealing them in a statistical analysis). The importance being described by these graphs lies in the role

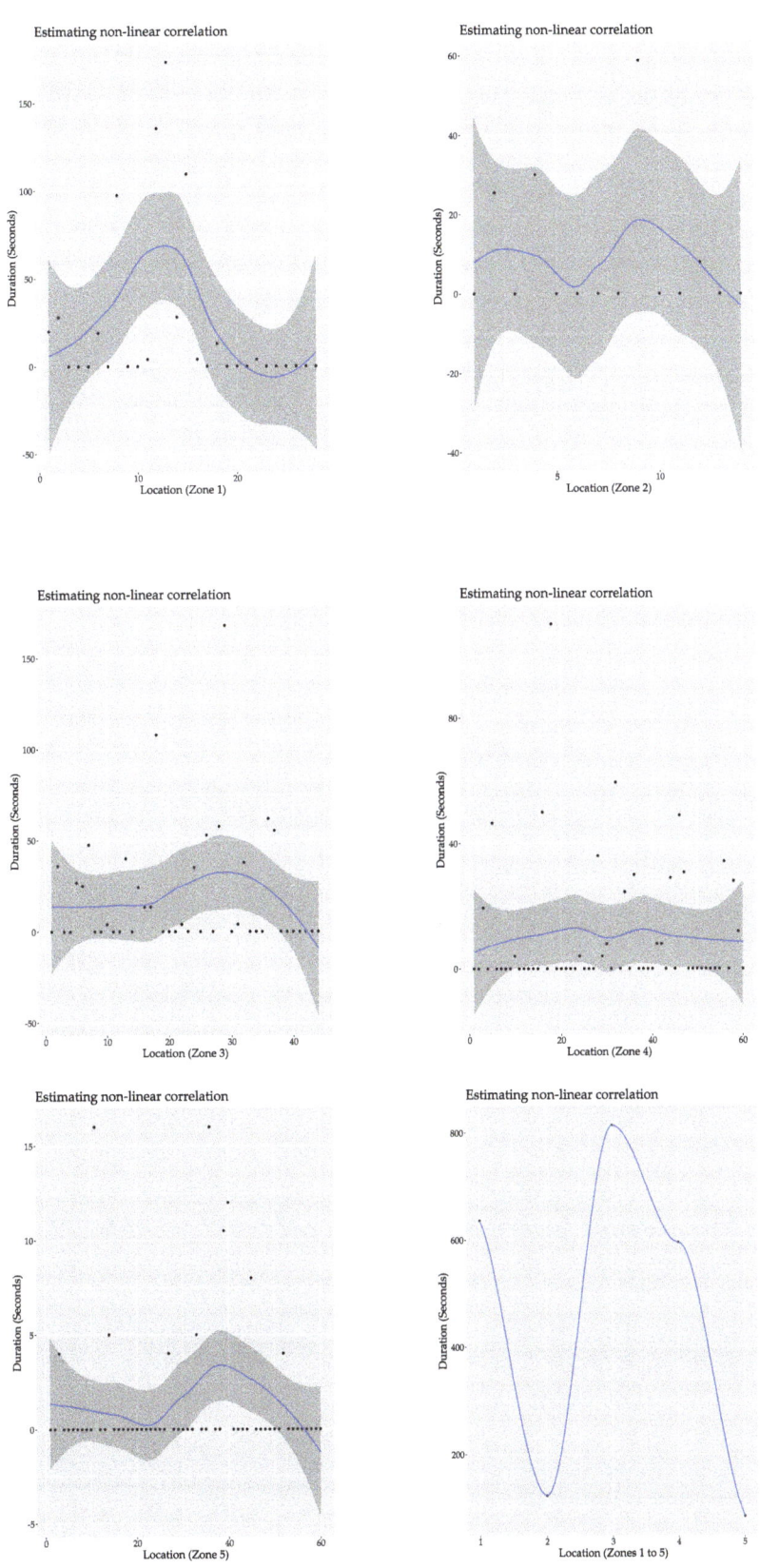

Figure 40. Estimating non–linear correlation: detecting non–linear variables using Location (Zones) and Duration.

Using 'nlcor' in R: Correlation estimate should be between 0 and 1 and the higher the value, the greater the non–linear correlation. In Figure 39, the linear correlations are all small, while non–linear correlation of Zone 2 to Zone 5 are pronounced.

ZONE 1. Top-left:
Linear correlation = -0.1851469.
Non–linear correlation estimate = 0.1851469
Adjusted p–value 0.35

ZONE 2. Top-right:
Linear correlation = -0.1270004.
Non–linear correlation estimate = 0.5022795
Adjusted p–value 0.48

ZONE 3. Middle-left:
Linear correlation = 0.003014066.
Non–linear correlation estimate = 0.4867128
Adjusted p–value 0.89

ZONE 4. Middle-right:
Linear correlation = 0.006229569.
Non–linear correlation estimate = 0.3648401.
Adjusted p–value 0.96.

ZONE 5. Bottom-left:
Linear correlation = -0.003341135.
Non–linear correlation estimate = 0.4548198
Adjusted p–value 0.74

ZONES 1–5. Bottom-right:
Linear correlation = -0.3040341.
Non–linear correlation estimate = 0.3040341
Adjusted p–value 0.62

CHAPTER 5 THE IMPORTANCE OF VISUAL SUSTAINABILITY

that interaction types might play, and for their potential to, in combination, produce emergent conditions that describe a phenomenon which appears to be indescribable: the phenomenon of visual sustainability. This is because the rates of change in variables is not constant, for example, as we have seen with the sixteenth variable of 0.25 seconds ("Interim summary 2" on page 102): the more there are of the SIXTEENTH interaction type, the less there is of any other interaction type. Which means that these short glances appear to signify alienating conditions because longer (more meaningful) engagements are prevented from occurring due to the poor urban conditions signified by the over–dominant rapid glances of the SIXTEENTH type. In other words, the conditions are such that low levels of visual sustainability compromise the visual relationship people hold dear to their surroundings.

In Figure 40 on page 115, Bottom-right, we can see the difference in duration across the transect from Zone 1 to Zone 5. There are several important things to take note of.

- Firstly, these data (Figure 40 on page 115) mirrors pie chart E in Table 5 on page 86, but of this representation we get a different sense of these data by way their non–linearity.
- The busiest zone, in terms of the length of time people were engaged with their surroundings, was Zone 3 and yet it is surprising that Zone 1 has the highest urban density and Zone 3 the lowest (equally with Zone 5).
- Zone 3 and Zone 5 are the least dense zones and yet they are the most different in terms of the length of time people were engaged.
- Zone 1 and Zone 4 have the same amount of attention paid to them (duration in seconds) but are also very different in character and have quite different urban densities. Zone 4 is significantly less dense than Zone 1. There are reasons why Zone 4 can be argued to have this effect. It is much higher ground and therefore prominent and secondly, it is home to the Royal Observatory which is a magnet for tourists. But the same amount of time was spent in every other area as was spent walking through the Royal Observatory area so these data should not be abnormally skewed in favour of activity in this area.
- Zone 3 however is the biggest surprise. It is where the most attention is paid but it is the least dense as a built up environment, although medium density in terms of activity levels or 'busyness.' The argument here for why there is this discrepancy is that zone 3 distributes people in a way that the other zones do not. For example,

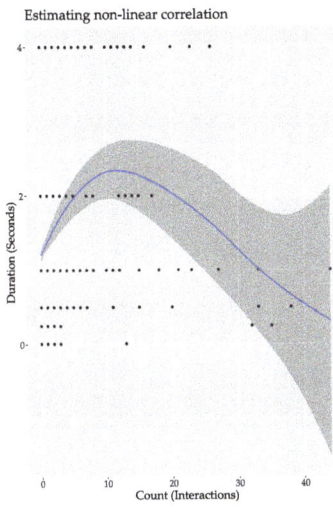

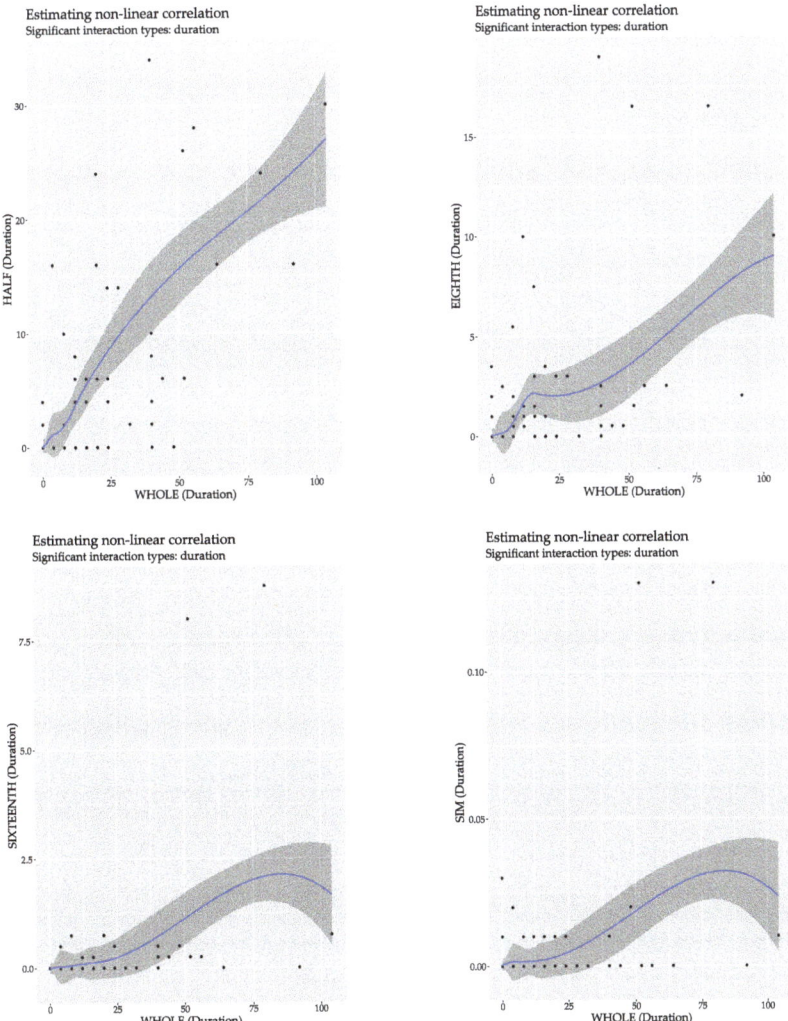

Top–left: Non–linearity in the occurrence of duration (0.01 seconds to 4 seconds), of interaction types.

Figure 41. Estimating non–linear correlation: detecting non–linear association in variables with p= <0.05 from the pairwise comparison.

Using 'nlcor' in R: Correlation estimate should be between 0 and 1 and the higher the value, the greater the non–linear correlation. In Figure 40, while the initial data was discrete ratio (counts), their duration is continuous and as continuous dependent variables are suitable for non–linear correlation analysis. All correlation coefficients are taken from the pairwise comparison (Figure 38 on page 111) and are significant at least at p<0.05 level.

Top-left:
Linear correlation = 0.093.
Non–linear correlation estimate = 0.093
Adjusted p–value 0

Middle-left: WH–HA
Linear correlation = 0.75
Non–linear correlation estimate = 0.75
Adjusted p–value 0

Middle-right: WH–EI
Linear correlation = 0.58
Non–linear correlation estimate = 0.58
Adjusted p–value 0

Bottom-left: WH–SI
Linear correlation = 0.43
Non–linear correlation estimate = 0.43
Adjusted p–value 0

Bottom-right: WH–SIM
Linear correlation = 0.41
Non–linear correlation estimate = 0.41
Adjusted p–value 0

CHAPTER 5 THE IMPORTANCE OF VISUAL SUSTAINABILITY

it is, firstly, the channel from town up to the Royal Observatory, although the same can be said of the role played by Zone 5. Secondly, it facilitates activity and movement crossways, east to west and vice versa. And last, but not least, there is the effect of the dominating architectural feature of the Royal Observatory complex upon the hill in Zone 4 — a tourist attraction and an object to which much attention appears to be paid.

- My suggestion here is that urban density plays less of a role than we might expect and what is more influential are the things that hold people's attention. In the quiet areas of Zone 4, for example, despite the presence of the Royal Observatory as a destination landmark, we should be careful not to ignore the positive effects of nature, trees, water, green vista's and the like. Zone 3, on the other hand, appears to be visually sustainable for its role in distributing attention towards surrounding attractors and points of interest.

Section summary

There appears to be, from an urban design point of view, a consistent level shown in the duration of engagement by people with their surroundings on this site i.e., the 4–second look and the 2–second look. The two exceptions are the very quiet Zone 5, and the anomaly of Zone 2 (which has been discussed). In urban design strategy, therefore, it appears that we need to pay attention at the scale of zones in an urban transect for information about visual sustainability characteristics. In Figure 41 on page 117 we can see what appears to be high levels of non–linearity in the relationship between WHOLE and the following: HALF, EIGHTH, SIXTEENTH, and SIM respectively, which are derived from the results of the pairwise comparison in Figure 38 on page 111. In the other relationships there isn't enough data, that was not zero, to calculate non–linearity in the same way. This appears to have been the problem when trying to analyse non–linearity at block level. But for WHOLE, we can see how the significance ($p = < 0.05$) in the relationships between variables, can be thought of in terms of a non–linear system.

LOCATIONS (BLOCKS) WHICH CONTAIN
A SUSTAINABLE MIX OF INTERACTION TYPES.

5 A digital tapestry

The digital tapestry presented in this study (Figure 44 on page 121) provides us with a canvas with which to help explain and further explore interaction mix. We have seen how, if interaction–type is satisfied, an interaction takes

IN URBAN DESIGN STRATEGY   FINDINGS

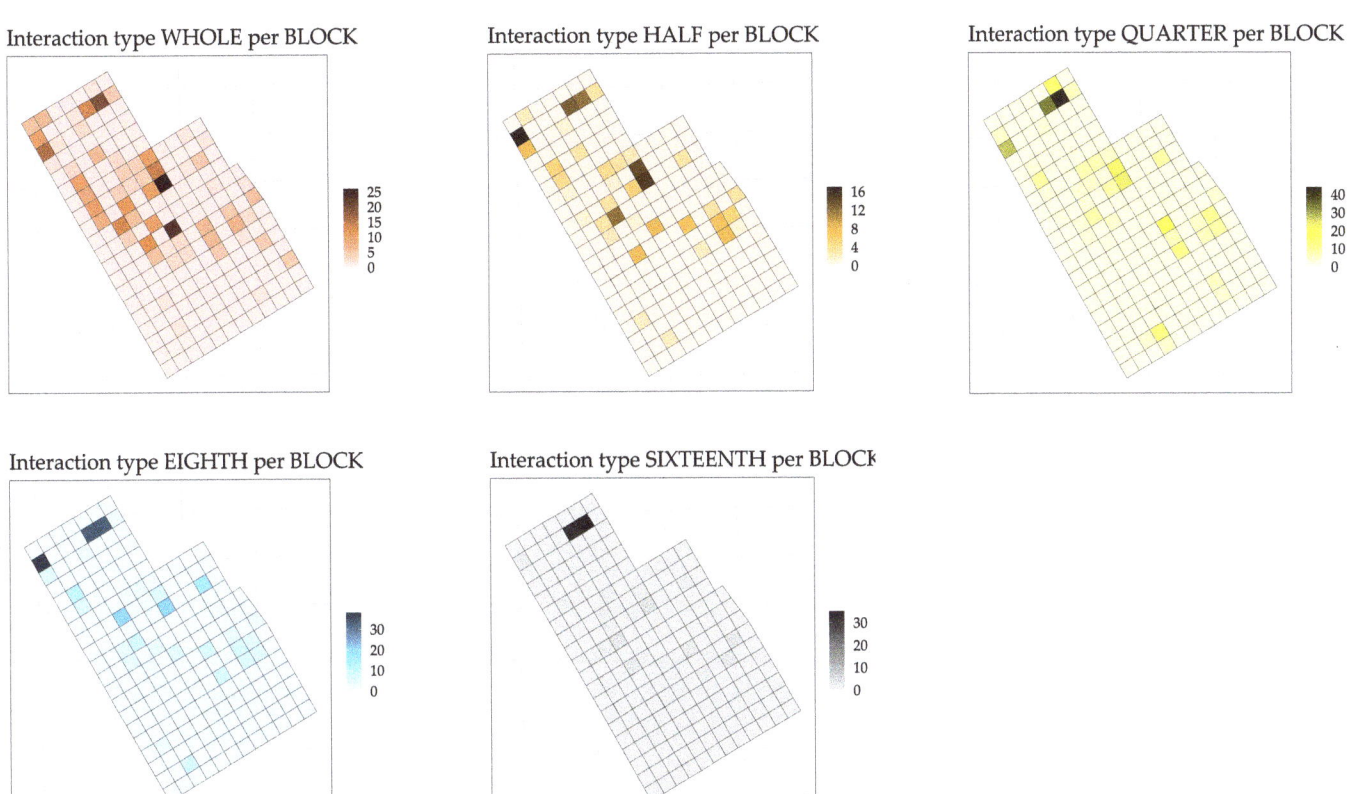

Figure 42. Study Area showing the relationship between location (blocks/zones) and interaction type (WH–SI).

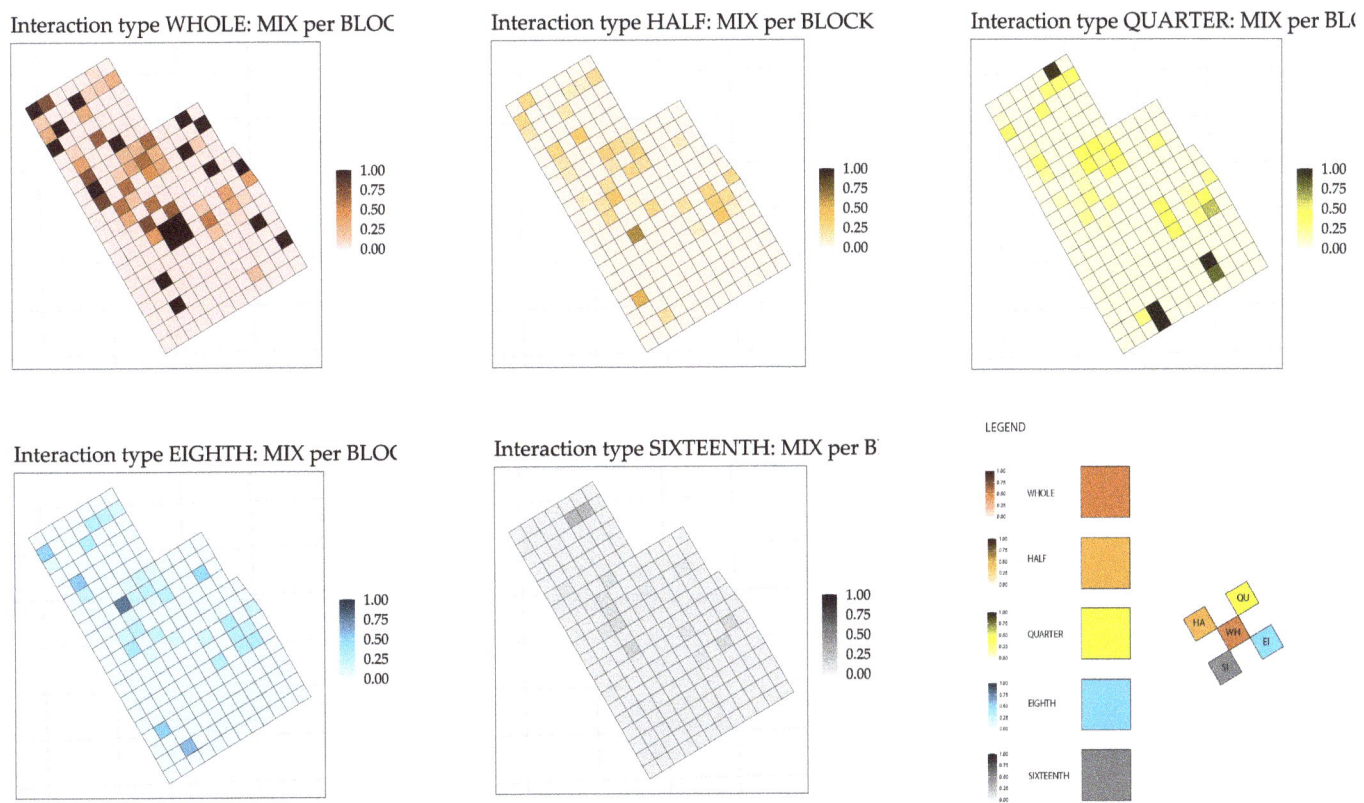

Figure 43. This diagram shows the mix of interaction types for each block. The darker the shade, the more active an interaction–type is in a block. The lighter the colour, the less represented an interaction–type is. In many cases an interaction–type may not be active in a block. In some cases, only one interaction–type may be present.

CHAPTER 5 — THE IMPORTANCE OF VISUAL SUSTAINABILITY

place either trending towards visual sustainability or towards alienation. I have proposed a *visual definition* in this study of alienation using the representation of sounds to represent time values (De Kock, 2023, p.4, Figure 3) and as a stacked bar chart (Figure 33 on page 103). Visual sustainability, as proposed, is the opposite of that scale of values by way of some special mix of interaction type and is, in my argument thus far, dominated by WHOLE and HALF interaction types. The locations (which are the blocks and zones) may then be viewed simply as containers of data relevant to that location (no matter where these data physically reside). Because, as I have argued, the interaction is in the same location from which it's experienced (see "Interaction mix and non–linear characteristics" on page 112). My contention in this study is that location is therefore privileged over everything else. We fetch what we see into our memory, just as we see with memory in a 'Bergsonian' sense. And, in that sense, what we fetch belongs to our unique perspective in time in the location we are in. We do not fetch a 'chunk of space' and store it in our brain. Instead, *we are* the time–extended event as described by Robbins (2014) and for us memory/ *redintegration occurs 'in situ' or as part of the unfolding events.

*Redintegration: the law of redintegration in Gibsonian terms would be: A current event, E' redintegrates a previous event, E, when E' and E share the same invariance structure. Derived from "a term coined already in 1732 by Wolff, a disciple of Leibniz, in his Psychologia Empirica. It is defined roughly as "a part of a current event retrieves the whole of a past event," or as Klein (1971) puts it, a pattern in a current event retrieves a past event with a similar pattern" (Robbins, S. E., 2021, p.21).

For these data collected then, let us try and see which block most closely represents a state of visual sustainability (and therefore which is the opposite of, or at least, most unlike alienation) and why. An accurate depiction of the relationship between interaction type and location can be seen in Figure 42 on page 119. The question then is, *which of these blocks contain a mix of interactions which represents the opposite of alienation*? Figure 45 on page 123 attempts to answer this by suggesting combinations that may support high levels of visual sustainability as opposed to its opposite effect, which is alienation. The answer proposed is the following: the upper row (black frame) represents conditions in which robust levels of visual sustainability may exist. The lower row (grey frame) represents combinations which I am suggesting introduces mild forms of alienation. The 'right mix' in these data is a more harmonious balance of interaction types where, much like our experience of music (De Kock, 2020a), even if we experience a full range of notes, it is the intensity of the notes which we are drawn to. Applying Bergson's theory of qualitative multiplicity, the suggestion therefore is that the answer lies in intensity of effect i.e., the darker the shade, the stronger the effect. We can see this intensity of effect in Figure 43 on page 119, where the darker the shade, the more ACTIVE an interaction–type is in a block. The lighter the shade, the less represented an interaction–type is *in relation to the other interaction types*. And in Figure 44 on page 121, we see an accurate depiction of the mix of interaction types

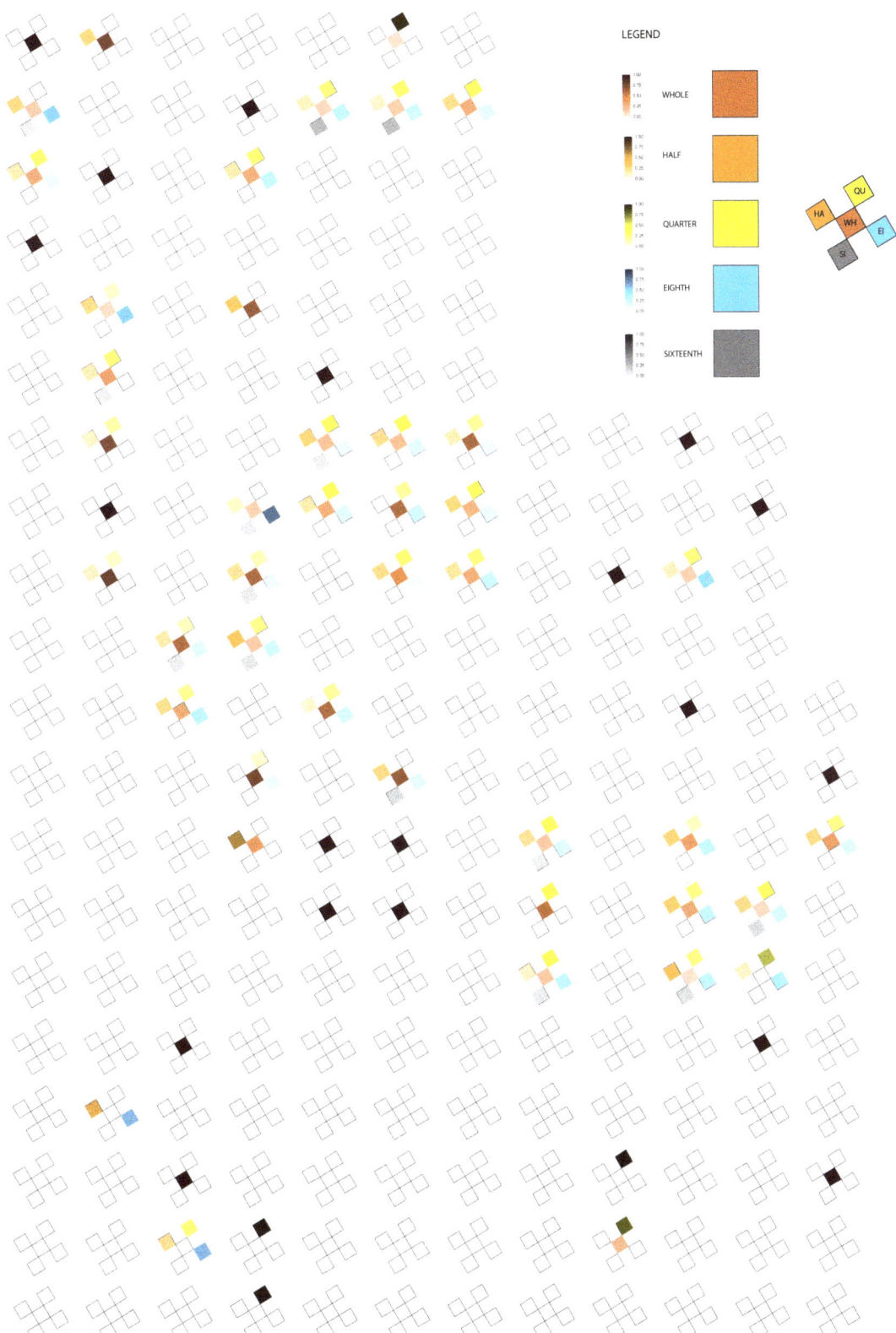

Figure 44. Digital tapestry. Percentage mix: the darker the values for each shade, the stronger the effect. For visual sustainability, the premise is that the orange and yellows are dominant. For alienation, the blues and greys are dominant.

for each block as they are situated in the study area. While all these colour patterns are a little overwhelming in an analytical sense, the tapestry does afford us the opportunity to have an appreciation for conditions that point to the general trend of levels of visual sustainability. Figure 44 on page 121, Figure 45, and Figure 46 on page 123 (in video format) provide a good overview of conditions of visual sustainability. There do not seem to be any areas where severe alienation in the study area exists.

Interim summary 3

- Interaction mix is a valuable aid in understanding more about visual sustainability levels.
- There is some evidence of non–linearity in these data especially in the zones of this urban transect, which points to conditions that appear to be sympathetic to dynamic and unpredictable phenomena described by complexity theory.
- We can infer with a certain amount of confidence that a predominance of QUARTER and EIGHTH types (yellow and blue colours) are visual indicators of an urban of declining quality.
- Dominant blue and grey colours (eighth and sixteenth) are strong indicators of poor visual sustainability, most likely requiring urban design intervention at a strategic level.
- The variables comparison results point to the proposal that interaction type serves as the building block of visual sustainability.
- If we look at Figure 33 on page 103 again, it is entirely conceivable that the urban environment can deteriorate and begin to resemble the stacked bar for Heygate (see the red outline denoting this comparison). It is also conceivable that where the yellow (QUARTER 1–second) variable is dominant, alienating conditions have the potential to escalate and resemble the Heygate example (dotted black outline).
- The WHOLE interaction type is significant in its relationship with every interaction type except QUARTER.
- The findings so far suggest that visual sustainability i.e., THE PROCESS OF CONNECTING TO WHAT WE HOLD DEAR, is strongest where WHOLE, and HALF notes are dominant.
- It appears that urban density (in built up terms) plays less of a role than we might expect and what is more influential is the 'busyness' or levels of activity and thus the things that hold people's attention. The positive effects of nature, trees, water, green vista's and the like in the quietness of Zone 4

Figure 45. A mix of interaction–types. The premise is that the upper row represents conditions in which robust levels of visual sustainability may exist. The lower row represents combinations which introduce mild forms of alienation.

Figure 46. Data as a digital tapestry (video). See video at https://doi.org/10.6084/m9.figshare.24996215.v1.

matches the duration in seconds of Zone 1, while Zone 3 has the lowest built density but enjoys the most attention in terms of length of engagement.
- The digital tapestry is a valuable aid in understanding more about visual sustainability levels of a study area at a macro level.

§. 21 *Commercial application*

6 Commercial relevance

In this section I will take a look at how interaction types may be a useful tool from a commercial point of view. The laws of non–linearity still apply, in the sense that, for example, where one shop in a high street sells x value of goods or services, does not mean the ten shops on either side of it sell ten times the value of x. Or, to put it in terms of visual interactions, the effect of 5 WHOLES, 2 HALF's, and 3 EIGHTH's in one block can not be expected to be the same as 10 WHOLE's, 4 HALF's, and 6 EIGHTH's in another. There is, it is argued, tension and compression (concepts described in more detail on page 132) at work in a high street producing uneven, unpredictable results, just as there are in how we are engaged with our surroundings. This means that there may be a real effect from the non–linearity of the mix of variables that make up visual sustainability. The point being made is that it is likely that interaction types are useful when considered in a commercial setting.

VALUE AS A RESULT OF INTERACTION TYPE

In a rhetorical sense, I am interested in whether a location's VALUE is generated, or influenced, by interaction types and by extension of the argument, by levels of visual sustainability. From an urban design point of view then, let us assume that the two conditions in Table 7 on page 125 are equally true and value is attached to a location because we pay for something with our attention. If we pay for something with our attention, then it follows logically that businesses will find value in those locations because it is where we prefer to be. For this analogy I would like to propose that there are elements in urban design that are similar to visual sustainability. Consider a mixed–use high street where some shops are anchors, most are line shops, and a few are niche/ luxury outlets. Suppose these yellow blocks (Figure 47 on page 125 and Figure 48 on page 125) represent 64 trading and active 'shops', meaning, blocks where interaction has been observed, counted, and categorised *Why do we transact with some of these and not others*? The answer appears to be that it depends on our needs, some of which are physical (related to object identification and problem solving) while others are visual, that is, wrapped up in *feeling*. Most are a combination of the two. Sometimes physical use is an

1	A block (Independent variable)	Influences	Interaction–type (Dependent variable)
	In other words:		*in other words:*
	Location; where you are	Influences	What you see & interact with.
Conversely:			
2	Interaction–type (Independent variable)	Defines/ affects	The quality of location (block) (dependent variable)
	Because…		
	If you do not have these types of interaction present	then	The location is less effective as an urban space.

Table 7. Location and interaction type are interdependent.

Figure 47. Blocks and interaction.

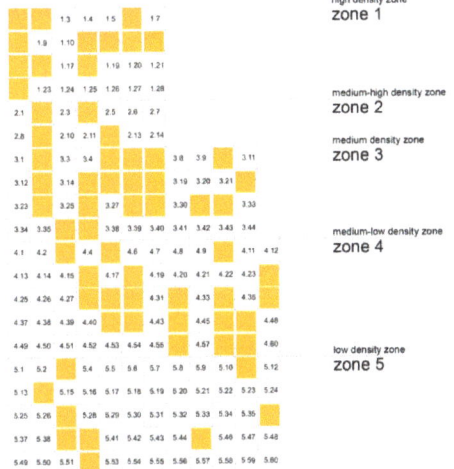

- Each block (shop) 'sells' interactions
- The currency used is time
- We exchange our time for an interaction
- The value is in the length of time we're engaged
- An interaction may be thought of in musical terms
  - WH: WHOLE (4 seconds)
  - HA: HALF (2 seconds)
  - QU: QUARTER ((1 second)
  - EI: EIGHTH (half a second)
  - SI: SIXTEENTH (a quarter of a second)

Figure 48. Study area: blocks with observed interactions

CHAPTER 5 THE IMPORTANCE OF VISUAL SUSTAINABILITY

When weighted values are applied, to reflect more accurately the value of a longer engagement (the long look), the counts of EI and SI drop down to between 15 and 20. My argument here is that visual sustainability is robust in terms of representation in the upper range of interactions (WH, HA, QU). This weighting is what is meant by intensity or effect. (Compare this with Figure 34 on page 105).

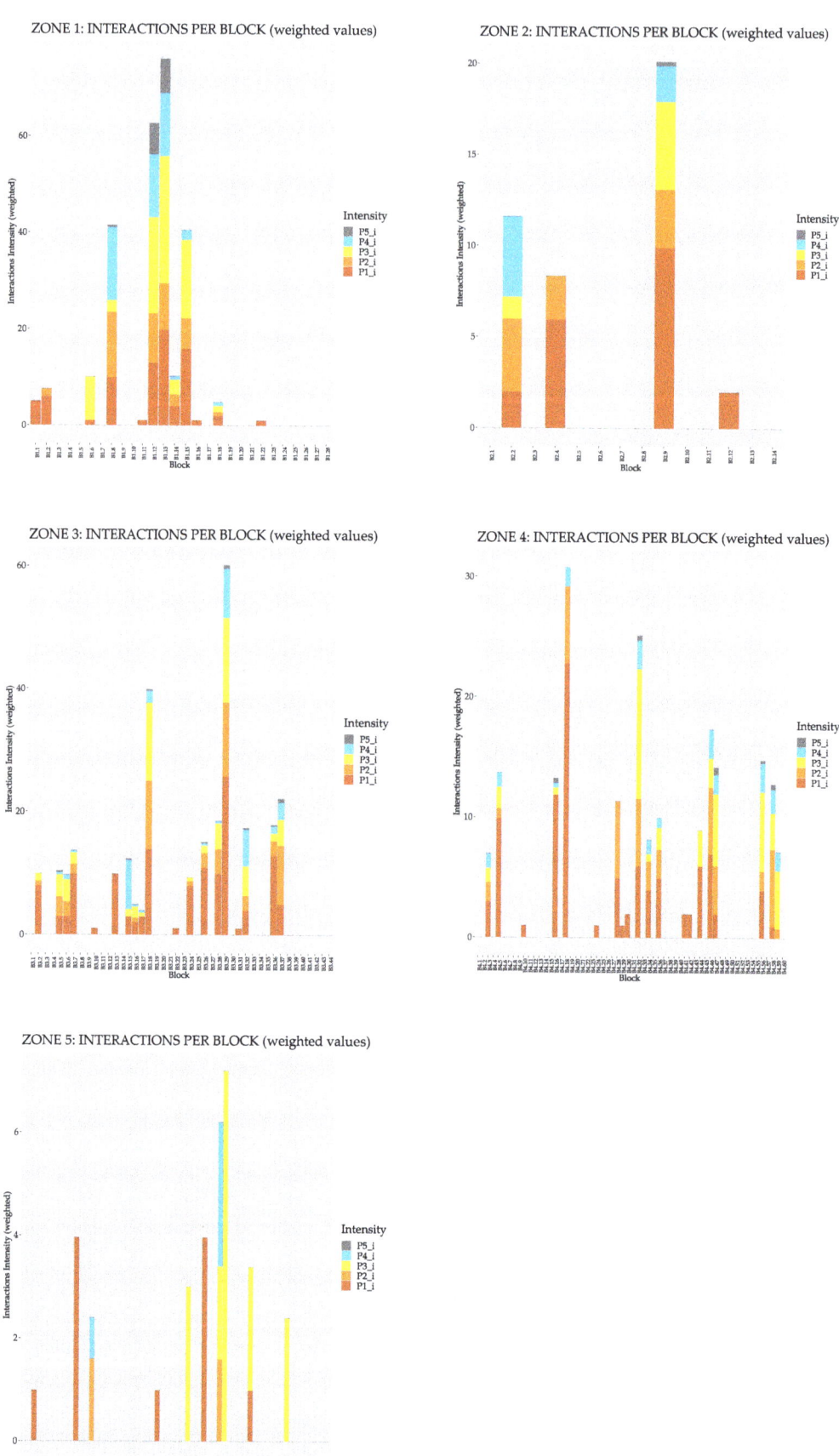

Figure 49. The distribution of interaction types at block level (weighted).

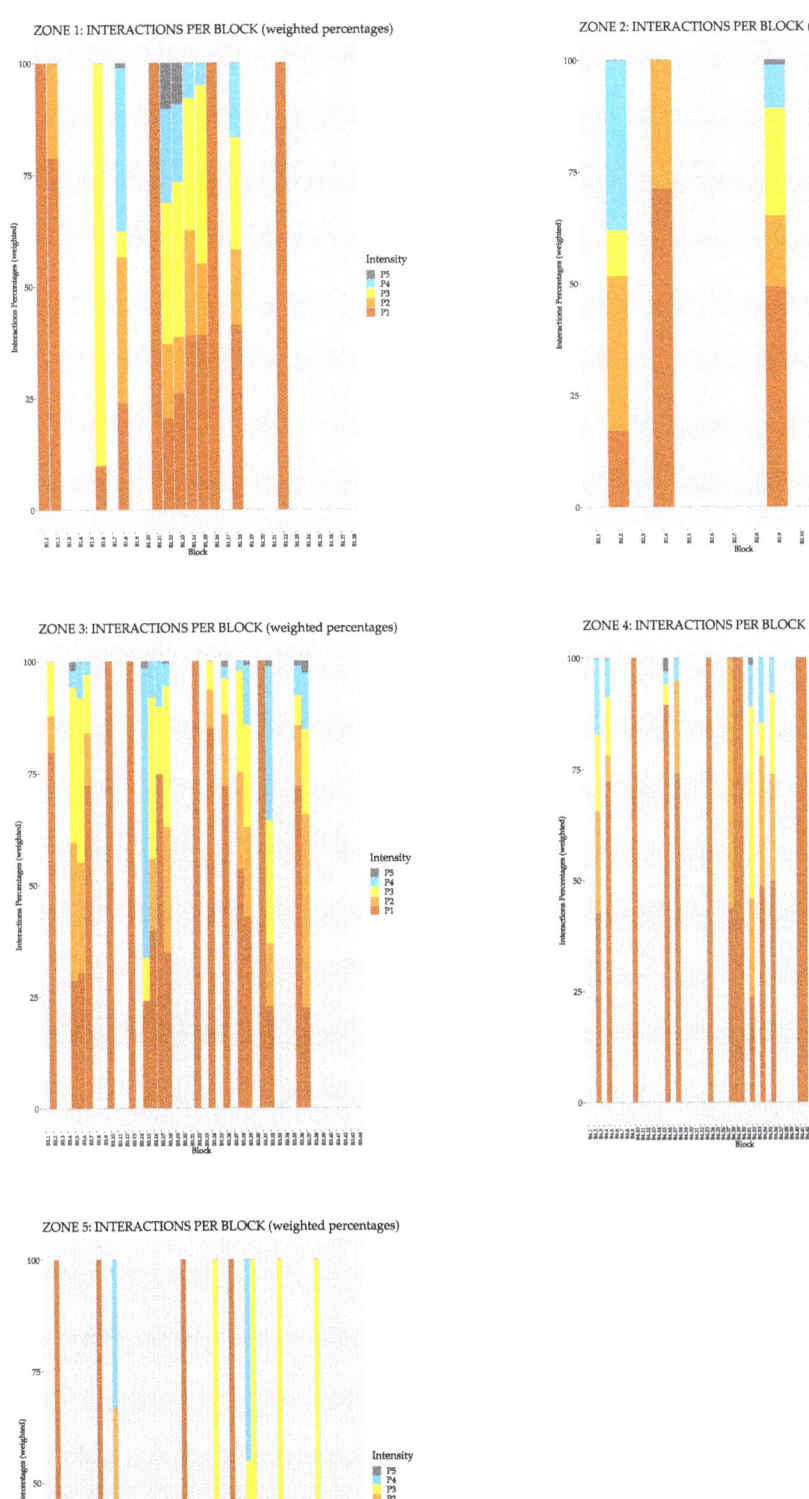

When viewed through the spectrum of values, the presence of alienating conditions (the blue and grey representing the lower range of interaction types) appears to be far less influential than we might have assumed from the un–weighted chart (Figure 35 on page 107).

Figure 50. Interaction percentages (weighted) per Block.

independent variable, sometimes a response or dependent variable. Likewise, sometimes visual use is an independent variable, sometimes a dependent variable. In the study area the blocks all vary in character as we have seen in these findings so far. One block provides more interaction than another block, just as one shop on a high street sells more than another. If I take the analogy further then it makes sense to also account for the price difference between shops — which is the same conceptually as the difference in length of engagement and, by extension of the argument, the quality of interaction. So just as with count and duration of interactions, there is also count and quality of the goods in shops. Because duration reflects the quality of an interaction. In this section I would like to propose the following:

The shops

- The study area consists of shops (Figure 48 on page 125) which are the blocks in the study area.
- In each block a sale is made where someone has transacted for a particular interaction with their time. The sales price is the length of interaction, from 4 seconds to 0.25 seconds.
- Time spent is thus the currency of our transaction, just as money is in shops.
- It is a person's time which they will never get back and therefore represents a thing of value. If I look at something for long enough it represents a positive engagement. It must mean something to me or else, I will quickly look away and look for something else to specify (in Gibson's terms).
- Some shops are more popular than others. This is equally true of the study area where some blocks are dominated by WHOLE and HALF interaction types and the 'price' we are willing to pay is higher in relation to other blocks (shops).

The sales

In terms of the importance of location being privileged over space, the value of location is proposed as follows:

- Example 1: Shop (Block) B_1.8 (highlighted in Figure 48 on page 125) sold the following items/ recorded the following interactions: 10 WHOLE's; 17 HA's; 4 QU's; 38 EI's; and 2 SI's. The collective relative value/ price paid/ market share amounts to approximately 4.8% of the total sale (i.e., total number of interactions per minute) in this study area. Let us now apply a value spectrum, where, for example, EI represents a 'product' selling for 25 pence (0.25 seconds) compared to say £4 for the WHOLE interaction–type (4 seconds). The EI sales of 38 items thus needs to be adjusted to reflect their inherent level of discomfort (in terms of the rationale explained earlier, of alienating conditions). *If we apply this weighting to all the values, would it not give us a better idea of the true value of levels of visual sustainability in any given part of the study area?*

Tracking visual sustainability

However, when thinking about visual sustainability, it does not follow that lower market share (score) necessarily represents a less important shop (block). We should be mindful that less visually sustainable areas might not necessarily lack that one transaction which is most dear to someone. And the more visually sustainable areas may not necessarily contain an object or event that is most dear to someone. The point being made here is that the most sustainable interaction we have is not discriminated by location, but as a general rule the most sustainable areas/ locations are a function of a more valuable mix of interaction types.

STATISTICAL ANALYSIS: COMMERCIAL VALUE

I am interested in the statistical significance of the relationship of value between interaction and location. Commercial relevance is explained in "Supplementary Terminology and Rationale" on page 82, by way of the application in this study of what I call: intensity or effect. The weighted values I have described define levels of intensity—which produce an effect.

Weighting

Data will be analysed differently in this section so that the commercial value of a location is better represented. I have proposed a weighting system for the interaction types that can be distinguished as follows.

- As we have seen in Figure 42 on page 119 and Figure 43 on page 119, data without weighting took the values from the original data in the observations in the study area i.e., WH to SI (WH – HA – QU – EI – SI).
- The proposal in this section, that speaks to commercial relevance, is to add weighting, and this is done using the notation 'P' tag (P1 – P2 – P3 – P5 – P6; or P1_I ; or P3W). Weighting is introduced by me to reflect levels of importance according to the length of engagement and therefore, the value of an interaction. A full explanation of this

CHAPTER 5 THE IMPORTANCE OF VISUAL SUSTAINABILITY

approach can be found in the section: "Value as a result of interaction type" on page 124.

There is a split between the range of values as follows: WH, HA, QU versus EI, SI, SIM for the upper and lower part of the spectrum respectively; or P1 to P3 versus P4 to P6. This split distinguishes between these data range in terms of length of engagement with the environment. The upper part of the spectrum reflects the 'stickiness' or how much glue there is in a location or zone compared with others; by which is meant: how engaging the environment appears to be. The notion of stickiness is applied in two ways: every location has a certain energy, but it also has a certain intensity, which can be described in the following two concepts: Tempo (Energy) versus Intensity (Effect). Energy derives its meaning from interaction count while intensity derives its meaning from interaction duration.

Effect of weighted values on urban design strategy
The effect on urban design strategy is as follows.

- Weighting changes the emphasis towards the upper range of interaction types (Figure 49 on page 126 and Figure 50 on page 127). This is because there is an inherent value in a more engaged look in comparison to a fleeting glance.
- I have established how alienation consists of a collection of fleeting glances in rapid succession and one reason may be that they *appear* to be stress related. Another reason may be indifference in that there is no value in holding our attention. And finally, they may simply be snippets of information whose value is over when understood, e.g. navigational.
- The main premise in terms of effect on urban design strategy is that the longer our engagement with an object or event lasts, the more visually sustained we are (and the less alienated we feel); until it is of some length where the object is 'lost' and the eye sees nothing (or in some sense one enters a state of simulacrum, where you can look at something but see something else).
- The suggestion is that blocks where there is a significant shift towards the upper range of interaction types (P1 and P2) are blocks where we are more visually sustained than we may realise. In urban design terms these are the blocks or nodes that need to be recognised and emulated in areas where interaction is poor.

The differences can be explained in another way. The colours in Figure 42 on page 119 are simply a reflection of the interaction COUNT. The darker

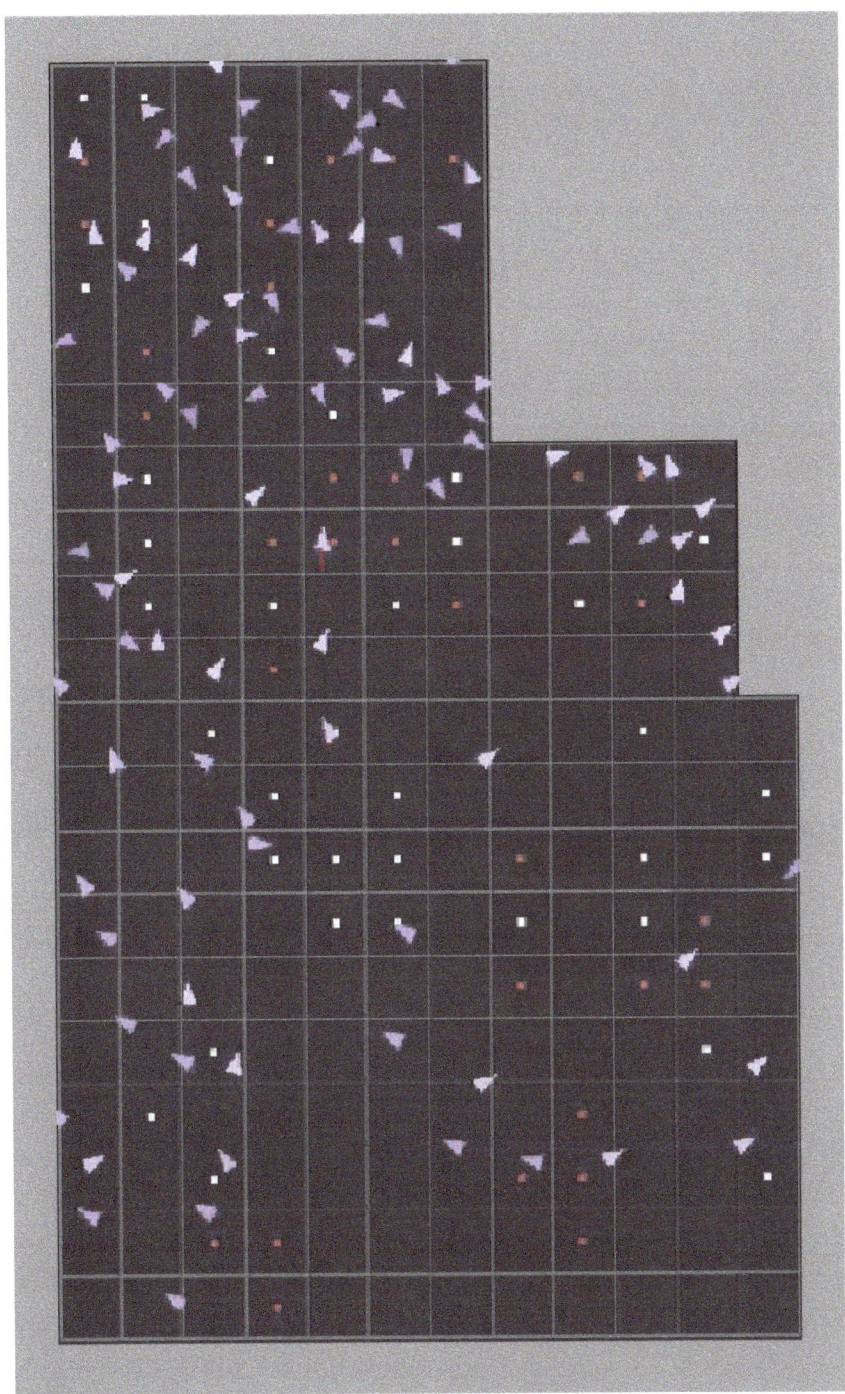

Figure 51. The commercial value of understanding urban compressive and tensile forces as the result of relationship between interaction type —because businesses follow people and people follow meaning (video). See video at https://doi.org/10.6084/m9.figshare.24996296.v1.

CHAPTER 5   THE IMPORTANCE OF VISUAL SUSTAINABILITY

the shade, the greater the interaction count for each interaction type in every block. But in Figure 43 on page 119, I took the analysis a step further and we saw how dominant each interaction type was in the MIX of every block. The darker the shade, the greater the percentage of the whole that particular interaction type enjoyed. These differences point to my argument that COMPRESSION and TENSION play a role in the study area and why it is an important pair of concepts to recognise in relation to commercial activity. Because I am interested in, not just COUNT or MIX, but in INFLUENCE. There is the question about how interaction types influence neighbouring blocks, which can be explored more by adopting an analysis similar to Schelling's model of segregation (Schelling, 1971) and an adaptation by me (in De Kock and Carta, 2020b, p.12–13) which looks at the effects of economic segregation in urban areas.

Effect of compression and tension
(Resulting from the comparison of interaction type means).

Compression and tension used in this study is basically an argument developed from network thinking and "focusing on relationships *between* entities rather than the entities themselves" (Mitchell, 2011, p.233, emphasis added). The rationale for *the space between various locations is based on Schelling as follows. The results of the variables comparison (Figure 38 on page 111) indicates that the value of a location is higher if WHOLE and HALF are active and dominant. Therefore, my argument is that if WHOLE and HALF total more than 50 percent of the block, the block can be considered an attractive location from which visual interactions can be enjoyed. In other words, the location acts in compression, attracting people towards it. On the other hand, if WHOLE and HALF make up less than 50 percent of the interaction type count, then the block can be considered less attractive and therefore acts in tension; that is, it repulses to some degree, trending towards alienating conditions. The QUARTER interaction type appears to be less statistically significant in relation to WHOLE and HALF and, as determined by the means comparison (Figure 38 on page 111), appears to be a better fit by association in the lower range of interaction types. I used 3dMax's crowd system with 'delegates' to simulate tension and compression in the study area. The resulting video (Figure 51 on page 131) shows the compressive and tensile forces at work. The red squares represent blocks where WHOLE and HALF make up less than 50 percent of the interaction types. The white squares represent the blocks where WHOLE and HALF are more dominant with more than 50 percent share. The light purple agents are a simulation of the population producing interactions

*For forces of urbanisation as they affect space between locations, see also Brenner, 2018.

with the surroundings. When we play the video, what we should observe is that the red blocks repel the delegate objects because their interaction mix is negatively biased. On the other hand, the white blocks should maintain or attract interactions because they are positively biased.

The commercial value of this simulation lies in understanding more about why some areas trend towards alienation, while others appear to be more resilient urban environments. As can be seen, with a few simple rules based on the results of the variables comparison, it is possible to understand how tensile forces could foster alienating conditions. This finding supports the idea that alienating conditions are, in a colloquial sense, 'bad for business.'

Commercial stakeholders and practical relevance
In the visual sustainability model we all benefit from understanding the importance of visual sustainability in urban design strategy. For a start there is a strong case to be made that a Local Council stands to benefit from increased revenue and reputation. Residents are bound to benefit from increased self–esteem and the levels of empowerment that goes along with that. The private sector will receive a boost because it is better for business. The public will receive a boost because of private sector investment. This visual sustainability model is well placed to rely on cooperation between the following proposed categories of stakeholders: *sponsors* (paying for this), *operators* (those carrying out the research), and *beneficiaries* (those who stand to gain). The following stakeholders are well suited to engaging with a programme which supports this analytical model.
- The National Lottery Community Fund (sponsor).
- Reaching Communities England (sponsor).
- People's Postcode Lottery (sponsor).
- Co-op Local Community Fund (sponsor).
- The Henry Smith Charity, Strengthening Communities (sponsor).
- The English Heritage Trust (sponsor).
- Local Council (sponsor, operator, beneficiary).
- Universities, tertiary education, and schools (sponsors, operator)
- Residents and visitors (beneficiaries).
- The vulnerable (beneficiaries).
- Successive generations (beneficiaries).

Commercial summary
While the primary value in visual sustainability arguably lies in spatial health and well–being of people in cities, this section focuses on commercial

CHAPTER 5 — THE IMPORTANCE OF VISUAL SUSTAINABILITY

value. The relationship between commercial reality and visual sustainability can be understood through the dynamics found in both the quantity and quality of the interactions we experience with the objects and events that surround us. The relevance to urban design strategy is that it centres around the things we are prepared to pay for, with our attention because that is the link in urban design strategy with the commercial drivers that produce our built environment: our interactions, the type, and the mix inform decisions around which areas are commercially more viable. An example of this is in store design, where merchandise is laid out along routes based on a retailer's prediction of levels of consumer interaction. In this study, it is not about the meaning. The important thing is only that meaning exists. And if meaning exists then certain parcels of land become commercially viable because businesses follow people and people follow meaning. Those visual transactions which we are prepared to 'pay for' with our time distinguish high levels of visual sustainability from low levels, where more physical and emotional discomfort is experienced in relation to other areas. It explains why some urban areas work, and others do not. Why there is lost space (Trancik, 1986) in some areas but not in others. If you spend most of your time having to transact with something you do not like, the result will be alienation, because your engagement will mirror the experience demonstrated by, for example, some of the interviewees in the qualitative analysis. On the other hand, transacting with things that are dear to you, will result in being enriched by the value of the product i.e., the quality of your engagement with the environment, which this study calls visual sustainability. All that remains is to determine the value. The value need only be relative since the point of the exercise is to determine the differences in commercial potential. Therefore, as long as value is consistently applied, a picture can emerge of opportunities and obstructions. But these opportunities and obstructions must be understood in terms of non–linearity. The variables in the form of interaction types may be considered to be dynamic and unpredictable. They do not appear to be linear. When combined, these variables produce a certain qualitative multiplicity (as described by Bergson) to which commercial value can be attached. And while no two sites are the same, this commercial value is arrived at because business follows people, people follow meaning, and meaning is the visual relationship which we hold dear to our surroundings.

To return to Bergson's theory: the process of being visually sustained — is in time. Time is the ultimate invariant. Memory is the transformation. Together they form the ultimate invariance structure. Which all points us to how it might be possible for Bergson and Robbins' theory of temporal metaphysics to shift the way we think about the commercial reality of our built environment. Because if we are the sound being made, then urban design needs to produce a beautiful sound in us.

Interim summary 4

We can now also see how:

- Non–linearity produces differences across a transect resulting in what can be termed compressive and tensile forces, where people may be attracted or repulsed by their surroundings. The key difference to be aware of in this study is that what we are repulsed by is not what we hold dear, it is a form of alienation because even if we stop and stare at, for example, some repulsive object or event or element, how do we differentiate through head movement, what this represents in relation to what we hold dear? This study was not able to determine a difference but neither was there any clear evidence of repulsion. However it is important to note that alienation in this study forms part of the concept of visual sustainability—it marks the one extreme of a spectrum, with *what we hold dear* being located at the opposite end. As discussed in "A report card" on page 156 this is a good question and requires further research into the effects repulsion has on head movement (see also suggested future research "Urban mental health" on page 155). But for now, in this study, there is no evidence, in these data collected, of repulsion of any significance or magnitude. These data collected in this study represent the full spectrum of visual sustainability, from alienation to high visual sustainabilty. Drawing a line between what we hold dear and what we are repulsed by is evident in, for example, the 0.25–second interaction type, which strongly suggests higher levels of repulsion because the more these increase, the less there are of any other type of interaction.
- There appears to be an association between commercial value and location as a result of interaction type.
- A weighting of the values of interaction types may be beneficial in explaining the potential differences in commercial value.

§. 22 *Findings summary*

The main points

The main points of interest from these findings can be summarised as follows.

1   The QUARTER type (yellow) appears to act as an early–warning

CHAPTER 5 THE IMPORTANCE OF VISUAL SUSTAINABILITY

       device for alienating conditions.

2   The null hypothesis, that interactions are evenly distributed and thus have no effect on visual sustainability or of being visually sustained in the act of seeing, is rejected.

3   A pattern has emerged which is suggestive of a scaling relationship between interaction type and interaction count (see "Interaction type characteristics" on page 96 and Figure 27 on page 99).

4   Higher counts of WHOLE and HALF interaction type coincide with areas of higher urban density, but for the compact range of data of QUARTER and EIGHTH the opposite is true.

5   The more SIXTEENTH interaction types there are in a block, the fewer interaction types are observed overall. This appears to confirm that the role played by alienation is highly influential where the SIXTEENTH interaction type is dominant.

6   Interaction mix is a valuable aid in understanding more about visual sustainability levels.

7   There is some evidence of non–linearity in these data especially between the zones of this urban transect, which points to conditions sympathetic to dynamic and unpredictable phenomenon described by complexity theory.

8   We can infer with a certain amount of confidence that a predominance of QUARTER and EIGHTH types (yellow and blue colours) are visual indicators of an urban environment of declining quality.

9   Dominant blue and grey colours (eighth and sixteenth) are strong indicators of poor visual sustainability, most likely requiring urban design intervention at a strategic level.

10   The variables comparison results point to the proposal that interaction type serves as the building block of visual sustainability.

11   If we look at Figure 33 on page 103 again, it is entirely conceivable that the urban environment can deteriorate and begin to resemble the stacked bar for Heygate (see the red outline denoting this comparison). It is also conceivable that where the yellow (QUARTER 1–second) variable is dominant, alienating conditions have the potential to escalate and resemble the Heygate example (dotted black outline).

12   The WHOLE and HALF interaction type appear to be statistically significant in relation to every interaction type except QUARTER

13   while QUARTER is only significantly related to SIXTEENTH and SIM. The findings so far suggest that visual sustainability i.e., THE PROCESS OF CONNECTING TO WHAT WE HOLD DEAR, is strongest where WHOLE, and HALF notes are dominant.

14   It appears that urban density plays less of a role than we might expect and what is more influential are the things that hold people's attention. The positive effects of nature, trees, water, green vista's and the like in the quietness of Zone 4 matches the duration in seconds of Zone 1, while Zone 3 has the lowest built density but enjoys the most attention in terms of length of engagement.

15   The digital tapestry is a valuable aid in understanding more about visual sustainability at a macro level and can lead to an understanding of emergence from the mix of interaction types.

16   The relationship between commercial reality and visual sustainability can be understood through the dynamics found in both the quantity and quality of interactions.

17   The commercial value lies in understanding more about why some urban areas trend towards alienation, while others are more successful for trading. The suggestion is that locations become commercially viable because businesses follow people, and people follow meaning. The meaning they seek is to be visually sustained.

18   Non–linearity produces differences across the site resulting in what can be termed compressive and tensile forces, where people may be attracted or repulsed by their surroundings.

19   There appears to be an association between commercial value and location as a result of interaction type.

20   A weighting of the values of interaction types may be beneficial in explaining the potential differences in commercial value.

Inspecting the parts or attending to their meaning

I have been cautious about making any claim in this study regarding *how* we are visually sustained because of

> the difficulty that we have in making sense of complex systems... and by complex systems I simply mean systems that are composed of many different [interacting] parts... without any centralised control... [such that] global patterns emerge from their interactions (Agent-Based Modeling: An Introduction from Uri Wilensky, 2018, 00:02:30),

But it does appear to be true from the findings, that we are dealing with

CHAPTER 5 THE IMPORTANCE OF VISUAL SUSTAINABILITY

a phenomenon which shows signs of non–linearity, unpredictability, and which has no central controlling agent or variable. We are the authors of this invisible city but we produce these data unconsciously, so in that sense then, we have no control over what is produced. We can only 'inspect' the results or, put another way, read the report card. The dilemma we're faced with is summed up by Polanyi:

> So long as you look at X, you are not attending from X to something else, which would be its meaning. In order to attend from X to its meaning, you must cease to look at X, and the moment you look at X you cease to see its meaning" (Polanyi and Grene, 1969, p.146).

This is because by analysing 'the parts', whether by hypothesis testing, pairs plot, or variables comparison, it appears to be impossible to single out the emergence produced by the mix of interactions. Perhaps the closest we get to seeing emergence is through the digital tapestry (when it functions as a visual synthesis of the parts in a durational sense) or in the sound played by these data themselves (because the sound through duration or melody may say something to us in another language). Whether it is a pleasant or an unpleasant experience is not the point, the point is as Polanyi asserts, to lift our gaze beyond the parts to the meaning.

The digital tapestry when attending to meaning

In the same sense that INTERACTION TYPE is a measurement of visual sustainability, the digital tapestry functions as a visual synthesis of the parts, in a durational sense, where: "In order to attend from X [i.e., the parts in the form of the individual interaction types, the blocks, or the zones] to its meaning, you must cease to look at X" because: "So long as you look at X, you are not attending from X to something else, which would be its meaning" (Polanyi and Grene, 1969, p.146). That 'something else' in this case is 'the effect' of the digital tapestry in conveying an overall sense of visual sustainability, or alienation. It is a *feeling* you get about the state of the urban from a tapestry of flashing light points. Its just a *feeling* which you cannot describe with words.

The parts which are of interest

But there are several areas that are interesting when inspecting 'the parts', as we have seen when considered as large networks of simple interacting elements called interaction types. The **first** is the variability of the QUARTER interaction type in Zone 1 and Zone 5. The **second**, is how, from the variables comparison, QUARTER appears to have no significance in relation to the other interaction types and yet appears to have an influence in a negative direction towards alienating conditions. The **third** is the SIXTEENTH interaction type which speaks to the "curtailment of meaning by alienation" (Polanyi and Grene, 1969, pp.146–147), because the greater the presence of the sixteenth type, the less (count) there are of every other interaction type. **Fourth**, if visual sustainability is the process by which we are sustained and enriched through the visual relationship we hold dear to our surroundings (De Kock, 2019, p.72), the logical conclusion is that we congregate, using the invariance of time, around processes of enduring visual stimulation. Which is why WHOLE and HALF interaction types appear, from these findings, to be most influential in producing emergent conditions that sustain us. **Fifth**, there appear to be three networks present in our study area. One is the human network, the other is the network which stimulates interactions, and the third is the resulting network of interaction. Each of these three networks appears to be a dynamic, unpredictable, non–linear, and *self–organising system. It may be that Lefebvre is right when he says that "the important thing is not to reconstruct a view… but rather to understand the grid that underlies it" (citing 'a Japanese philosopher', 2011, p.155) because we do need to comprehend the connectivity in these three underlying grids in our cities. But if we circle back to visual sustainability as a process: "It is the heat of the flame that causes the [sensation] pain… not the colour or not the shape" (The Perception of Causality (Part 1), 2013, 00:35:00). That thing that we don't see (the temperature) is, as Kelley points out, indivisibly part of the object (The Perception of Causality (Part 1), 2013, 00:34:30). So, the **sixth** area of interest, by way of this analogy, is that 'temperature' (in the analogy) represents a spectrum along which visual sustainability may be measured. And the suggestion is that temperature is produced by the mix of interaction types. It can be hot or cold or anywhere in between but at what point emergent conditions arise, or at what point there's a change in state, remains a mystery. Because "you see the leaves of the tree blowing in the wind… you feel the wind… and you see the wind moving the leaves… it's not just the wind blowing and the leaves moving" (The Perception of Causality (Part 2), 2013, 00:21:30). Therefore, the perception of our experience in being visually sustained, is "not that we're doing something but that something is doing something to us" (The Perception of Causality (Part 2), 2013, 00:26:50) and this appears to be true also of the phenomenon of visual sustainability. And if Polanyi were to have his say, it might be that visual sustainability is a function of an "external reality gradually accessible to knowing" (Polanyi and Grene, 1969, p.133)..

Self organising: Mitchell explains the self as "behaviour arises only due to interactions within the system," while organising refers to "the appearance of what we would call organized patterns" (Introduction to Complexity: Models of Biological Self-Organization, 2018, 00:01:00).].

At home in a complex system
So, in final contemplation of these findings, the idea that cities are complex

CHAPTER 5   THE IMPORTANCE OF VISUAL SUSTAINABILITY

systems is a given. Our urban is:
> made up of a large number of strongly interacting entities, and those entities are often heterogeneous... not only of people, of course, but also the networks and infrastructure, social and physical, that support those people (Fractals and Scaling: Reflections on urban scaling, 2019).

To that we could add the commercial relevance of the city as a complex system. The things that:
> drives GDP or wages or various consumption measures, measures of creativity... tend to be interactions. So, cities come together, people come together in cities, because there's a benefit to these interactions that one has... economic benefits, social benefits (Fractals and Scaling: Summary of course, 2019).

And, of course, one could add the benefits of being visually sustained, because without it all the other benefits appear to be marginal at best, as people are repulsed by alienating conditions and leave.

INDUSTRY STANDARDS: A COMPARISON

There may well be some curiosity around how this model of visual sustainability compares with, what is arguably the leading empirically based urban analytical model, namely, Space Syntax. Both appear to have something to say about how we're sustained, although Space Syntax (Hillier and Hanson, 2005; Hillier, 2015) has been around for some time. If we look at their website as it stands today, they
> forecast the social, economic & environmental impacts of development on mobility, land value & health at all scales... [through the use of] advanced digital technologies (Space Syntax Limited, 2024).

While an in–depth comparison is outside the scope of this study there are several interesting comparisons to make. The overview that follows is presented in the context of my findings in this study.

1   Essence

Space Syntax's contemporary tagline is "Thriving life in buildings & urban places" (Space Syntax Limited, 2024). Their strategy appears to be more interventionist in approach in the sense of analysing existing conditions and intervening or 'loosening up' the connectivity in cities to achieve the kind of result they want to achieve, or that their client wishes to achieve. They do so by 'channelling' human and human–related activity in a physical way. Nonetheless, the tagline of my study could easily be adapted from one of Hillier's earlier books such as 'The social logic of space' or 'Space is the machine: a configurational theory of architecture.' Except my tagline might

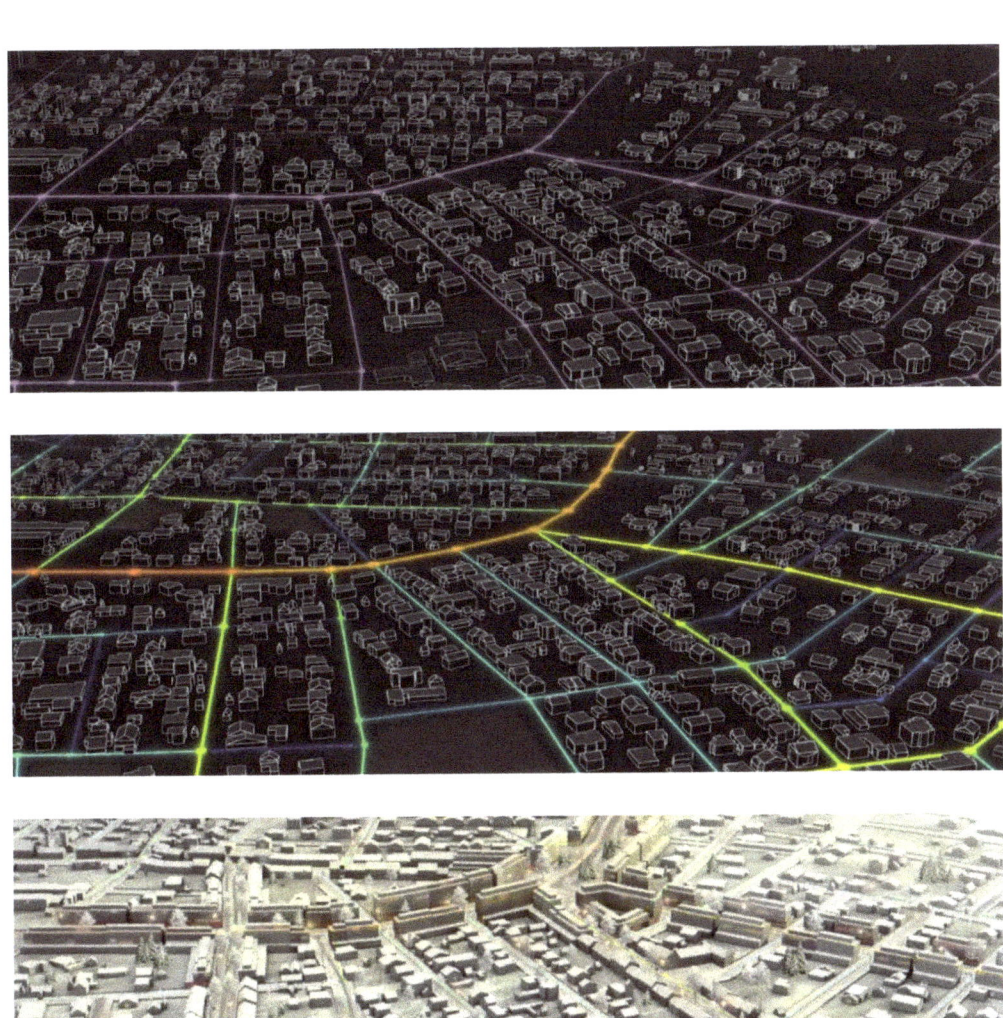

Figure 52. Planar characteristics of the space syntax model: improving connectivity in a physical city in two dimensions. (Images © Space Syntax Limited, 2024).

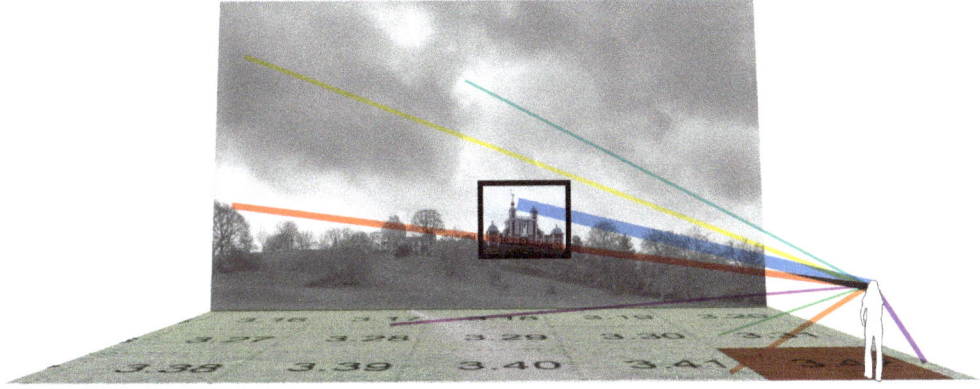

Figure 53. Visual sustainability model: interaction types as dynamic, time–extended, multi–dimensional events.

CHAPTER 5 THE IMPORTANCE OF VISUAL SUSTAINABILITY

be suited to something along these lines:

The social logic of time, or

Time is the machine: a configurational theory of our urban.

This is because my visual sustainability model is configurational theory in one sense, since it consists of a (dynamic) configuration of interaction types which reveal what was previously hidden. Time is a key differentiator, however, and I have presented a case for how space is really just depth of time. As for social logic, it may be said that, in this study, social connectivity is only ever fully realised when the invisible city is. There is, however, another type of 'visual corridor,' absent from the space syntax model, which embraces not only physical use but visual use i.e., how we feel about the use that we see and being defined by it. A more appropriate tagline to describe this research outcome might thus be something along the following lines:

Visually sustained by what we hold dear.

My argument in this research (in relation to the space syntax model) is that we need to understand another type of visual corridor, which can only be accessed by understanding the multi–dimensional qualities of visual interaction type (see Figure 53 on page 141).

2 Scope

My intuition is that the space syntax model complements the research in this study in terms of its use, as attending to an effect, the cause of which, I would argue, is more subtle in visual sustainability than it is in Space Syntax which attends to movement in urban corridors through integration analysis and directional changes (Hillier and Hanson, 2005; Hillier, 2015). The cause of alienation in the visual sustainability model is better flushed out at the level of what we can *not* see in the types of interaction we have with our surroundings, and therein lies the first major difference. Because our interaction—the way we see—while it is certainly established in the streets we walk or drive along, is not limited to the streets we walk or drive along. Nor is it limited by the physicality of the movement corridors, whether situated inside a building or outside.

3 Technology

The visual sustainability model is not reliant on advanced or expensive digital technologies to produce results, nor is the method of obtaining results the same. R is free open source software, the Adobe suite is accessible and relatively cheap, and there are now many excellent alternatives available which are inexpensive or free. All–in–all, the level of sophistication is modest compared to the space syntax model. The implication is of course, that the visual sustainability model is accessible to interested parties with meagre resources and limited training.

4   Interaction

Space Syntax relies on analysing movement corridors and then categorising these channels according to levels of physical connectivity, described by nodes and links. It therefore has limited understanding of human interaction in a visual sense because it chooses not to deal with the levels of subjectivity involved or with things such as beauty, facades, or site constraints like, setbacks, bulk, etc. There is an argument to be made that the visual sustainability model is also about connectivity. It is, but not in the same way. In the space syntax model the physical environment is privileged over the intangible. The focus is to improve the space between what is already built. The visual sustainability model is different in that space is not privileged, because it is a function of time. The interaction is dynamic, and connectivity is established with all sorts of things in all sorts of ways, both visible and invisible. And each interaction type has the levels of subjectivity 'baked in.' These data produced are human–centric, not object oriented. My argument is therefore that we get a better 'read' of the urban using the methods established in this research.

5   Subjectivity

An argument can be made that subjectivity is implied in the results of the space syntax method i.e., 'thriving life.' It does so through a completely different paradigm however and is therefore arguably less durable as a solution to urban alienation mainly because of its narrow range of focus.

6   The human condition

The space syntax model assumes meaning from the improvement of physical levels of connectivity, which is perfectly acceptable in terms of the rationale it has adopted, to improve "buildings & urban places" (Space Syntax Limited, 2024). My research also aims to improve buildings and urban places but from a different source and in a different way. It arguably goes further because it investigates human alienation at a more personal level and extends the solution beyond the potential offered by Space Syntax. For example, outcomes are inferred which reach well beyond the physical solutions offered by the space syntax model, due to the influence of Bergson and his rationalisation of the role we play in time–extended events. Because we do play a role in our cities, one which goes beyond simply improving buildings and urban places. *We* are the improvement and in this way, as we improve so does our environment, whereas for the space syntax model, the improvements are the physical corridors and they are then left to change us. The idea behind the visual sustainability model is that we improve our condition in a way which is resistant to forces of alienation, ambiguity, and confused meaning. Simply improving buildings and urban spaces i.e., 'the objects of the physical city', is not good enough because one man's improvement is often another man's distress. The person providing the money receives the desired outcome. In other words, the ambiguity remains because we also need to improve the objects that surround us, of the invisible city. The objects of the invisible city represent tangible as well as non–tangible elements. The case for visual sustainability then is that it transcends these conflicts of interest because, in my study, the most important thing is *the mix of interaction types*. Not space, not connectivity of streets and squares, not the insides of buildings. From the mix we can comprehend and take stock of the nature and quality of both visible and invisible objects that surround us. Because our interactions do not lie. It is at this point then, after this unbiased condition report, that I can see the benefit of adopting space syntax methods, after which a survey of interaction types could be carried out again, as a sort of report card, to better understand the urban environment in terms of the use we see and how we feel about the use that we see. The main idea is that we need to be able to first see what people see in an area of interest. Only then can we more fully appreciate potential as well as shortcomings.

7   Three–dimensional

This research produces a three–dimensional artefact of the invisible forces at work, which the space syntax model is unable to do in the same way since it deals with two–dimensional spatial relationships. The space syntax model is a product of classical metaphysics, employing Euclidean principles in a two–dimensional way. The 3D outcome shown in Figure 52 on page 141 (Bottom) is coincidental to the method used in that it is the proposed effect of strengthening the hierarchical connectivity characteristics of nominated physical movement corridors. For the space syntax model, connectivity is planar in that it is a function of a physical corridor of space running from a to b, in an x,y plane, which is not the case in the visual sustainability model. In the visual sustainability model (Figure 53 on page 141) connectivity is a function of memory and runs in all directions, x, y, z, and t (time). The currency we use in our interactions with our surroundings is time i.e., the longer we are engaged, the more meaningful the interaction. The network is only of interest for the emergent properties of the mix of interaction types. In that sense then, time is not a network, it is duration. In contrast, value in the space syntax model is a hierarchical network i.e., the more connected the more valuable.

8 Pedagogical

The space syntax model is arguably less intuitive, more time consuming, and less revealing than the visual sustainability model in terms of being able to quickly grasp the nature of challenges presented in contextual urban design analysis. The level of training and sophistication required appears to be the reason why it has naturally evolved into a professional consulting service with highly skilled staff, as evidence by their website (Space Syntax Limited, 2024). It did not start that way but it is a complex process to follow and has therefore evolved the way it has. There are several advantages of the visual sustainability model, the first of which is that it trains a student to see both visible and invisible objects in relation to tensile and compressive forces in an area of interest. It trains students to think about people. It also trains students to think about the threat to any urban environment, of alienation. It uses the same software familiar to architectural, urban design, and planning students and is ideally situated to be integrated early on because it is relatively quick (see "§. 14 Research design" on page 77), producing the results which would be invaluable when going from feasibility into the conceptual design phase. Ideally it would be a mandatory for students to have completed this kind of analysis so that their response to any design brief is both logical and intuitive because they know what is 'going on' in their chosen site. It would, arguably, be introduced in the third year of a five–year undergraduate course or immediately in a Masters. The whole point of making it a mandatory part of any built environment course (including planning) is so that students (and practitioners) are made aware and fully understand the site properly first, and for a student to present their understanding early on. It is critical for planners to adopt this method because architects and urban designers are in a sense dictated to by inputs further upstream (plans and policy as outlined by Sturzaker and Hickman, 2024). Designers thus need to empirically understand what types of interaction already exist, and this is true even on an empty site, because the things we interact with could be two centimetres away or two kilometres away, they could be visible or invisible, but they are all relevant, as my findings have shown. The good thing though, is that in this model we do not need to know the meaning or even what it is someone has looked at.

9 Top–own versus bottom–up

Space Syntax is more of a top–down model which is able, through interventions in the urban, to condition human behaviour. It is excellent as a tool for adding commercial value by strengthening commercial strips, high streets, and civic squares. It is also used in buildings to improve circulation and add value to spaces as destinations. By contrast, the visual sustainability model can be argued to be authentically bottom–up, such that it acts like a report card informing us of the level of well–being of everyone interacting with their environment, *including* the network of movement corridors which the space syntax model focuses on. But movement corridors are only one small part of the gamut of information contained in the visual sustainability model. The simplest way to put it perhaps, is that the space syntax method constructs part of the physical city but the visual sustainability model constructs the invisible city, and the building materials used are: *what we hold dear*, and *what we are repulsed by*.

IN URBAN DESIGN STRATEGY

CONCLUSION

§. 23 *Measuring our temporal urban*

The only thing really surprising about dark matter is that we should be surprised that it exists. And the same goes for 'urban dark matter.' The idea is not sensational in one sense, which is that it appears to exist everywhere. The challenge has been to find a convincing strategy that will uncover enough of the invisible city in order to make more sense of it. The analogy of interaction type as invisible dark matter is evident by the effect it has on the objects that we *do* see, which are the interactions people have. The fact that people were engaged with something around them for a certain amount of time is all the data we need to understand a little more about the concept of visual sustainability. The rejection of the null hypothesis should be equally

CONCLUSION THE IMPORTANCE OF VISUAL SUSTAINABILITY

unsurprising since we intuitively know that there is a difference in the types of interaction we have with our surroundings. The problem with human nature is that we are often driven to far–flung places (meant also in a metaphorical sense) in our search for answers to the things that gnaw at our souls, when the answers are much closer to home than we are often comfortable with. The overall aim of this study has been to explore the philosophy behind how we are sustained by what we see and its relevance to urban design. It has meant that I have had to understand more about the types of interactions we have with our environment, without knowing the exact meaning of what it is we interact with or even what was looked at. But it has not required artificial intelligence to provide an answer. The answer is much closer to home, using a simple technique called observation. In other words, I have used my own eyes to see how people use theirs. And I have, primarily using Bergson, Polanyi, Varela, and Gibson, explored the philosophical reasoning behind how and what we see; and why this is relevant to urban design strategy.

The exegesis or artefact produced—a digital tapestry—demonstrates the potential of the tactile nature of the invisible city we build. It provides a springboard to further explore the mix of interaction types. It has been argued that the invisible city is a reflection pool, and we see ourselves through the sounds of interaction being played, whether we are conscious of it or not. When we look into that pool of data, we even see in our own reflection the pain of alienation in certain circumstances. It is that 0.25–second long alarm bell of the SIXTEENTH interaction type which sounds so uncomfortably. It forces us to leave a location (which is really just a container holding these data which we are repulsed by). I have addressed, through the findings, how the strategy of using interaction type as a measuring device helps us understand more about the relationship between urban heterogeneity and how we are visually sustained through engagement with our surroundings. My research question (on page 6) has been answered because the philosophical concept of duration describes the types of interaction we have with our environment, and these interactions are descriptors for conditions of visual sustainability, or alternatively, visual indicators of an urban of declining quality. For visual sustainability to exist in this sense means it cannot be ignored by any of the built environment professionals if we are to ever produce effective, coordinated urban design strategy. Because we cannot produce effective solutions if we do not understand the quality of urban space we are trying to intervene in. The findings ("§. 22 Findings summary" on page 135), have demonstrated the significance of the relationship between variables (Figure 38 on page 111), their non–linear characteristics, and the general research results pointing to how the number, the types, the mix, and the intensity of interactions help describe the quality of the urban environment (Figure 42 on page 119 and Figure 43 on page 119). The number and duration of interactions appear to be privileged criteria that help explain how (the process by which) "we are sustained and enriched in daily life through the visual relationship we hold dear to our surroundings" (De Kock, 2019, p.72).

THESIS STATEMENT

The use of VISUAL INTERACTION TYPE as a measuring device, is an effective strategy for understanding the relationship between urban heterogeneity and how we are visually sustained through engagement with our surroundings.

§. 24 *Response overview*

Condensed outcome of this study
By considering interaction in the design of our cities we can, through an appreciation of the influence of the full gamut of types of visual interactions we have with our surroundings, make a difference to our experience of the built environment. My interest has been in the relationship between being visually sustained and how we interact with our environment, without knowing the exact meaning, or even what it is we interact with. The study has produced several interesting findings without having to negotiate the ambiguous, contradictory, fluid, theoretically dense subject of the act of seeing which has traditionally underpinned much of architectural and urban design theory. In this sense there is an endless amount of literature available about how we see but nothing that *directly* addresses the process of visual sustainability, which is why my decision to research this topic using a mixed methods approach has allowed me to understand more about the act of seeing through triangulation between qualitative and quantitative methods. The overall protocol followed was as follows:

1. I adopted a philosophical approach, bracketing existing theory, and looked for the ESSENCE of the problem in a phenomenological sense.
2. I started with the theory of Bergson because he was the only philosopher I encountered who differentiated himself along temporal lines. His concept of duration aligned with my research interest about how time might explain the way we interact with our surroundings.
3. I then forced myself to look beyond the philosophy to statistical analysis for evidence of emerging patterns and clues pointing to the relationship between visual sustainability and interactions with our environment.

CONCLUSION THE IMPORTANCE OF VISUAL SUSTAINABILITY

What has transpired is greater clarity about the nature of the building blocks of visual sustainability and this constitutes my contribution to knowledge. What I found was that the number, the types, the mix, and the intensity of interactions help describe the quality of the urban environment. If interaction–type is satisfied, then an interaction takes place, either trending towards visual sustainability, or towards alienation. The significance of understanding interaction–type therefore appears to be fundamental to any consideration of urban design strategy in the built environment.

A summary of the difference made by my research
There are three considerations to take into account regarding the difference this research makes: 1. Embodied mind, 2. Urban design strategy, and 3. External stakeholders.

Firstly, the long–term difference is that we are able to understand ourselves — and our role in society — better, when mindful of the types of interaction that take place around us. That is what I mean by the phrase 'embodied mind' borrowed from Varela et al.. Because our bodies are the centre of action (Bergson, 1988, p.48) and the centre of action is where we are grounded when we interact with our surroundings. It is the ever–present past that Bergson alludes to, which holds us together and which binds us, one to the other. And this, when taken into account in urban design strategy, has the potential to produce environments that are less alienating because it reflects a functioning society. We can not, in these terms, be the result of anything other than an embodied mind in a certain location at a certain moment in time, and the value of transacting with things that are dear to us will result in being enriched by the quality of our engagement with the environment, which this study calls visual sustainability.

Secondly, insofar as urban design strategy is concerned, is that we 'lift the lid' on the idea of 'urban dark matter' i.e., the invisible, and the effect it might have on us through the visual interactions we have with our surroundings. Urban dark matter is thus important to any claim made about how we are visually sustained. This is because how we are visually sustained lies at the heart of strategic urban design. Not understanding how we are visually sustained points directly to a lack of understanding of urban design strategy. It is my argument, therefore, that it is only by way of the number, type, mix, and intensity of interactions that we are enabled to firstly, understand how to correctly interpret the quality of the urban environment; secondly, to properly describe the quality of the urban environment in an unbiased way; and thirdly, to implement a strategy which protects, enhances, or else fixes shortcomings in the urban environment. The relevance to urban design strategy is that it centres around the things we are prepared to pay for, with our attention and it is this transaction which should be emphasised in any discussion that occurs in relation to stakeholders.

As for external stakeholders, while the significance of my findings are qualified by the limitations of my research design (see "§. 27 Study limitations" on page 156), my suggestion is that visual interaction type is the building block of visual sustainability. And to the extent that this research is validated by future research (see "§. 26 Future research" on page 153), it would appear that visual interaction types *are* 'the dark matter' in cities. In terms of practical implementation of the principles of this observational technique, it has the potential to be useful not only in pedagogical environments but also in investment circles where the performance/health of real estate is able to withstand a more perceptive and robust level of scrutiny, able to be well understood by all. Beneficiaries include (but are not limited to) what I consider in the current climate to be competing interests, such as Community Action Groups, Urban Design Teachers & Practitioners, and Property Portfolio & Asset Managers. Competing, because it appears to me that none of these groups fully understand what is going on in the parcels of land in which there is a common interest. But by understanding interaction type and the findings of this and future studies, any attempt at clouding the issues at stake is likely to fail.

§. 25 *Outcomes*

My findings chapter concluded that any strategy in an urban design context has to be framed around the premise that visual sustainability is measured by a mix of interaction types, the majority of which are in the upper range of WHOLE and HALF notes; while QUARTER notes appear to share a more significant relationship with the lower range of notes, trending towards alienation. The findings suggest that visual sustainability i.e., the process of connecting to what we hold dear, is strongest where WHOLE, and HALF interaction types are dominant. There is also the observation that higher counts of WHOLE and HALF interaction types coincide with areas of higher urban density, but for the compact range of data of QUARTER and EIGHTH the opposite is true. WHOLE and HALF therefore appear to thrive in lively areas while the less dense locations appear to be more susceptible to developing alienating conditions. These findings appear to satisfy the idea that the type of interaction we have with

CONCLUSION   THE IMPORTANCE OF VISUAL SUSTAINABILITY

our environment is indeed a descriptor for conditions of visual sustainability, be they high, low, or non–existent in the form of alienation. The visual interactions we have with our environment provide a rich source of data which I believe is currently untapped. Interaction analysis is proposed as a useful tool that can be used to measure what might be referred to as 'spatial health.' Spatial health is arguably more important than commercial value. Commercial value can be thought of as a down–stream effect of spatial health because, it can be argued, it succeeds in vibrant, positive communities. There is little to gain from commercial activity in a depressed or poorly–functioning population (except perhaps for the pharmaceutical industry). Spatial health is focused on people's well–being and ultimately is consequential to urban health and safety, through the prevention of urban alienation in our cities.

Interaction analysis is a tool that appears to be able to resist theoretical contradiction and unsettled discourse. There is thus, as indicated by my rejection of the null hypothesis (on page 93), a difference in the type of interaction, and this difference is informative in terms of how we interact with our environment, especially in our cities. The importance therefore to architecture, and the resulting urban spaces we produce, should not be underestimated because the number and duration of our interactions act as a litmus test for urban forces that we are attracted to and repulsed by. The number, the type, the mix, and the intensity of interactions help describe urban quality. In its exteriority, this is visually evidenced by interaction type, and when these data are played as sound ("Appendix C" on page 221), it spills over into the intangible qualities normally associated with interiority (De Kock, 2020a). Together, through this bridging effect of sound, Bergson's theory comes alive and contributes to understanding, in a unique way, how (the process by which) we are sustained and enriched. We have also seen how the mix of interactions is an attribute of location. This is because, if visual sustainability is an emergence or a by–product of non–linearity in surrounding events—as posited by Frankl (Man's Search for Meaning, 2017)—then such emergence, in the sense described by complexity theory, may best be seen by way of a certain mix of interaction types. It is, as posited by Frankl (2003), meaning which cannot be manufactured, and therefore resistant to advances in artificial intelligence/AI. But the conditions need to be 'right' for the effect to be realised, which, in this case, refers to emergence from the 'right' mix of interaction–types. The proposal therefore is that visual sustainability, through the analysis of interaction types, informs urban design strategy. And as a shared asset, in the sense that data are collected and a database or library of validated conditions or classifications are stored, it may

IN URBAN DESIGN STRATEGY

be useful for evaluation and comparison. The significance of understanding interaction–type therefore appears to be fundamental to any consideration of urban design strategy in the built environment.

The relationship of the visual interaction types can be presented in two ways. Firstly, through their potential to help code how we look at our surroundings, and, secondly, through the sound from the time stamps that describe time–extended events. There lies in these two parameters the promise of both statistical significance and relevance of Bergson's theory of duration. Both of these refer back to the two principles derived from Bergson's theory which I have concentrated on, namely, the reciprocity between Principle 3 and Principle 7: invariance structures in relation to dynamic form (Table 4 on page 65). The urban invariance structure proposed may be argued as follows: Statistical significance is a structural invariant and may be thought of as *use*, while duration is, of course, transformation. It is *the feeling* of that use. The structure of the basic building block (Figure 38 on page 111) is the device by which an endless array of permutations is possible. The permutations within that structural device represent transformation similar, one could argue, to a Rubik's Cube. The cube, in this analogy, is the structural invariance; the permutations are the transformation. Together they form the invariance structure of the invisible city. It is both device and *feeling*, physical use and visual use. Each possible permutation represents a level of visual sustainability. But the invisible city is more than just a Rubik's Cube. It is not simply an abstraction for it exists, just as much as a physical city exists. The invisible city represents the sound that *we* make through visual interaction type: it is a record of our reaction to the physical city. And this sound, or duration from time values, can be said to be recorded in the same way the built environment that we see is—in layers, levels, and floors—existing in memory somewhere as time–extended events in that vast universal interference pattern that is Bergson's photographic plate. Because "*... is it not obvious that the photograph, if photograph there be, is already taken, already developed in the very heart of things and at all the points of space?*" (Bergson, Matière et mémoire, 1896, translated, emphasis added).

§. 26 *Future research*

Sound and music

One avenue that warrants exploration is the sound these data make, how and what type. Sound is a tool which, through qualitative multiplicity, speaks to the process itself, in this case of alienation or visual sustainability. Sound speaks to Bergson's time–extended event, not to spatial chunks frozen in time

CONCLUSION THE IMPORTANCE OF VISUAL SUSTAINABILITY

(Robbins, 2014, 2021). Xenakis is famous for using musical notation to design the 1958 Phillips Pavilion (Parthenios et al., 2016). A sample of my use of the musical notation, using only length of time, is included in "The sound of data" on page 221 of "Appendix C" and has been produced out of curiosity because it appears naturally from my data, in the form of emergence. It is entirely logical—especially grounded as I am in this study, in Bergson—for me, after having seen these data and drawn conclusions from the findings, to have asked the question: "*I wonder what* these *data* sound *like*?" There is also an opportunity to track head movement using a 'pen–down' feature or simply by transposing data points (changes in movement/direction at points along the video time–line) on to a (musical) bar. This enactment of visual experimentation of harmonious interpretations and associated durational effects, represent further exploration of what alienation may sound like in relation to being visually sustained.

Context
However, the main serviceable emphasis in future research should arguably be on obtaining data from other urban areas. My study area represents an urban transect which contains five urban environments, each quite distinct in character from the other. It is a study area which functions as an urban exemplar in the sense that one expects to find more robust levels of visual sustainability because it is a World Heritage Site. What is required now in future research is to measure, using the device proposed in this study—of sounds as a metric—urban areas which are more representative of urban heterogeneity. In doing so, it will serve as a daily reminder of the ordinary—in other words 'that which we have to put up with'—and to acknowledge (as concluded in Chapter Two) how extraordinary we are for *seeing* the ordinary.

Practitioners and students
There is also the aspect of future research into what many believe to be the problem of the professions. Planners, architects, urban designers, and associated professionals are arguably all experiencing an identity crisis of some sort. If globalisation has hollowed out nation states then the trickle down effect is bound to devastate these actors in the built environment. Power shifts remain at an all time high but political dominance, less so. Corporations appear to be firmly in control and private enterprise is emboldened by all manner of AI and associated arsenal capable of orchestrating technologically driven, dominance–seeking strategies. But if there is one area, modest in its character though it is, where an opportunity exists, it lies in the uneasy

IN URBAN DESIGN STRATEGY

ground identified by Sturzaker and Hickman (2024), at the interface between an introverted system geared towards inputs (plans, policy) versus outcome based consulting. The findings in this research suggest that there is an unbiased, unambiguous way to measure urban health. For example, the problem highlighted by Sturzaker and Hickman with respect to the high turnover of professionals before any meaningful contextual engagement has taken place 'on the ground,' can largely be overcome with the right urban design strategy in place, one that recognises interaction type as a metric for establishing the status condition of any parcel of land of interest. Because if it is true of urban design, then not understanding how we are visually sustained equally directs us towards what appears to be a fundamental lack of understanding in strategic planning efforts.

Urban mental health

Urban mental health is an important avenue for research because it has serious consequences (Bhugra et al., 2019). Interaction type provides an excellent platform for understanding urban well–being especially, as seems to be the case, where meaning has become an obstruction to understanding, because people are obsessed with identifying meaning above everything else. If we instead try to get a read on the types of interaction and levels of visual sustainability, then the problem of alienation i.e., the pain of not having a connection to what is held dear, can be dealt with at the heart of the problem, at the locations where it exists. Because this research has shown that we do not have to know meaning to be able to build a profile of alienation in any part of the city. There is also scope for further research into the effects repulsion has on head movement when compared to attraction (which is outside the scope of this study). In urban mental health the variable of interest is in what disgusts us or, put another way, elements which we are repulsed by. Future research will need to look at ways to account for these phenomena in relation to what we are attracted to.

Ontology, epistemology, and pedagogical

The final area of future research belongs to ontology. It is a domain that easily gives way to simulacrum as different realities can be charged with obscuring and obstructing relevance, causing confused meaning. It is the domain which informs pedagogical relevance. Because an architectural school should not become a manufacturing company, nor should a manufacturing company become an architectural school. What is needed is not more training necessarily, but more thought. Planners, architects and urban designers spend a decade

CONCLUSION THE IMPORTANCE OF VISUAL SUSTAINABILITY

before there's any sense of the practical nature of the globalist arena into which they have been or will be thrust. It is inconceivable how even more training, technology, or deepfake will help produce better built environments. In reality, the opposite is arguably the case because as we have become 'cleverer', the quality of our urban environment has arguably become more chilling in its alienation. We cannot ever be sure now where public space begins and ends and with it some of the inalienable rights we as humans treasure. The pedagogical relevance of this study lies in a return to our human–centric existence where a city is built by thoughtful discourse. As the findings of this research has hopefully shown, there is no value in endlessly throwing technology at the objects that surround us, but instead, through the ability we have to *think…deeply, to concentrate on what resides *in* us. What my research is suggesting is that *if* the visible city has been built by thoughtful discourse, then the invisible city will provide material evidence of the quality of that thoughtfulness, through the metric used of interaction type. And future research should focus on architectural materialism for the role it is capable of playing in shaping that outcome, by which is meant, having a bearing on the quality of thoughtfulness. One sub–theme of this research direction may be in how architecture and urban design (as seen in "Object and experience as a map" on page 46) seem to play a role, where their presence is implied and their materialism impactful, but neither are ever articulated explicitly. Because, as we have seen from this research, it seems that they are only able to be revealed through a metric such as interaction type.

See "Object and experience as a map" on page 46.

§. 27 *Study limitations*

The following points provide an overview of some of the limitations of this study, with suggestions where improvements can be made.

A report card
The visual sustainability model only provides information *about* levels of visual sustainability. Its value lies in the role it plays in understanding non–linear urban systems. Visual sustainability is produced by the way we interact with our surroundings but we (and/or the method) cannot *manufacture* visual sustainability. It is a by–product of our interactions with the environment and is naturally occurring, for example, we cannot insist on carrying out an interaction type. We are, as it were, reflected in an environmental condition state describing levels of visual sustainability or alienation. These levels point to levels of urban quality and associated mental health. Nor can a

person point a finger at something and lay claim to a high level of visual sustainability. A person could look at head movement, as I have done in this study, and speculate about its importance in terms of count and duration, but the contextual value of levels of visual sustainability (and any emergence) can only be understood when the interaction types have been fully analysed and the statistical analysis completed. When it comes to repulsion as opposed to attraction we should remind ourselves that these are all *levels* of visual sustainability. Some environments are rich and some are poor in these levels of visual sustainability. The key difference to be aware of in this study (as has been noted in "Interim summary 4" on page 135, first bullet point) is that what we are repulsed by is not what we hold dear, it is a form of alienation because even if we stop and stare at, for example, some repulsive object or event or element, how do we differentiate through head movement, what this represents in the relationship between what we hold dear as opposed to what we do not hold dear but still engage with (even if involuntarily)? This study was unable to determine this difference. But it is important to remember that alienation in this study forms part of the concept of visual sustainability—the only difference is that it marks the one extreme of a spectrum, with *what we hold dear* being located at the opposite end. So this is a possible limitation in our understanding the quality of environment but not insurmountable and can easily be triangulated by using follow–up surveys or interviews. What we still get is a measure of *levels* visual sustainability. The other point is that this application depends on the urban *arena* our research is located in, for example, if one were to carry out this observation in a war zone or in a football stadium, the results would reflect their context—as should the conclusion we reach about what it is we are seeing and reporting on. In these types of scenarios context 'is king,' and by this meant that our analysis must adapt to the conditions of enquiry. For this study, the site (as with every study area) has its own particular characteristics and these are 'baked in,' meaning that we are interested in the site as it functions in front of us, regardless of, for example, the number of visitors/tourists, demographics, personalities, etc. because our interest should lie in the 'totality' of the site, 'warts and all.'

One–dimensional typology
While the transect is composed of different urban conditions, it is essentially still part of a well maintained world heritage site. The same method applied to other areas would provide a more robust understanding of the mix of interactions types from different socio–economic environmental typologies, for example, in areas of deprivation, segregated areas, infrastructural interface e.g., near railway corridors, or in semi–urban and country areas.

THE IMPORTANCE OF VISUAL SUSTAINABILITY

Individual versus team effort
A small team of researchers criss–crossing the site in a more methodical manner could produce a stronger analysis, especially in terms of continuity of research, where the same team is commissioned to complete entire neighbourhoods. For example, the Royal Borough of Greenwich could employ one, or all of the universities in Greenwich, to undertake a borough–wide evaluation of existing visual conditions, as part of their course.

Specialisation
It would be better for several reasons, if each team member specialised in one of the skills required to collect and analyse these data. For example, problems can be identified and resolved quickly, the work can be completed faster, and the work would, in all likelihood, be forensically more stable.

Data
On the technical side I noticed a problem (but not insurmountable) in some instances of too much data. The digital tapestry, for example had a few cases of where there were too many of the longest note to fit into 60 seconds (WHOLE interaction type of 4–seconds) i.e., there is a limit of the number of times it can flash per minute which for the WHOLE type is 15 times. So, when producing a digital tapestry it would appear that the sample optimum is about 1,000, before having to carry out some kind of evening out of these data such as a log–transformation, or breaking the study area up into smaller parts. Nevertheless, the point of the digital tapestry is to give us a flavour of the type of activity observed through rhythm (tempo/energy versus intensity/effect), and perhaps a sense of the emergence in the accurate rendition of data as moving image and sound.

§. 28 *Final word*

One of the analogies proposed in this conclusion has been a Rubik's Cube, except the invisible city is not a problem to be solved. It is a by–product in the sense proposed by Frankl (2003) in the form of emergence. It may be said that we sustain the invisible city, but we do not inform it. It informs us. Future research ought to understand more about our invisible city before we start producing the kind of visible city from which there is no return.

BIBLIOGRAPHY

35% Campaign, 2012 *Elephant & Castle – Greenest Regeneration Scheme in London.* [video online]. Available at: https://www.youtube.com/watch?v=M9H K3msMSc .

35% Campaign, 2013. *Revisiting the Heygate.* [video online] Available at: https://www.youtube.com/watch?v=zffKMFTbrBk.

Agent-Based Modeling: An Introduction from Uri Wilensky. 2018. Directed by U. Wilensky. Available at: https://www.youtube.com/watch?v=ocp3OdOvrZM [Accessed 15 Mar. 2022].

Alexander, C., Ishikawa, S. and Silverstein, M., 1977. *A pattern language: towns, buildings, construction.* New York: Oxford University Press.

Altamirano–Allende, C. and Selin, C., 2016. Seeing the city: photography as a place of work. *Journal of Environmental Studies and Sciences*, [online] 6(3), pp.460–469. Available at: http://link.springer.com/10.1007/s13412-015-0273-5 [Accessed 20 Sep. 2022].

Anon. 2018. *Six Things I Learned From World Urban Forum 9.* [online] Available at: https://nextcity.org/daily/entry/six-things-i-learned-from-world-urban-forum-9 [Accessed 31 August 2022].

Anzoise, V., 2017. Perception and (re)framing of Urban Environments: A Methodological Reflection toward Sentient Research. *Visual Anthropology*, [online] 30(3), pp.191–205. Available at: https://www.tandfonline.com/doi/full/10.1080/08949468.2017.1296285 [Accessed 20 Sep. 2022].

Ballantyne, A., 2007. *Deleuze and Guattari for architects.* Routledge.

Batty, M., 2007. *Cities and complexity: understanding cities with cellular automata, agent–based models, and fractals.* 1. paperback ed ed. Cambridge, Mass. London: MIT Press.

Batty, M. and Marshall, S., 2012. The Origins of Complexity Theory in Cities and Planning. In: J. Portugali, H. Meyer, E. Stolk and E. Tan, eds. *Complexity Theories of Cities Have Come of Age: An Overview with Implications to Urban Planning and Design.* [online] Berlin, Heidelberg: Springer Berlin Heidelberg. pp.21–45. https://doi.org/10.1007/978-3-642-24544-2_3.

Baudrillard, J., 1983. *Simulations.* Foreign agents series. New York City, N.Y., U.S.A: Semiotext(e), Inc.

Beinart, J., 2013. *Lec 21: Form Models III and IV: Rationality and Memory | Video Lectures | Theory of City Form | Architecture | MIT OpenCourseWare.* [online] Available at: https://ocw.mit.edu/courses/architecture/4-241j-theory-of-city-form-spring-2013/video-lectures/lec-21-form-models-iii-and-iv-rationality-and-memory/ [Accessed 27 Aug. 2022].

Bell, S. and Morse, S., 1999. *Sustainability indicators: measuring the immeasurable?* London: Earthscan.

Ben-Zeev, A., 1981. J.J. Gibson and the ecological approach to perception. *Studies in History and Philosophy of Science Part A*, [online] 12(2), pp.107–139. Available at: http://linkinghub.elsevier.com/retrieve/pii/0039368181900169 [Accessed 31 Aug. 2022].

Bergson, H., 1988. *Matter and Memory.* Translated by N.M. Paul and W.S. Palmer New York: Zone Books.

Bergson, H., 1965. *Duration and Simultaneity.* The Bobbs-Merrill Company, Inc.

Bergson, H., 2001. *Time and free will: an essay on the immediate data of consciousness.* Mineola, N.Y: Dover Publications.

Berleant, A. 1997. *Living in the landscape: Toward an aesthetics of environment.* University Press of Kansas.

Bhugra, D., Ventriglio, A., Castaldelli-Maia, J. and McCay, L. eds., 2019. *Urban mental health.* 1st edition ed. Oxford cultural psychiatry series. New york, NY: Oxford University Press.

Brenner, N., 2018. Debating planetary urbanization: For an engaged pluralism. *Environment and Planning D: Society and Space*, [online] 36(3), pp.570–590. Available at: http://journals.sagepub.com/doi/10.1177/0263775818757510 [Accessed 20 Jan. 2022].

Complexity a Guided Tour - Melanie Mitchell. 2013. Directed by M. Mitchell. Available at: https://www.youtube.com/watch?v=GYChwJq0310&feature=youtu.be [Accessed 27 February 2022].

Complexity Explorer Lecture: David Krakauer. What is Complexity?. 2023. Directed by Complexity Explorer. Available at: https://www.youtube.com/watch?v=FBkFu1g5PlE [Accessed 18 January 2024].

Cullen, G., 1995. *The concise townscape.* Oxford ; Boston: Butterworth-Heinemann.

Daemi, M. and Crawford, J.D., 2015. A kinematic model for 3-D head-free gaze-shifts. *Frontiers in Computational Neuroscience*, [online] 9. https://doi.org/10.3389/fncom.2015.00072.

David Hockney – The Art of Seeing. 2018. Available at: https://www.youtube.com/watch?v=Cdqch3-D94A&feature=youtu.be [Accessed 13 April 2022].

de Kock, P., 2024. Architecture: Hurtling Towards an Irrelevant Conclusion; or Skilfully Shifting the Paradigm ? archiDOCT & Anglia Ruskin University, pp.118–122. https://doi.org/10.25411/aru.c.7115281.

De Kock, P.M., 2023b. Unifying Object With Experience: Heritage in a Temporal Setting. AMPS Proceedings Series 35 Prague – Heritages: Past and Present - Built and Social. Czech Technical University. 28-30 June (2023), 3, pp.467–476.

De Kock, P. M., 2023. *Joyful vs joyless expenditure: Relevance, real estate, and the voice of urban data*. 7664147 Bytes. https://doi.org/10.6084/M9.FIGSHARE.23834781.V1.

De Kock, Pieter, 2022a. *The importance of visual sustainability in urban design strategy*. https://doi.org/10.6084/M9.FIGSHARE.21311427.V1.

De Kock, Pieter, 2022b. *Visual sustainability– hypothetical synopsis*. https://doi.org/10.6084/M9.FIGSHARE.18526436.V1.

De Kock, P.M., 2020a. Buildings, faces, songs of alienation: how interiority transforms the meaning out there. *Interiority*, 3(1), pp.41–60. https://doi.org/10.7454/in.v3i1.68.

De Kock, P.M., 2020b. Modern–day sustainability: managing the parts or looking beyond to the meaning? [online] https://doi.org/10.6084/m9.figshare.12229427.v1.

De Kock, P.M. and Carta, S., 2020b. Trojans of ambiguity vs resilient regeneration: visual meaning in cities. *Construction Economics and Building*, 20(2), pp.6–24. https://doi.org/10.5130/AJCEB.v20i2.6605.

De Kock, P.M., 2020c. *Visually dissecting sustainability*. Available at: https://figshare.com/articles/preprint/Visually_dissecting_sustainability/13095578.

De Kock, P.M. and Carta, S., 2020a. *SDG 18 Visual Sustainability: dream or reality?* [online] Figshare. https://doi.org/10.6084/M9.FIGSHARE.12702320.V1.

De Kock, P.M., 2019a. Data, data everywhere, not a lot in sync: reconciling visual meaning with data. *ENQUIRY: The ARCC Journal | Special Edition: Urban Data Assemblage*, 16(2), pp.32–49. https://doi.org/10.17831/enq:arcc.v16i2.582.

De Kock, P. M., 2019. The Meaning in Seeing: Visual Sustainability in the Built Environment. *AMPS Proceedings Series 17.1. Education, Design and Practice – Understanding Skills in a Complex World*. Stevens Institute of Technology, USA. 17 – 19 June (2019), 69–77.

Deal, S., 2017. The Urban Transect: One of the Planning Profession's Most Powerful Tools. *Water Log*, 37(1), p.4.

De Landa, M., 2006. *A new philosophy of society: assemblage theory and social complexity*. London ; New York: Continuum.

De Landa, M., 2016. *Assemblage Theory. Speculative realism*. Edinburgh: Edinburgh University Press.

Designed to Hesitate: Consciousness as Paying Attention. 2010. Directed by B.M. Stafford. Available at: https://www.youtube.com/watch?v=2BF6UaI7HGA&feature=youtu.be [Accessed 13 April 2022].

Erem, Ö. and Gür, E., 2008. Complexity versus sustainability in urban space: The case of Taksim Square, Istanbul. *ITU AZ*, 5(1), pp.54–73.

Evans, J. and Jones, P., 2008. Rethinking Sustainable Urban Regeneration: Ambiguity, Creativity, and the Shared Territory. *Environment and Planning A*, 40(6), pp.1416–1434. https://doi.org/10.1068/a39293.

Fractals and Scaling: Reflections on urban scaling. 2019. Directed by D. Feldman. Available at: https://www.youtube.com/watch?v=XblKRr6AcFY [Accessed 18 Jul. 2022].

Fractals and Scaling: Summary of course. 2019. Directed by D. Feldman. Available at: https://www.youtube.com/watch?v=-pynRkP-UfY [Accessed 26 Mar. 2022].

Frankl, V., 2003. *Man's Search for Meaning*. [online] Blackstone Publishing. Available at: https://www.blackstonelibrary.com/man-s-search-for-meaning [Accessed 31 December 2023].

Gibson, J.J., 1983. *The senses considered as perceptual systems*. Westport, Conn: Greenwood Press.

Gibson, J. J. 2015. *The ecological approach to visual perception: Classic edition*. Psychology Press, Taylor & Francis Group.

Gigerenzer, G., 2000. *Adaptive thinking: rationality in the real world*. Evolution and cognition. New York: Oxford University Press.

Golembiewski, J.A., 2022. Salutogenic Architecture. In: M.B. Mittelmark, G.F. Bauer, L. Vaandrager, J.M. Pelikan, S. Sagy, M. Eriksson, B. Lindström and C. Meier Magistretti, eds. *The Handbook of Salutogenesis*. [online] Cham: Springer International Publishing.pp.259–274. https://doi.org/10.1007/978-3-030-79515-3_26.

Guy, S. and Farmer, G., 2001. Reinterpreting Sustainable Architecture: The Place of Technology. *Journal of Architectural Education,* [online] 54(3), pp.140–148. Available at: https://www.tandfonline.com/doi/full/10.1162/10464880152632451 [Accessed 31 Aug. 2022].

Haun, A.M., Tononi, G., Koch, C. and Tsuchiya, N., 2017. Are we underestimating the richness of visual experience? *Neuroscience of Consciousness,* [online] 2017(1). https://doi.org/10.1093/nc/niw023.

Havel, V., 2010. *Remarks at the Opening Ceremony*. [online] Available at: https://www.catholiceducation.org/en/culture/catholic-contributions/remarks-at-the-opening-ceremony.html.

Hillier, B., 2015. *Space is the machine: a configurational theory of architecture*. London: Space Syntax.

Hillier, B. and Hanson, J., 2005. *The social logic of space*. Repr ed. Cambridge: Cambridge Univ. Press.

Hollander, J.B., Sussman, A. and Carr, H.C., 2018. Seeing the 'Unseen' in Devens. p.40.

Ingold, T., 2002. *The Perception of the Environment: Essays on Livelihood, Dwelling and Skill*. 1st ed. [online] Routledge. Available at: https://www.taylorfrancis.com/books/9780203466025 [Accessed 25 Sep. 2022].

Introduction to Complexity: Models of Biological Self-Organization. 2018. Directed by M. Mitchell. Available at: https://www.youtube.com/watch?time_

continue=2&v=YFnQUdk6bGQ [Accessed 1 Mar. 2022].

In Our Time: S21/34 Bergson and Time (May 9 2019). 2019. Directed by In Our Time. Available at: https://www.youtube.com/watch?v=pK8N47RFRd8 [Accessed 26 May 2022].

James Gibson – Ohio – 1974 – Part 1. 1974. Directed by J.J. Gibson. Available at: https://www.youtube.com/watch?v=hwRxUyuQEgc&list=PLtoX6L88vjkdj8HfxaYRtLkuR-yY0ZYu3 [Accessed 13 Dec. 2022].

John Searle on Perception & Philosophy of Mind. 2015. Directed by J. Searle. and Directed by R. Pollie. Available at: https://www.youtube.com/watch?v=Oh2NylJZRHs&feature=youtu.be [Accessed 15 December 2022].

Kádár, B., 2013. Differences in the spatial patterns of urban tourism in Vienna and Prague. *Urbani izziv*, 24(2), pp.96–111. https://doi.org/10.5379/urbani-izziv-en-2013-24-02-002.

Kothari, R., Yang, Z., Kanan, C., Bailey, R., Pelz, J.B. and Diaz, G.J., 2020. Gaze-in-wild: A dataset for studying eye and head coordination in everyday activities. *Scientific Reports*, 10(1), p.2539. https://doi.org/10.1038/s41598-020-59251-5.

Kröger, J.L., Lutz, O.H.-M. and Müller, F., 2020. What Does Your Gaze Reveal About You? On the Privacy Implications of Eye Tracking. In: M. Friedewald, M. Önen, E. Lievens, S. Krenn and S. Fricker, eds. *Privacy and Identity Management. Data for Better Living: AI and Privacy: 14th IFIP WG 9.2, 9.6/11.7, 11.6/SIG 9.2.2 International Summer School, Windisch, Switzerland, August 19–23, 2019, Revised Selected Papers*, IFIP Advances in Information and Communication Technology. [online] Cham: Springer International Publishing. pp.226–241. https://doi.org/10.1007/978-3-030-42504-3_15.

Kromm, J. and Bakewell, S.B. eds., 2010. *A history of visual culture: Western civilization from the 18th to the 21st century*. English ed ed. Oxford [England] ; New York: Berg.

Larry And Janet Move Out, 2016. *Larry And Janet Move Out: a documentary about the Heygate Estate, Elephant and Castle*. [video online] Available at: https://www.youtube.com/watch?v=MvSmC7susNI .

Lawlor, L. and Moulard-Leonard, V., 2021. Henri Bergson. *The Stanford Encyclopedia of Philosophy* (Fall 2021 Edition).

Lefebvre, H., & Nicholson-Smith, D. (2011). *The production of space* (Nachdr.). Blackwell.

Le Corbusier, 1991. *Precisions on the present state of architecture and city planning*. Cambridge, Mass: MIT Press.

Leopold, D., 2018. Alienation. *The Stanford Encyclopedia of Philosophy*, p.20.

LSBUACCOUNT, 2013. *Heygate Estate: A Troubled Story*. 2013. [video online] Available at: https://

www.youtube.com/watch?v=GQXkbBzkT28&feature=youtu.be [Accessed 19 Apr. 2022].

Lynch, K., 2005. *The image of the city*. Nachdr. ed. Publication of the Joint Center for Urban Studies. Cambridge, Mass.: MIT PRESS.

Makin, A. D. J. (2018). *The Gap Between Aesthetic Science and Aesthetic Experience*. 30.

Man's Search for Meaning. (2017). https://www.youtube.com/watch?v=vsRXR1SJCHs&feature=youtu.be

Manuel DeLanda. Assemblage Theory, Society, and Deleuze. 2011. 2012. Directed by M. De Landa. Available at: https://www.youtube.com/watch?v=J-I5e7ixw78&feature=youtu.be [Accessed 2 February 2022].

Martinez-Conde, S., Macknik, S. L., & Hubel, D. H. (2004). The role of fixational eye movements in visual perception. *Nature Reviews Neuroscience*, 5(3), 229–240. https://doi.org/10.1038/nrn1348.

McLeod, S.A., 2008. *Visual perception theory*. [online] Available at: https://simplypsychology.org/perception-theories.html [Accessed 31 August 2022].

Merleau-Ponty, M., 1968. *The Visible and the Invisible*. Translated by A. Lingis Northwestern University Press, Evanston IL.

Merquior, J.G., 1987. *Foucault*. Berkeley: University of California Press.

Merriam Webster Dictionary, 2023. *Definition of BRACKET*. [online] Available at: https://www.merriam-webster.com/dictionary/bracket [Accessed 2 January 2024].

Mirzoeff, N. ed., 2010. *The visual culture reader*. 2. ed, repr ed. London: Routledge.

Mitchell, M., 2011. *Complexity: a guided tour*. 1. paperback ed ed. Oxford: Oxford Univ. Press.

Motevalian, N. and Yeganeh, M., 2020. Visually meaningful sustainability in national monuments as an international heritage. *Sustainable Cities and Society*, [online] 60, p.21. Available at: https://linkinghub.elsevier.com/retrieve/pii/S2210670720301943 [Accessed 20 Sep. 2022].

Moustakas, C.E., 1990. *Heuristic research: design, methodology, and applications*. Newbury Park: Sage Publications.

Narayan, J., Hu, K., Coulter, M., Mukherjee, S., Hu, K. and Mukherjee, S., 2023. Elon Musk and others urge AI pause, citing 'risks to society'. *Reuters*. [online] 5 Apr. Available at: https://www.reuters.com/technology/musk-experts-urge-pause-training-ai-systems-that-can-outperform-gpt-4-2023-03-29/ [Accessed 2 January 2024].

Nora, P., 1989. Between Memory and History: Les Lieux de Mémoire. *Representations*, [online] (26), pp.7–24. Available at: http://rep.ucpress.edu/cgi/doi/10.2307/2928520 [Accessed 27 Aug. 2022].

Ortman, S.G., Lobo, J. and Smith, M.E., 2020. Cities: Complexity, theory and history. *PLOS ONE*, 15(12), p.e0243621. https://doi.org/10.1371/journal.pone.0243621

Owen, C. and Dovey, K., 2008. Fields of sustainable architecture. *The Journal of Architecture*, 13(1), pp.9–21. https://doi.org/10.1080/13602360701865373.

Parthenios, P., Petrovski, S., Chatzopoulou, N. and Mania, K., 2016. Reciprocal transformations between music and architecture as a real-time supporting mechanism in urban design. *International Journal of Architectural Computing*, 14(4), pp.349–357. https://doi.org/10.1177/1478077116670743.

Periton, D., 2018. Generative history: Marcel Poëte and the city as urban organism. *The Journal of Architecture*, 23(4), pp.580–594. https://doi.org/10.1080/13602365.2018.1479227.

Polanyi, M., 1966. *The tacit dimension*. Doubleday.

Polanyi, M., & Grene, M. (1969). *Knowing and being*. Routledge and Kegan Paul.

Qualtrics, 2023. *Sample Size Calculator*. [online] Qualtrics. Available at: https://www.qualtrics.com/blog/calculating-sample-size/ [Accessed 11 January 2024].

Ramachandran, V. S., & Hirstein, W. (1999). The science of art: A neurological theory of aesthetic experience. *Journal of Consciousness Studies*, 6(6–7), 15–51.

Ramachandran, V.S. and Hirstein, W., 1997. Three laws of qualia: What neurology tells us about the biological functions of consciousness. *Journal of Consciousness Studies*, 4(5–6), pp.429–457

Rapoport, A. (1990). *The meaning of the built environment: A nonverbal communication approach*. University of Arizona Press.

Reading Ancient Minds: Metaphor, Culture, and Complexity. 2012. Directed by S. Ortman. Available at: https://www.youtube.com/watch?v=fOlYyh3dk8c&feature=youtu.be [Accessed 16 March 2022].

Robbins, S.E., 2004. On time, memory and dynamic form. *Consciousness and Cognition*, 13(4), p.26. https://doi.org/10.1016/j.concog.2004.07.006.

Robbins, S.E., 2013. Form, Qualia and Time: The Hard Problem Reformed. *Mind & Matter*, 11(2), p.29.

Robbins, S.E., 2006a. Bergson and the holographic theory of mind. *Phenomenology and the Cognitive Sciences*, 5(3–4), pp.365–394. https://doi.org/10.1007/s11097-006-9023-1.

Robbins, S. E. (2006b). *New developments in consciousness research: On the Possibility of Direct Memory* (V. W. Fallio, Ed.). Nova Science Publishers.

Robbins, S.E., 2014. *Collapsing the singularity: Bergson, Gibson and the mythologies of artificial intelligence*. CreateSpace Independent Publishing Platform.

Robbins, S.E., 2015. Talk at The Anatomy of Matter and Memory: Bergson and Contemporary Theories of Mind, Perception and Time. p.15.

Robbins, S. E., 2021. Is Experience Stored in the Brain? A Current Model of

Memory and the Temporal Metaphysic of Bergson. *Axiomathes*, 31(1), 15–43. https://doi.org/10.1007/s10516-020-09483-x.

Robbins, S.E., 2002. *Semantics, experience and time.* Cognitive Systems Research, 3(3), pp.301–337. https://doi.org/10.1016/S1389-0417(02)00045-1.

Robbins, S.E., 2000. Bergson, Perception and Gibson. *Journal of Consciousness Studies*, (7(5)), pp.23–45.

Robbins, S.E., 2023. Gibson and Time: The Temporal Framework of Direct Perception. *Ecological Psychology*, 35(1–2), pp.31–50. https://doi.org/10.1080/10407413.2023.2170234.

Robinson, H., 2020. Dualism. *Stanford Encyclopedia of Philosophy*, p.30.

Rodaway, P. (2011). *Sensuous geographies: Body, sense, and place* (1. iss. in paperback). Routledge.

Rose, G., 2007. *Visual methodologies: an introduction to the interpretation of visual materials*. 2nd ed ed. London ; Thousand Oaks, Calif: SAGE Publications.

Rydin, Y., 2011. *The purpose of planning: creating sustainable towns and cities*. Bristol: Policy Press.

Salingaros, N.A., 1999. Urban space and its information field. *Journal of Urban Design*, 4(1), pp.29–49. https://doi.org/10.1080/13574809908724437.

Scarantino, A., & de Sousa, R. (2018). Emotion. *The Stanford Encyclopedia of Philosophy*, 43.

Schelling, T.C., 1971. DYNAMIC MODELS OF SEGREGATION. *Journal of Mathematical Sociology*, 1, pp.143–186.

Scruton, R. (2007). In Search of the Aesthetic. *The British Journal of Aesthetics*, 47(3), 232–250. https://doi.org/10.1093/aesthj/aym004.

Sheena, 2010. *Heygate Lives: Demo of interactive locative narrative on iPod*. [video online] Available at: https://www.youtube.com/watch?v=y4T_1KHw1EU.

Singh, N.D. and M., 2023. *Sample Size Calculator for Estimating a Proportion*. [online] Available at: https://statulator.com/SampleSize/ss1P.html [Accessed 12 January 2024].

Something Rich and Strange: The Life and Music of Iannis Xenakis. 2022. Directed by Anthoney Hart. Available at: https://www.youtube.com/watch?v=2p_uhmOIsnQ [Accessed 7 January 2024].

Space Syntax Limited, 2024. *Homepage - Space Syntax*. [online] Space Syntax. Available at: https://spacesyntax.com/ [Accessed 12 March 2024].

Stack Overflow, 2017. How to fix an error with zero-inflated Poisson regression. [Forum post] *Stack Overflow*. Available at: https://stackoverflow.com/q/41702368 [Accessed 31 December 2023].

Statista Research Department, 2024. *Royal Museums Greenwich: visitor numbers 2022*. [online] Statista. Available at: https://www.statista.com/statistics/508072/royal-museums-greenwich-visitor-numbers-uk/ [Accessed 11 January 2024].

Stevens, S. S. (1946). On the Theory of Scales of Measurement. *Science*, 103(2684), 677–680. https://doi.org/10.1126/science.103.2684.677.

Sturzaker, J. and Hickman, H., 2024. Planning's value, planners' values: defining and redefining for contemporary practice. *Planning Practice & Research*, 39(2), pp.157–170. https://doi.org/10.1080/02697459.2024.2316988.

Sussman, A. and Chen, K., 2017. *The Mental Disorders that Gave Us Modern Architecture*. [online] Common Edge. Available at: http://commonedge.org/the–mental–disorders–that–gave–us–modern–architecture/ [Accessed 31 August 2022].

Sussman, A. and Hollander, J., 2018. *Three fundamental errors in architectural thinking and how to fix them*. [Text] CNU. Available at: https://www.cnu.org/publicsquare/2018/07/19/three–fundamental–errors–architectural–thinking–and–how–fix–them [Accessed 31 August 2022].

Sussman, A. and Ward, J.M., 2016. *Planning for the Subconscious*. [online] American Planning Association. Available at: https://www.planning.org/planning/2016/jun/subconscious/ [Accessed 31 August 2022].

Sussman, A. and Ward, J.M., 2017. *Game–Changing Eye–Tracking Studies Reveal How We Actually See Architecture – Common Edge*. [online] Available at: http://commonedge.org/game–changing–eye–tracking–studies–reveal–how–we–actually–see–architecture/ [Accessed 30 August 2022].

Tam, J., 2019. *Visual Tracking: What Eye Tracking Can and Can't Do*. [online] Gazepoint. Available at: https://www.gazept.com/blog/visual–tracking/the–capabilities–and–limitations–of–eye–tracking/ [Accessed 22 December 2023].

Tavernor, R., 2007. Visual and cultural sustainability: The impact of tall buildings on London. *Landscape and Urban Planning*, [online] 83(1), pp.2–12. Available at: https://linkinghub.elsevier.com/retrieve/pii/S0169204607001399 [Accessed 3 Sep. 2022].

TEDxWaterloo - Colin Ellard - Getting Lost. 2011. TEDx Talks and Directed by C. Ellard. Available at: https://www.youtube.com/watch?v=UHdlG_KMAv0 [Accessed 31 Aug. 2022].

Terranova, C.N., 2008. Marcel Poëte's Bergsonian Urbanism: Vitalism, Time, and the City. *Journal of Urban History*, 34(6), pp.919–943. https://doi.org/10.1177/0096144208317587.

The ecological approach to perception & action. 2013. Directed by H. Heft. Available at: https://www.youtube.com/watch?v=k4fKBqu–Ris&feature=youtu.be [Accessed 12 Dec. 2022].

The Perception of Causality (Part 1). 2013. Directed by D. Kelley. Available at: https://www.youtube.com/watch?v=Bz9QoCnG5to&feature=youtu.be [Accessed 3 May 2022].

The Perception of Causality (Part 2). 2013. Directed by D. Kelley. Available at: https://www.youtube.com/watch?v=olPZSgs9pAo&feature=youtu.be [Accessed 4 May 2022].

Tobii, 2023. *Tobii Customer Portal*. [online] Available at: https://connect.tobii.com/s/article/does-head-movement-affect-eye-tracking-data?language=en_US#:~:text=Please%20refer%20to%20the%20user,within%20the%20%22track%20box%22. [Accessed 22 December 2023].

Torraco, R.J., 2005. Writing Integrative Literature Reviews: Guidelines and Examples. *Human Resource Development Review*, 4(3), pp.356–367. https://doi.org/10.1177/1534484305278283.

Varela, F. J., Thompson, E., & Rosch, E., 2016. *The Embodied Mind: Cognitive Science and Human Experience* (Second Edition, Revised ed.). The MIT Press. https://muse.jhu.edu/book/49607.

Voyatzaki, M., 2018. *Architectural Materialisms: Nonhuman Creativity*. In: Architectural Materialisms. [online] Edinburgh University Press. pp.1–28. https://doi.org/10.3366/edinburgh/9781474420570.003.0001.

World Commission on Environment and Development, 1987. *Report of the World Commission on Environment and Development: Our Common Future*. [online] Available at: http://www.un-documents.net/our-common-future.pdf [Accessed 22 March 2022].

Xenakis, I. and Kanach, S., 1992. *Formalized music: thought and mathematics in composition*. Rev. ed ed. Harmonologia series. Stuyvesant, NY: Pendragon Press.

Yuill, C., 2017. The use of abduction in alienation research: A rationale and a worked example. *Social Theory & Health*, 15(4), pp.465–481. https://doi.org/10.1057/s41285-017-0038-1.

LIST OF FIGURES

Figure 1. Theoretical premise. This diagram illustrates the connection between Bergson's temporal metaphysics and epistemological approaches from other domains of knowledge pertaining to the visual world (De Kock, 2022a, p.18). — 15

Figure 2. The paradox of Buridan's donkey: Architecture versus Heritage or, stated differently, Object versus Experience. — 39

Figure 3. Perception as an event in time. — 39

Figure 4. The event is part of our location, not of depth of space, but in space as depth of time. — 39

Figure 6. Direct–environment versus memory–environment. — 41

Figure 5. Tourists and locals mingle indiscriminately using different forms of perception: direct–environment versus memory–environment. — 41

Figure 7. Person A's record of most meaningful locations visited in Prague (yellow accents). — 41

Figure 8. Use patterns premise, adapted using the concept by Robbins of patterns as invariance structures of events, to describe the environmental transaction between physical use and visual use (De Kock, Pieter, 2022, p.21). — 43

Figure 9. Unifying object with experience. — 43

Figure 10. How data is represented in this person's experience. — 43

Figure 11. Interaction dominance: the stronger the shade, the more dominant the interaction type in that location. — 45

Figure 12. Greenwich Town Centre and Greenwich Park observation data: interactions per minute (video) https://doi.org/10.6084/m9.figshare.24996215.v1. — 45

Figure 13. Top: The visible city: what we see is what we get. Buildings represent the most visible elements of a city, where location is an expression of 'space.' Bottom: The invisible city: contextual strength is evidenced by visual interaction type; where location as an experience and expression of 'time.' — 57

Figure 14. Urban design relevance. — 59

Figure 15. Urban transect: the invisible city when combined with the visible city. — 59

Figure 16. Theoretical principles. This diagram shows the ten key principles derived from the literature review, which will be used to more fully describe the application of physical use and visual use in urban design (De Kock, 2022a, p.18). — 65

Figure 17. Nvivo coding references comparison highlights the dominance of the following three themes: Memory, Perception, and Psychic States. 67

Figure 18. Differentiating interaction type through rhythm: beats per minute (video). See video at https://doi.org/10.6084/m9.figshare.25391047.v1. 69

Figure 19. Differentiating interaction type through time values in sound, where markers of time–extended events are used to signify durational qualities (video). See video at https://doi.org/10.6084/m9.figshare.25391044.v1. 69

Figure 20. Interaction type analysis from YouTube video 'Revisiting the Heygate' showing timestamps as markers of a time–extended event (pink blocks). 71

Figure 21. Interaction type analysis from YouTube video 'Larry And Janet Move Out' with timestamps as markers of interaction types with time values as a metric (see *Appendix B* "Youtube: Larry And Janet Move Out" on page 208). 71

Figure 22. The study area: Greenwich Town Centre and Greenwich Park, divided into Zones and Blocks. 75

Figure 23. Study Area with observed visual interactions. 75

Figure 24. Histograms: LHS: incl. zeros, SIM; Middle: excluding zero rows; RHS: excl. zero rows after log transform. 91

Figure 25. Boxplots. LHS: including zero rows; RHS: excluding zero rows and SIM. 91

Figure 26. Distribution: histogram of interaction count. 99

Figure 27. Interaction type characteristics: spread by count. 99

Figure 29. Interaction type characteristics: spread by block. 99

Figure 28. Interaction type characteristics: spread by zone. 99

Figure 30. Poisson model: used to understand the data containing so many zero values. 101

Figure 31. Negative binomial (NB) model versus zero–inflated negative binomial (ZINB) model. 101

Figure 33. What is alienation? A depiction of conditions of alienation (far left dashed black outline) can be compared with each of the five zones in the study area. 103

Figure 32. Interactions per minute in each zone. Zone 1 is high density; Zone 2 medium–high; Zone 3 medium; Zone 4 medium–low; Zone 5 is low density. 103

Figure 34. A visual description of the relationship between interaction and location. This shows the distribution of interaction types at the block level, for each zone. 105

Figure 35. A visual description of the relationship between interaction

IN URBAN DESIGN STRATEGY

and location. This shows the interaction percentages per block, for each zone. — 107

Figure 36. Linear model diagnostics plot to check for violations of the assumptions of linearity, homogeneity of variance and normality of residuals. The data appear to be conducive to further analysis using regression methods. — 109

Figure 37. Pairs plot between blocks and each interaction type. — 109

Figure 38. The building block: diagram showing interaction types with significantly different means: therefore, reject the null hypothesis at the 5% level of significance. — 111

Figure 39. Estimating non–linear correlation: Location (Blocks) and Duration. — 113

Figure 40. Estimating non–linear correlation: detecting non–linear variables using Location (Zones) and Duration. — 115

Figure 41. Estimating non–linear correlation: detecting non–linear association in variables with p= <0.05 from the pairwise comparison. — 117

Figure 42. Study Area showing the relationship between location (blocks/zones) and interaction type (WH–SI). — 119

Figure 43. This diagram shows the mix of interaction types for each block. The darker the shade, the more active an interaction–type is in a block. The lighter the colour, the less represented an interaction–type is. In many cases an interaction–type may not be active in a block. In some cases, only one interaction–type may be present. — 119

Figure 44. Digital tapestry. Percentage mix: the darker the values for each shade, the stronger the effect. For visual sustainability, the premise is that the orange and yellows are dominant. For alienation, the blues and greys are dominant. — 121

Figure 45. A mix of interaction–types. The premise is that the upper row represents conditions in which robust levels of visual sustainability may exist. The lower row represents combinations which introduce mild forms of alienation. — 123

Figure 46. Data as a digital tapestry (video). See video at https://doi.org/10.6084/m9.figshare.24996215.v1. — 123

Figure 47. Blocks and interaction. — 125

Figure 48. Study area: blocks with observed interactions — 125

Figure 49. The distribution of interaction types at block level (weighted). — 126

Figure 50. Interaction percentages (weighted) per Block. — 127

Figure 51. The commercial value of understanding urban compressive and tensile forces as the result of relationship between interaction type —because businesses follow people and people follow meaning (video). See video at https://doi.org/10.6084/m9.figshare.24996296.v1. — 131

Figure 52. Planar characteristics of the space syntax model: improving connectivity in a physical city in two dimensions. (Images © Space Syntax Limited, 2024). — 141

Figure 53. Visual sustainability model: interaction types as dynamic, time–extended, multi–dimensional events. — 141

Figure 54. Randomised selection of postcodes for distribution of the survey form. — 179

Figure 55. Postcode address verification using public online data. — 181

Figure 56. Digital tapestry with sound: The sounds made along the transect between zones 1 and 5 (video watch at https://doi.org/10.6084/m9.figshare.24996428.v1. — 224

Figure 57. Alienation produced in sound form: low entropy; low complexity (sound). Hear sound at https://doi.org/10.6084/m9.figshare.24996347.v1. — 225

Figure 58. Block 1.12: urban sound with SIM interaction type (sound). Hear sound at https://doi.org/10.6084/m9.figshare.24996326.v1. — 225

Figure 59. The sounds we make Zone 3. High entropy; high complexity (sound). Hear sound at https://doi.org/10.6084/m9.figshare.24996377.v1. — 225

LIST OF TABLES

Table 1. An example of the complexity in and between just four architectural theories.	15
Table 2. This table compares Bergson with three key theories relating to visual interaction, namely, by Polanyi, Gibson, and Varela.	21
Table 3. The physical city is a proxy for memory; the invisible city is that memory.	56
Table 4. Theoretical principles (De Kock, 2022a, p.28–29).	65
Table 5. Data summary: square pie charts (LHS); tabulated data (RHS).	86
Table 6. Percentage duration of interaction type, per zone.	87
Table 7. Location and interaction type are interdependent.	125

THE IMPORTANCE OF VISUAL SUSTAINABILITY

APPENDICES

APPENDIX A THE IMPORTANCE OF VISUAL SUSTAINABILITY

SE3 7RD
1 Leamington Court, Restell Close
2 Leamington Court, Restell Close
3 Leamington Court, Restell Close
4 Leamington Court, Restell Close
5 Leamington Court, Restell Close
6 Leamington Court, Restell Close
7 Leamington Court, Restell Close
8 Leamington Court, Restell Close
9 Leamington Court, Restell Close
10 Leamington Court, Restell Close
11 Leamington Court, Restell Close
12 Leamington Court, Restell Close
13 Leamington Court, Restell Close
14 Leamington Court, Restell Close
15 Leamington Court, Restell Close
16 Leamington Court, Restell Close
17 Leamington Court, Restell Close
18 Leamington Court, Restell Close
19 Leamington Court, Restell Close
20 Leamington Court, Restell Close
21 Leamington Court, Restell Close
22 Leamington Court, Restell Close
23 Leamington Court, Restell Close
24 Leamington Court, Restell Close
25 Leamington Court, Restell Close
26 Leamington Court, Restell Close
27 Leamington Court, Restell Close
28 Leamington Court, Restell Close
29 Leamington Court, Restell Close
30 Leamington Court, Restell Close
31 Leamington Court, Restell Close
32 Leamington Court, Restell Close
33 Leamington Court, Restell Close
34 Leamington Court, Restell Close
35 Leamington Court, Restell Close
36 Leamington Court, Restell Close
37 Leamington Court, Restell Close
38 Leamington Court, Restell Close
39 Leamington Court, Restell Close
40 Leamington Court, Restell Close
41 Leamington Court, Restell Close
42 Leamington Court, Restell Close
43 Leamington Court, Restell Close
44 Leamington Court, Restell Close
45 Leamington Court, Restell Close
46 Leamington Court, Restell Close
47 Leamington Court, Restell Close
48 Leamington Court, Restell Close
49 Leamington Court, Restell Close
50 Leamington Court, Restell Close
51 Leamington Court, Restell Close
52 Leamington Court, Restell Close
53 Leamington Court, Restell Close
54 Leamington Court, Restell Close
55 Leamington Court, Restell Close
56 Leamington Court, Restell Close
57 Leamington Court, Restell Close
58 Leamington Court, Restell Close
59 Leamington Court, Restell Close
1 Seren Park Gardens
2 Seren Park Gardens
3 Seren Park Gardens
4 Seren Park Gardens
5 Seren Park Gardens
6 Seren Park Gardens
7 Seren Park Gardens
8 Seren Park Gardens
9 Seren Park Gardens
10 Seren Park Gardens
11 Seren Park Gardens
12 Seren Park Gardens
13 Seren Park Gardens
14 Seren Park Gardens
15 Seren Park Gardens
16 Seren Park Gardens
17 Seren Park Gardens
18 Seren Park Gardens
19 Seren Park Gardens
20 Seren Park Gardens
21 Seren Park Gardens
22 Seren Park Gardens
23 Seren Park Gardens
24 Seren Park Gardens
25 Seren Park Gardens
26 Seren Park Gardens
27 Seren Park Gardens
28 Seren Park Gardens
29 Seren Park Gardens
30 Seren Park Gardens
31 Seren Park Gardens
32 Seren Park Gardens
33 Seren Park Gardens
34 Seren Park Gardens
35 Seren Park Gardens
36 Seren Park Gardens
37 Seren Park Gardens
38 Seren Park Gardens
39 Seren Park Gardens
40 Seren Park Gardens
41 Seren Park Gardens
42 Seren Park Gardens
43 Seren Park Gardens
44 Seren Park Gardens
45 Seren Park Gardens
46 Seren Park Gardens
47 Seren Park Gardens
48 Seren Park Gardens
49 Seren Park Gardens
50 Seren Park Gardens
51 Seren Park Gardens
52 Seren Park Gardens
53 Seren Park Gardens
54 Seren Park Gardens
55 Seren Park Gardens
56 Seren Park Gardens
57 Seren Park Gardens
58 Seren Park Gardens
59 Seren Park Gardens
60 Seren Park Gardens
61 Seren Park Gardens
62 Seren Park Gardens
63 Seren Park Gardens
64 Seren Park Gardens
65 Seren Park Gardens
66 Seren Park Gardens
67 Seren Park Gardens
68 Seren Park Gardens
69 Seren Park Gardens
70 Seren Park Gardens
71 Seren Park Gardens
72 Seren Park Gardens
73 Seren Park Gardens
74 Seren Park Gardens
75 Seren Park Gardens
76 Seren Park Gardens
77 Seren Park Gardens
78 Seren Park Gardens
79 Seren Park Gardens
80 Seren Park Gardens
81 Seren Park Gardens
82 Seren Park Gardens
83 Seren Park Gardens
84 Seren Park Gardens
85 Seren Park Gardens
86 Seren Park Gardens
87 Seren Park Gardens
88 Seren Park Gardens
89 Seren Park Gardens
90 Seren Park Gardens
91 Seren Park Gardens
92 Seren Park Gardens
93 Seren Park Gardens
94 Seren Park Gardens
95 Seren Park Gardens
96 Seren Park Gardens
97 Seren Park Gardens
98 Seren Park Gardens
99 Seren Park Gardens
100 Seren Park Gardens
101 Seren Park Gardens
102 Seren Park Gardens
103 Seren Park Gardens
104 Seren Park Gardens
105 Seren Park Gardens
106 Seren Park Gardens
107 Seren Park Gardens
108 Seren Park Gardens
109 Seren Park Gardens
110 Seren Park Gardens
111 Seren Park Gardens
112 Seren Park Gardens
113 Seren Park Gardens
114 Seren Park Gardens
115 Seren Park Gardens
116 Seren Park Gardens
117 Seren Park Gardens
118 Seren Park Gardens
119 Seren Park Gardens
120 Seren Park Gardens
121 Seren Park Gardens
122 Seren Park Gardens
123 Seren Park Gardens
124 Seren Park Gardens
125 Seren Park Gardens
126 Seren Park Gardens
127 Seren Park Gardens
128 Seren Park Gardens
129 Seren Park Gardens
130 Seren Park Gardens
131 Seren Park Gardens
132 Seren Park Gardens
133 Seren Park Gardens
134 Seren Park Gardens
135 Seren Park Gardens
136 Seren Park Gardens
137 Seren Park Gardens
138 Seren Park Gardens
139 Seren Park Gardens
140 Seren Park Gardens
141 Seren Park Gardens
142 Seren Park Gardens
143 Seren Park Gardens
144 Seren Park Gardens
145 Seren Park Gardens
146 Seren Park Gardens
147 Seren Park Gardens
148 Seren Park Gardens
149 Seren Park Gardens
150 Seren Park Gardens
151 Seren Park Gardens
152 Seren Park Gardens
153 Seren Park Gardens
154 Seren Park Gardens
155 Seren Park Gardens
156 Seren Park Gardens
157 Seren Park Gardens
158 Seren Park Gardens
159 Seren Park Gardens
160 Seren Park Gardens
161 Seren Park Gardens
162 Seren Park Gardens
163 Seren Park Gardens
164 Seren Park Gardens
165 Seren Park Gardens
166 Seren Park Gardens
167 Seren Park Gardens
168 Seren Park Gardens
169 Seren Park Gardens
170 Seren Park Gardens
171 Seren Park Gardens
172 Seren Park Gardens

IN URBAN DESIGN STRATEGY

APPENDIX A

APPENDIX A

SURVEY STRATEGY AND SURVEY FORM

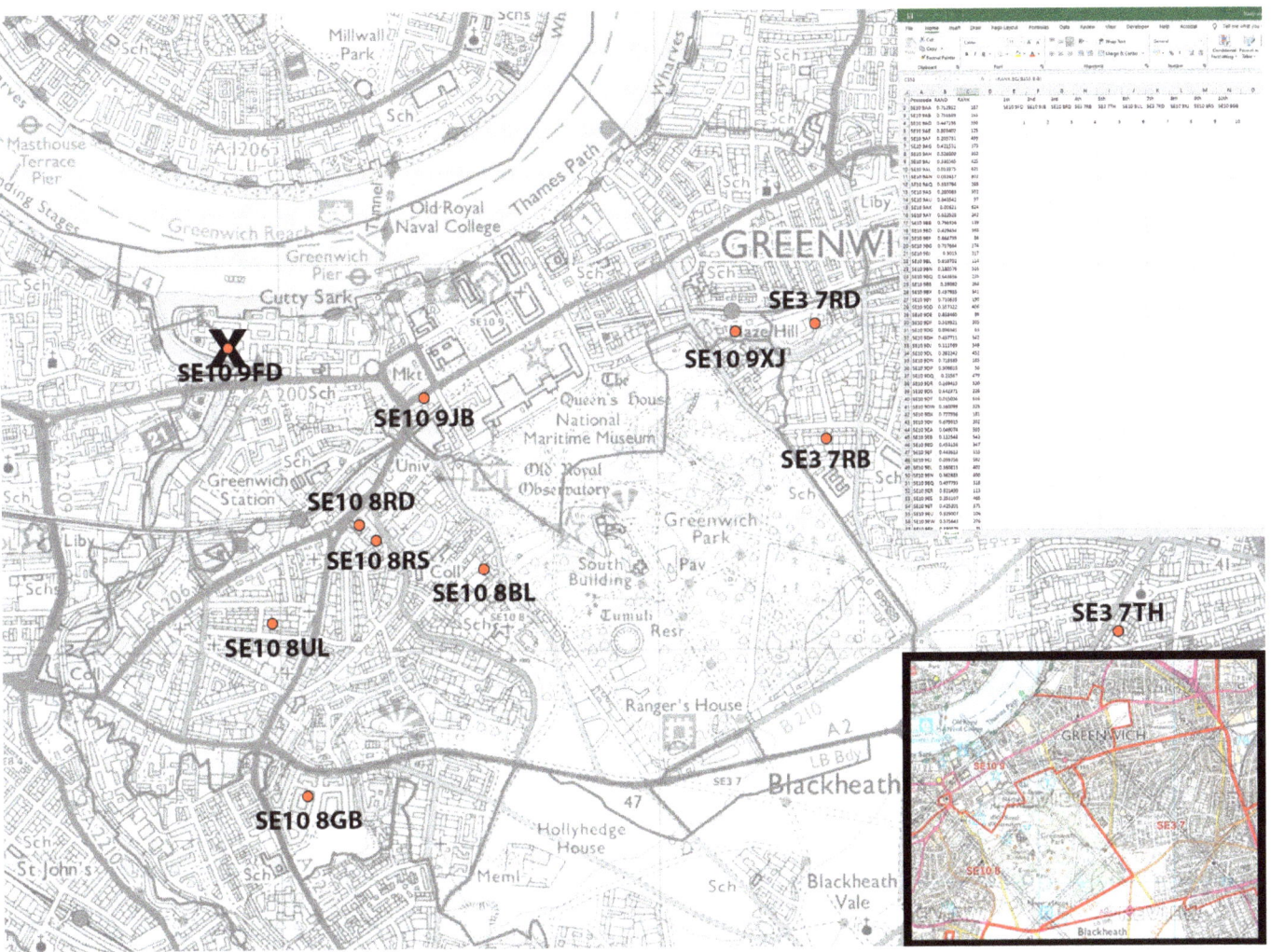

Figure 54. Randomised selection of postcodes for distribution of the survey form.

173 Seren Park Gardens	188 Seren Park Gardens	203 Seren Park Gardens	218 Seren Park Gardens
174 Seren Park Gardens	189 Seren Park Gardens	204 Seren Park Gardens	
175 Seren Park Gardens	190 Seren Park Gardens	205 Seren Park Gardens	SE10 8UL
176 Seren Park Gardens	191 Seren Park Gardens	206 Seren Park Gardens	26 Ashburnham Grove
177 Seren Park Gardens	192 Seren Park Gardens	207 Seren Park Gardens	27 Ashburnham Grove
178 Seren Park Gardens	193 Seren Park Gardens	208 Seren Park Gardens	28 Ashburnham Grove
179 Seren Park Gardens	194 Seren Park Gardens	209 Seren Park Gardens	29 Ashburnham Grove
180 Seren Park Gardens	195 Seren Park Gardens	210 Seren Park Gardens	30 Ashburnham Grove
181 Seren Park Gardens	196 Seren Park Gardens	211 Seren Park Gardens	31 Ashburnham Grove
182 Seren Park Gardens	197 Seren Park Gardens	212 Seren Park Gardens	32 Ashburnham Grove
183 Seren Park Gardens	198 Seren Park Gardens	213 Seren Park Gardens	33 Ashburnham Grove
184 Seren Park Gardens	199 Seren Park Gardens	214 Seren Park Gardens	34 Ashburnham Grove
185 Seren Park Gardens	200 Seren Park Gardens	215 Seren Park Gardens	35 Ashburnham Grove
186 Seren Park Gardens	201 Seren Park Gardens	216 Seren Park Gardens	36 Ashburnham Grove
187 Seren Park Gardens	202 Seren Park Gardens	217 Seren Park Gardens	37 Ashburnham Grove

APPENDIX A — THE IMPORTANCE OF VISUAL SUSTAINABILITY

38 Ashburnham Grove
39 Ashburnham Grove
40 Ashburnham Grove
41 Ashburnham Grove
42 Ashburnham Grove
43 Ashburnham Grove

SE3 7RB
2 Westcombe Park Road
4 Westcombe Park Road
6 Westcombe Park Road
8 Westcombe Park Road
10 Westcombe Park Road
12 Westcombe Park Road
14 Westcombe Park Road
16 Westcombe Park Road
18 Westcombe Park Road
20 Westcombe Park Road
22 Westcombe Park Road
24 Westcombe Park Road
26 Westcombe Park Road
28 Westcombe Park Road
30 Westcombe Park Road
32 Westcombe Park Road
34 Westcombe Park Road
36 Westcombe Park Road
38 Westcombe Park Road
SE3 7TH
11 Stratheden Road
13 Stratheden Road
Top Floor Flat, 13 Stratheden Road
13a Stratheden Road
13b Stratheden Road
13c Stratheden Road
13d Stratheden Road
Garden Flat, 13 Stratheden Road
21 Stratheden Road
21a Stratheden Road
21b Stratheden Road
21c Stratheden Road
25 Stratheden Road
27 Stratheden Road
29 Stratheden Road
30a Stratheden Road
31 Stratheden Road

SE10 8RD
CHRISTOPHRITTERSTUDIO LTD, MERIDIAN HOUSE ROYAL HILL
FURNITUBES INTERNATIONAL LTD, Meridian House, Royal Hill
GREENWICH COLLEGE, Meridian House, Royal Hill
G S M LONDON, Meridian House, Royal Hill
SE10 8GB
Flat 1 Blossom House, Hillside Ave
Flat 2 Blossom House, Hillside Ave
Flat 3 Blossom House, Hillside Ave
Flat 4 Blossom House, Hillside Ave-
Flat 5 Blossom House, Hillside Ave
Flat 6 Blossom House, Hillside Ave
Flat 7 Blossom House, Hillside Ave
Flat 8 Blossom House, Hillside Ave
Flat 9 Blossom House, Hillside Ave
Flat 10 Blossom House, Hillside Ave
Flat 11 Blossom House, Hillside Ave
Flat 12 Blossom House, Hillside Ave
Flat 13 Blossom House, Hillside Ave
Flat 14 Blossom House, Hillside Ave
Flat 15 Blossom House, Hillside Ave
Flat 16 Blossom House, Hillside Ave
Flat 17 Blossom House, Hillside Ave
Flat 18 Blossom House, Hillside Ave

SE10 8RS
1 Peyton Place
1a Peyton Place
2 Peyton Place
3 Peyton Place
4 Peyton Place
5 Peyton Place
6 Peyton Place
7 Peyton Place
Ernest Cottage, Peyton Place
Flat 1, Linear House, Peyton Place
Stanley Cottage, Peyton Place
Development Solution Ltd, The Hall, Peyton Place
Hards P R, The Hall, Peyton Place
Medical Centre Holdings Ltd, The Hall, Peyton Place
The Old Coach House, Peyton Place
The Hall, Peyton Place

SE10 9JB
Flat 1, 1a Nelson Road
Flat 2, 1a Nelson Road
2a Nelson Road
3–4 Nelson Road
5a Nelson Road
6a Nelson Road
7a Nelson Road
7b Nelson Road
2a Nelson Road
8a Nelson Road
8a–8b Nelson Road
8b Nelson Road
12a Nelson Road
12b Nelson Road
12c Nelson Road
13a Nelson Road
Flat 1, 14 Nelson Road
Flat 2, 14 Nelson Road
Flat 3, 14 Nelson Road
15a Nelson Road
Flat 1, 17 Nelson Road
Flat 2, 17 Nelson Road
Flat 3, 17 Nelson Road
Flat 4, 17 Nelson Road
Flat 1–4, 17 Nelson Road
19a Nelson Road
19b Nelson Road
20a Nelson Road
Flat 1, 20a Nelson Road
Flat 2, 20a Nelson Road
Flat 3, 20a Nelson Road
Flat 1, 21a Nelson Road
Flat 2, 21a Nelson Road
Flat 3, 21a Nelson Road
Second Floor Flat, 21 Nelson Road
22a Nelson Road
23a Nelson Road
24a Nelson Road
First Floor Flat, 23a Nelson Road
Second Floor Flat, 23a Nelson Road
Third Floor Flat, 23a Nelson Road

SE10 8BL
1 Mays Court 54 Crooms Hill
2 Mays Court 54 Crooms Hill
3 Mays Court 54 Crooms Hill
4 Mays Court 54 Crooms Hill
5 Mays Court 54 Crooms Hill
6 Mays Court 54 Crooms Hill
7 Mays Court 54 Crooms Hill
8 Mays Court 54 Crooms Hill
9 Mays Court 54 Crooms Hill
10 Mays Court 54 Crooms Hill
11 Mays Court 54 Crooms Hill
12 Mays Court 54 Crooms Hill
13 Mays Court 54 Crooms Hill
14 Mays Court 54 Crooms Hill
15 Mays Court 54 Crooms Hill
16 Mays Court 54 Crooms Hill
17 Mays Court 54 Crooms Hill
18 Mays Court 54 Crooms Hill
19 Mays Court 54 Crooms Hill
20 Mays Court 54 Crooms Hill
21 Mays Court 54 Crooms Hill

SE10 9XJ
1 Tom Smith Close
2 Tom Smith Close
3 Tom Smith Close
4 Tom Smith Close
5 Tom Smith Close
6 Tom Smith Close
7 Tom Smith Close
8 Tom Smith Close
9 Tom Smith Close
10 Tom Smith Close
11 Tom Smith Close
12 Tom Smith Close
13 Tom Smith Close
14 Tom Smith Close
15 Tom Smith Close
16 Tom Smith Close
17 Tom Smith Close
18 Tom Smith Close
19 Tom Smith Close
20 Tom Smith Close
21 Tom Smith Close
22 Tom Smith Close
23 Tom Smith Close
24 Tom Smith Close
25 Tom Smith Close
26 Tom Smith Close
27 Tom Smith Close
28 Tom Smith Close
29 Tom Smith Close
30 Tom Smith Close
31 Tom Smith Close
32 Tom Smith Close
33 Tom Smith Close
34 Tom Smith Close
35 Tom Smith Close
36 Tom Smith Close
37 Tom Smith Close
38 Tom Smith Close
39 Tom Smith Close
40 Tom Smith Close
41 Tom Smith Close
42 Tom Smith Close
43 Tom Smith Close
44 Tom Smith Close
45 Tom Smith Close
46 Tom Smith Close
47 Tom Smith Close
48 Tom Smith Close
49 Tom Smith Close
50 Tom Smith Close
51 Tom Smith Close
52 Tom Smith Close
53 Tom Smith Close
54 Tom Smith Close
55 Tom Smith Close
56 Tom Smith Close
57 Tom Smith Close
58 Tom Smith Close
59 Tom Smith Close
60 Tom Smith Close
61 Tom Smith Close
62 Tom Smith Close
63 Tom Smith Close
64 Tom Smith Close
65 Tom Smith Close
66 Tom Smith Close
67 Tom Smith Close
68 Tom Smith Close
69 Tom Smith Close
70 Tom Smith Close
71 Tom Smith Close
72 Tom Smith Close

Figure 55. Postcode address verification using public online data.

APPENDIX A   THE IMPORTANCE OF VISUAL SUSTAINABILITY

Visual Sustainability Research Initiative
INVITATION TO PARTICIPATE   Page 1 of 12

University of Hertfordshire UH   Ethics Committee

This is an official notification by a student of the University of Hertfordshire in respect of a study involving human participants.

Title of study: The importance of visual sustainability in urban design strategy
Protocol Number: CTA/PGR/UH/05780
Approving Committee:
    The University of Hertfordshire Social Sciences, Arts and Humanities Ethics Committee with Delegated Authority

If you have any queries concerning this document, please contact me Pieter de Kock, email: visual.sustainability@outlook.com or my supervisor Dr Silvio Carta, email: s.carta@herts.ac.uk

Activity and Location: (map provided)	Unaccompanied walk in the area of Greenwich Town Centre and Greenwich Park (PARTs 1 and 2); and immediate surrounds (PART 3).

If you're a regular walker within the Greenwich Town Centre, including Greenwich Park and immediate surroundings, we'd like to know more about what and how you see. We're particularly interested in the object(s) that you're most attracted to during your normal daily walk. This should take place in your favourite area and one in which you are familiar and comfortable. We'd like to know what you most hold dear. It could be anything, large or small, for example but not limited to: an entrance door, a statue, a view of something in particular, a special place, a favourite tree or bench. A building or some part of a building. Perhaps an ornamental feature. A certain stretch in your walk, foliage, architecture or microclimate. Sounds or a sound associated with an object, whether related or not. Laughter, a passing train, a bell, a car, a bicycle. Patterns of light and shade.

Your participation is hereby requested for PART 1 and PART 2 of this study. After your reply to accept this invitation is received, we'll send you more information about the study area, along with the Participant Information Sheet and a Consent Form to complete. Here is a short summary describing your involvement (duration: 45 to 90 minutes):

In PART 1—for the walk—we'll ask you to take photos and make some notes to describe any objects that you feel most attracted to during your walk. As an optional exercise, we'll also ask you to use a simple free smartphone App to record aspects of your walk.

In PART 2, we'll ask you several questions, for example, to remember a day later what you experienced; how you would feel if that object disappeared or that unique experience was no longer possible; and to identify one single event or memory that stands out—one that is most valuable or vivid and which, for whatever reason, is *most dear to you*.

For participation forms please reply to: Visual Sustainability Research Initiative
Email: visual.sustainability@outlook.com

PART 3 will involve those participants who are happy to continue with the study after Part 2 and will consist of semi-structured interviews. Anticipated duration: 45 minutes to 90 minutes. Please complete the following if you're interested in participating in PART 3.

    Email (or preferred contact): _____

Thank you very much for your support in this study!

University of Hertfordshire. Protocol number: CTA/PGR/UH/05780. Approved by the Social Sciences, Arts and Humanities ECDA. Questions, further information and contact details: Pieter de Kock, Researcher at the University of Hertfordshire | College Lane | Hatfield | Herts | AL10 9AB | E: visual.sustainability@outlook.com

IN URBAN DESIGN STRATEGY APPENDIX A

Visual Sustainability Research Initiative
PARTICIPANTS INFORMATION Page 2 of 12
Part 1 & 2 study area: Greenwich Town Centre and Greenwich Park

(2 copies provided)

University of Hertfordshire. Protocol number: CTA/PGR/UH/05780. Approved by the Social Sciences, Arts and Humanities ECDA. Questions, further information and contact details: Pieter de Kock, Researcher at the University of Hertfordshire | College Lane | Hatfield | Herts | AL10 9AB | E: visual.sustainability@outlook.com

APPENDIX A — THE IMPORTANCE OF VISUAL SUSTAINABILITY

Visual Sustainability Research Initiative
PARTICIPANTS INFORMATION Page 3 of 12
PART 1

1. In PART 1 we would like you to please:

   1.1. On your walk, take photos of object(s) that you feel most attracted to (**major attractions**), so that we can understand more about your point of view and your feelings while observing your favourite feature(s).
   1.2. Draw a line of the route you took on the map provided. It would also be helpful if you could indicate the location of each **major attraction** on the attached map.
   See examples below:

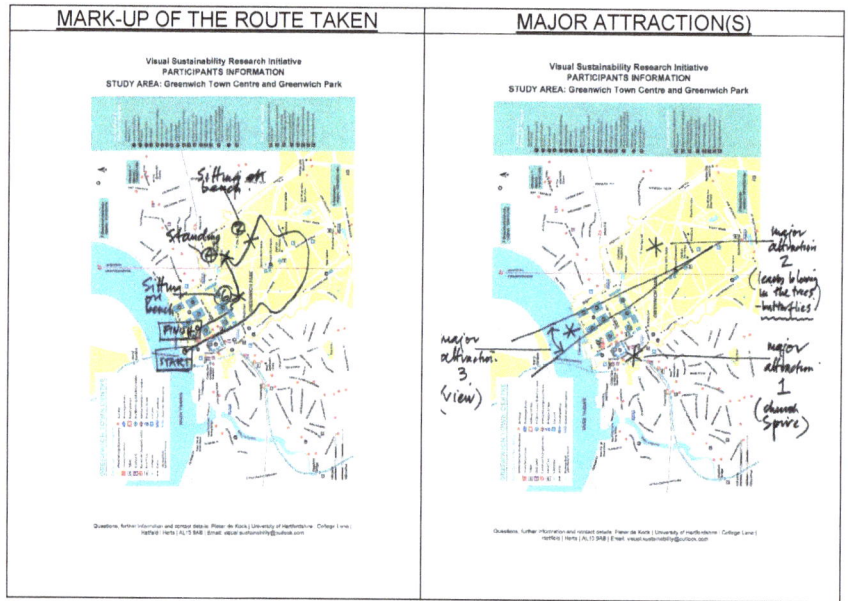

*It is important to understand that there are no rights or wrongs. This is simply your experience and unique to you. The meaning you see along this walk is your meaning. There are no rules as to what you see and don't see. So, relax, enjoy your walk and when you see that thing that is useful to you and you are able describe how you feel about that use, don't forget to record it! Even if you can't find words to describe how you feel about it, please note it down; no matter how strange or insignificant it may seem to others. We're interested in how **you** engage with your environment.*

Please use the survey sheets which follow to provide your answers

University of Hertfordshire. Protocol number: CTA/PGR/UH/05780. Approved by the Social Sciences, Arts and Humanities ECDA. Questions, further information and contact details: Pieter de Kock, Researcher at the University of Hertfordshire | College Lane | Hatfield | Herts | AL10 9AB | E: visual.sustainability@outlook.com

Visual Sustainability Research Initiative
PARTICIPANTS INFORMATION Page 4 of 12
PART 1 NOTES

Rating for the physical object or event | Rating for level of emotion attached to object

PHYSICAL FEATURE OR EVENT					ASSOCIATED FEELING				
strong		neutral		weak	Strong		Neutral		weak
5	4	3	2	1	5	4	3	2	1
E.g.: Butterflies, leaves, dappled sunlight [5]					Peace and calm [5]				
E.g.: Church spire [3]					Time, sandstone, the sky [4]				
E.g.: Takeaway storefront [2]					Feeling of being rushed, stress, hunger [3]				

APPENDIX A THE IMPORTANCE OF VISUAL SUSTAINABILITY

Visual Sustainability Research Initiative
PARTICIPANTS INFORMATION Page 5 of 12

University of Hertfordshire. Protocol number: CTA/PGR/UH/05780. Approved by the Social Sciences, Arts and Humanities ECDA. Questions, further information and contact details: Pieter de Kock, Researcher at the University of Hertfordshire | College Lane | Hatfield | Herts | AL10 9AB | E: visual.sustainability@outlook.com

Visual Sustainability Research Initiative
PARTICIPANTS INFORMATION — Page 6 of 12

1.3. (OPTIONAL)

On your walk, please use a simple, easy to use, smart phone App:

Clickr for Android, available on Google Play or at: https://rdq.cz/clickr.html

or

Counter Tally Count for iPhone, available at the App Store or at:
https://apps.apple.com/us/app/counter-tally-count/id1144352844?platform=iphone

The premium version for each is required and will be provided free of charge to you to record your walk. Both these Apps are able to export to Excel compatible .csv files.

An example of a walk using the Android App is illustrated below.

HOW TO USE THE APP

Using the **New Counter** button while you're walking, divide your walk into as many sections as feels comfortable to you. Each section should represent a change in activity from, say walking, to sitting, or to standing while observing, etc. Please label each new counter with a name that describes your activity. After completion, the .csv file that you export show times, so it will be easy for us to order these sections afterwards.

WHAT TO DO

Once you have created a new counter, start your activity and click the + button every time you see something that you visually engage with, or you find interesting. This can be an object, an event, or an experience such as a feeling or emotion related to your walk. As you can see in the picture to the left, this person experienced 126 separate visual experiences or engagements while walking during the first section they called: *1-Started walking*. This activity took 25 minutes. We know this from the exported .csv file they provided us. The entire walk with pauses and stoppages took 1 hour and 25 minutes. This person walked in an area from the Town Centre to an area in Greenwich Park, and back along a different route (which is their favourite walk). We know this because they marked their route out with a pen on the map provided by us. They were also kind enough to mark the spots where each activity changed, for example, from walking to sitting on a bench—and then when they started walking again. **In this example we received exactly what we had wished for from the participant.**

University of Hertfordshire. Protocol number: CTA/PGR/UH/05780. Approved by the Social Sciences, Arts and Humanities ECDA. Questions, further information and contact details: Pieter de Kock, Researcher at the University of Hertfordshire | College Lane | Hatfield | Herts | AL10 9AB | E: visual.sustainability@outlook.com

APPENDIX A   THE IMPORTANCE OF VISUAL SUSTAINABILITY

Visual Sustainability Research Initiative
PARTICIPANTS INFORMATION
PART 2

2A). When you get home, try, after at least 24 hours, to remember what you saw without referencing your notes. Then write down, in the notes section 2A below, those events which are most easily recollected and which stand out for you, even if it differs from your earlier experience.

2B). If, when thinking about the memory of the previous day's walk, you are reminded of another event or emotion, please write down, in the notes section 2B below, the associated memory.

2C). If a scenario such as the New Zealand earthquake of 2010
https://interactives.stuff.co.nz/2020/08/munted/
were to destroy the area that you most hold dear (as it did in large parts of Christchurch in New Zealand), how do you think you would feel? In other words, how you would feel if that one object most dear to you on your walk, disappeared; or that unique experience was no longer possible?

Please rate your reaction below:

1. Inconsolable
2. Very upset
3. Concerned
4. Not really concerned
6. Not concerned at all

Please also add any additional response in the notes section 2C below.

2D). Finally, in the notes section 2D below, please identify which one single event or memory stands out as the most valuable or vivid and which, for whatever reason, is *most dear to you*. It would be helpful if you could also indicate the location of each event on the attached map.

PART 2 NOTES

PART 2A. Only what you **remember** from the previous day's experience (without looking at your notes); and give it a rating.

WHAT YOU SAW AND RATING					HOW YOU FELT AND RATING				
strong		neutral		weak	Strong		Neutral		weak
5	4	3	2	1	5	4	3	2	1

University of Hertfordshire. Protocol number: CTA/PGR/UH/05780. Approved by the Social Sciences, Arts and Humanities ECDA. Questions, further information and contact details: Pieter de Kock, Researcher at the University of Hertfordshire | College Lane | Hatfield | Herts | AL10 9AB | E: visual.sustainability@outlook.com

Visual Sustainability Research Initiative
PARTICIPANTS INFORMATION Page 8 of 12

University of Hertfordshire. Protocol number: CTA/PGR/UH/05780. Approved by the Social Sciences, Arts and Humanities ECDA. Questions, further information and contact details: Pieter de Kock, Researcher at the University of Hertfordshire | College Lane | Hatfield | Herts | AL10 9AB | E: visual.sustainability@outlook.com

APPENDIX A
THE IMPORTANCE OF VISUAL SUSTAINABILITY

Visual Sustainability Research Initiative
PARTICIPANTS INFORMATION Page 9 of 12

PART 2B. What other memories are associated with the dominant memory of yesterday's walk; and give each memory a rating of intensity

YESTERDAY'S MEMORY					NEW ASSOCIATED MEMORY				
strong		neutral		weak	Strong		Neutral		weak
5	4	3	2	1	5	4	3	2	1
E.g.: police on horseback [3]					An ice-cream on the beach [5]				
E.g.: afternoon sun on a rose [4]					Your favourite shampoo [4]				
E.g.: grass beyond a deep shaded area [5]					A friend [3]				

University of Hertfordshire. Protocol number: CTA/PGR/UH/05780. Approved by the Social Sciences, Arts and Humanities ECDA. Questions, further information and contact details: Pieter de Kock, Researcher at the University of Hertfordshire | College Lane | Hatfield | Herts | AL10 9AB | E: visual.sustainability@outlook.com

Visual Sustainability Research Initiative
PARTICIPANTS INFORMATION Page 10 of 12

University of Hertfordshire. Protocol number: CTA/PGR/UH/05780. Approved by the Social Sciences, Arts and Humanities ECDA. Questions, further information and contact details: Pieter de Kock, Researcher at the University of Hertfordshire | College Lane | Hatfield | Herts | AL10 9AB | E: visual.sustainability@outlook.com

APPENDIX A THE IMPORTANCE OF VISUAL SUSTAINABILITY

Visual Sustainability Research Initiative
PARTICIPANTS INFORMATION

PART 2C. Notes expanding on how you would feel if that object disappeared or that unique experience was no longer possible.

PART 2D. SINGLE EVENT OR MEMORY What is that one memory most held dear?

Congratulations!

This completes PARTS 1 and 2. Thank you for your support!

Please email the results of the data collected from the App as well as the map with route indication, any photos, and comments/ notes to: visual.sustainability@outlook.com

Or, if you prefer, we can collect these from you at a convenient time and place.

University of Hertfordshire. Protocol number: CTA/PGR/UH/05780. Approved by the Social Sciences, Arts and Humanities ECDA. Questions, further information and contact details: Pieter de Kock, Researcher at the University of Hertfordshire | College Lane | Hatfield | Herts | AL10 9AB | E: visual.sustainability@outlook.com

Visual Sustainability Research Initiative
PARTICIPANTS INFORMATION

I would like to receive a summary of the results of the study	Yes / No

ADDITIONAL EXPLANATORY NOTES OR SKETCHES

APPENDIX B THE IMPORTANCE OF VISUAL SUSTAINABILITY

APPENDIX B

INTERVIEWS

Semi-structured interview

1. Interview question

What's a typical day for you?.

[This is to establish a baseline. TONE. This goes to help understand how much they vary from their initial register during the rest of the conversation].

PM

Ahhh, take the dog for a walk first thing in the morning. Come back. Tidy up. Talk to some friends. Take the dog for another long walk in the afternoon. Think about something to eat. And maybe plan something for the evening. Go out, uhhh, watch some TV, listen to the radio. But my joy is probably audiobooks and listening to books and that sort of stuff.

2. Interview question

Do you have a favourite urban space?

[Trying to get the person straight into thinking about special places: i.e., matter and associated memory. So, I need the person to start mixing both worlds as they try to answer this. Is there a certain reciprocity at work between the visible and invisible?]

PM

Umm. Brecon Beacons in Wales.

Interviewer

Which one?

PM

Brec... uh, probably have a uh, an urban one.

Interviewer

Well, which is the one you've just mentioned, because...?

PM

Brecon Beacons. It's a National Park.

Interviewer

Oh, ok.

PM

Ahh umm.

Interviewer

That's fine.

PM

Urban space in London? Probably around the British Library. I like that area.

3. Interview question

What's it like? [+] This favourite space? It could be either of the two, the first one you mentioned, or the second.

[Simple questions. This will lead to dialogue, not monologue. Again, is there a certain reciprocity at work between the visible and invisible].

PM

Well, the, I think the one, lets stick with the urban in London, I think it's the architecture. Its design. Its historical value. Umm. I think it's interesting when you look at something like Victorian design and Victorian building, and that we then come along and change it into this [pause] grey battleship, prefabricated nonsense that [pause] architects and designers hide behind the idea that every generation should design its own environment and therefore it doesn't have to last forever. Whereas, I think, particularly the Victorians, believed in building, something that's was going to be everlasting, because they thought that, I guess the Empire would be everlasting.

Interviewer

And your first choice of favourite place?

PM

Hmm... would be the Brecon Beacons in Wales.

Interviewer

Yes, what's it like?

PM

Its [pause] desolate. Its [indistinct] pine forest, Forestry Commission land, uhm, its got the three highest peaks in South Wales, umm, its just somewhere you can walk and relax and [long pause] just [pause] admire nature. And be inspired by Nature.

Interviewer

Great. Now between the two of them do you find yourself at odds... [indistinct] between the two? [wind noise].

PM

One is the natural habitat which has its own value and its own protection...
[wind noise]
It inspires, and, it makes you reflect. I think it's the reflection. On Life... [indistinct].

4.   Interview question
Is context Important to you?
[Here I want to know how important relational networks are to this person].

PM

Yes. If you don't have a context, if you don't have context, its difficult to, well I find it difficult to understand the rationale or what was trying to be achieved. To me you have a set of values that you try to, whether is building or living, that you try to [long pause] well, you try to achieve. So, architecture should be inspiring, it should be, not for a generation, but should inspire the next generation, to build better, to build [pause] for the future.

Interviewer

When you talk about those values, do you see a difference between, and a distinction between, your first choice and your second choice? In other words, one is abstract, and one is more concrete.

PM

No...

Interviewer

The second one is building, the first one is abstract...

PM

There's no difference in my mind.

Interviewer

There's no difference in your mind?

PM

No.
[pause] it's the emotion, it's ...

Interviewer

Do you feel transformed more by one than the other or the same?

PM

It depends on the mood. It, it can be, its different, you know, you [pause] sometimes I'll be walking through, say, through London, and you'll see something and think, wow I've never noticed that before, and, that's tremendous. And wonder... then it triggers: I wonder why we built it like that. And who designed it. And what was the rationale. Whereas if you're out in the wild, as I call it, in Brecon, its nature left alone to get on and do what nature wants to do. Which is also inspiring. Man hasn't come along with a bulldozer and changed the shape of a mountain, or...

Interviewer

But there's... there are still objects there in front of you aren't there?

PM

Absolutely.

Interviewer

That there's space between them, and there's a sense of discernment...

PM

Yeah, you can touch them, you can walk on them, you can... feel them.

5.   Interview question
What kind of things do you do in this space? [+] when you're there? When you're physically there?
[Physical use: how we see the use (action/ virtual action/ affordance)].

PM

Ahh–ah–ah, well, it depends, Brecon Beacons you can walk, aaaand just fill your lungs with clean fresh air. Its, in London, again, its about, it's probably more people–watching and building–watching to see the interaction between people and buildings. And [long pause] to see how difficult some people seem to have, with, managing a relationship with a building. Intimidation. Oh, I'm not going in there. It's not for the likes of us. It's, uh, what's the word? Posh. It's a posh person's place. It's not for us. Greasy spoon versus, five–star restaurants still serving food.

Interviewer

Do you feel that space has been privatised too much, so you don't know whether you're on public land or not?

PM

Yeah… that's blurred, completely now.

6. Interview question

How do you feel when you're in your favourite space? [+] well, we've got two now in this interview.

[Visual Use: how we feel about the use that we see (memory/ past–present/ spirit)].

PM

Yeah, Uh… [long pause] Usually very relaxed and calming. Aaand [pause] contemplating the past, thinking about the future. Seeking inspiration. Umm…

Interviewer

Even in the urban one?

PM

In the urban one as well. And the urban one is kind of [pause] we can do this when you've got a good team, and you've got a good design, when you've got money, when you've got the will. And it's not being done on the cheap. Whereas the other one is nature in all its glory, saying, you don't actually have to spend all this money and have all this planning. This is what it would, may have, looked like a thousand years ago. You know, when

London was a foggy marsh. Until Romans came along and started to design nature out, and put Man in his place. Or to manage nature. One is managed, and one isn't.

Interviewer

But in both cases, you seem to feel a sense of, not enlightenment, but you're not thinking about the basics, like Maslow's hierarchy. You're there right at the top.

PM

No. Not right at the top, but I mean its… sometimes I feel like I am at the top. Of Maslow's pyramid. And that's quite strange. But its very rare. Umm. But certainly, sort of like, a fair way up the pyramid, I think. In a way that I look at, look at things and I think that's to do with part of my career, when we were looking at funding projects, and design, and putting things in place, which work for the next a hundred years and not for a year.

Interviewer

Is it theme of foresight coming through in the sense of looking forward?

PM

Yeah. Some of the stuff I've worked on is now just breaking the first sod.

7. Interview question

Is the space always a constant and dependable environment that you feel secure in? + I think you've answered that by…
[Here I'm moving on to understanding more about where the invariance lies i.e., Structural Invariant (SI)].

PM

Yeah, … it… I think a lot of its down to the individual and how confident they are in themselves, but… I can't think of a space that intimidates me, not even a dark alley and some of the… the less salubrious areas, particularly of London. But, I can't think of anywhere that actually makes me feel [indistinct]. Most places, maybe it's about the choice of where I go to, tend to be something interesting in there, that

I would find interesting. Just to look at a building.

Interviewer
Where you've struck up a relationship with an event or object or something?

PM
Yeah.

Interviewer
And when you go back, do you strike up that relationship again, or do you find something new, and you forget about the old relationship?

PM
Yeah, I tend, I tend, I tend to build on it, and so if I go back again, I will look at it, and then you will find something different. Or, I am by nature a curious person, and, um, uh, if I see something that's not all that nice, and just carry on, and I think, I wonder why, and, um, earlier on I was saying that the Tories built something that was going to last forever because they thought the Empire was going to last forever. I don't know whether that's true, just my take on it, I think there was a certain amount of arrogance, and, um, but the core values, uhh, that poor will remain poor and the rich will remain rich, haven't changed.

8. Interview question
Describe how your relationship or affinity with this space started. [+] Do you remember that moment that you struck up a relationship with, say, either…
[Here I'm looking to identify an EVENT. What caused this relationship and are there other events embedded in memory].

PM
Umm, when I was very, very small, my grandfather took me down to Cardiff Docks. Which used to be docks in those days, with boats and ships and [indistinct]. You know, a real Port. And I can remember he, he took me along and there were all these ships at the docks and the scale of them and the size of them, and I was only, probably about four or five. Just amazed me. I was struck at the big cranes and how they all worked and how clever it was to have railway lines running, and that was in the days when trains, and planes, and boats all seem to go inside one another.

Interviewer
So, is it fair to say that the Docks was actually your favourite space?

PM
It was my father's, my grandfathers favourite place and because of my grandfather, that I was the apple of my grandfather's eyes, he would take me… we always ended up going down to the docks to see the ships because, a. that's where all his mates were, I think, but it was also, he's not going to get into trouble down there because he can, you know, the, the guys would look out for him. And it was busy. There were steam engines, there was coal being exported, goods being imported. So, it was a really busy port.

Interviewer
But it wasn't just your grandfather's space. It sounds like it was yours as well.

PM
It was our space.

Interviewer
Yeah, it was your space, but together.

PM
Yeah.

Interviewer
Interesting.

PM
It, it, and that, that triggers my [pause] because people say, oh, its terrible down there, and I'd say, no, its really fascinating, do you know, and that's where the 'Do You Know', the curiosity thing came from about immigration into Cardiff, the Somali community and the first riots were in Cardiff, the race riots, and Seaman and [indistinct], Butes, and… there's a whole sort of like storyline and history line that goes with it.

Interviewer

So, you got caught up in that story.

PM

Yeah. Yes. I wonder why it's called, Bute docks, I discovered because the Marquess of Bute paid for the damn thing. And, you know, he was the richest man in the world at the time and owned most of the coal exports and set the price of coal in the world... because he married a woman called Sophie who brought with her the Brecon Beacons, that just happened to be full of iron, iron–ore, trees and water, and coal. And because he married the right woman who brought with her the right land, they exported out, uhm, good quality coal, high value, carry on steam value, or something, what's it called. So, the whole British navy brought Bute's coal. Um, and you were part of that, as a little kid, you were being dragged around by your grandfather, who was explaining all this to you. He was trying to set the context for me and I, well it obviously sank in, because I'm able to give you a narrative now.

Interviewer

So, for you, the docks, the narrative, is the more important event and its not so much just the single objects or an assemblage that you saw, it was more the story that was developing...]

PM

It's the... yeah, it's the narrative [my note: see song]. The, I wondered why that happened, or, I was curious as to...

Interviewer

And you still look back on that.

PM

Yeah.

Interviewer

So that space, is still there with you?

PM

Yeah. One of my jobs was to it was regenerating Cardiff Bay, so it was destroying the docks and building flats. That's the irony. You know you; you think...

Interviewer

Did you feel guilty at the time? Did you feel a sense of, I'm not doing the right thing?

PM

Yeah, we're not doing the right thing. Its too dense, its not right, its not for local people. But the markets turned and this is what's wanted. And politicians... demanded, this is what we want, we're not interested, its all very well [interviewee's name] but, I want half a million–pound flats built there please. OK.

9. Interview question

Do you feel that over the years the space has changed you? [+] I'm talking about now the three spaces. You've got the first two, and then you've got the Docks. I've got the feeling the Docks are more important but, I mean, I'm not sure. Do you feel as if the space has changed you.
[Here I'm looking to identify TRANSFORMATION (Tx) in an Invariance Structure, where I.S. = SI +Tx].

PM

Yes [long pause]. Yeah. Its because, I think its because of my curious nature. There is a relationship between, if you take you take Brecon Beacons, and if you take, London, and you take the Docks, there is a storyline that actually weaves its way through all those three developments. And when you take a step back you realise that there is this, probably the same storyline in every single country in the world. That takes to do with trying to make things better, if it's about exploitation of the working class. Its about design. Beautiful things for people who are, in inverted commas, educated to appreciate beauty and not for A.N. Other.

Interviewer

Do you sometimes find that a memory linked with one, jogs you to think about memory with another [indistinct].

APPENDIX B THE IMPORTANCE OF VISUAL SUSTAINABILITY

PM
Oh yes.

Interviewer
Sort of backwards and forwards thing or…?

PM
Oh yeah.

Interviewer
Often?

PM
Often. But the older I get…

Interviewer
Do you find you get new memories?

PM
Yeah, the older you get, the more it happens, uhm, you begin to, well I find what happens, is ah yes, it does seem to make sense. Like a jigsaw. Life has always been a jigsaw puzzle for me. And you're constantly putting the pieces, you don't have the full picture, but you have these pieces that you know, must go together eventually.

Interviewer
Is it fair to say that you, as we all do, that you live…

PM
In the past.

Interviewer
You live in it because the memory is the past?

PM
Yeah, yeah, yeah, you, but the past, for me, its like the past lays the foundations for the future. Um, and that can have a massive impact on your life. You know, positive impact or negative impact.

Interviewer
And the present isn't that important, in the sense because…

PM
Well, what is the present? The present is only here and now. You blink, it's gone. You know, this, is now the past. So, what, you… the present is…

Interviewer
What?

PM
What.

Interviewer
Exactly.

PM
That's why I'm feeling relaxed about the future.

10.   Interview question
So, you feel over the years, space has changed you. How have you changed the space over the years? [+] I mean not only the physical space but the memory, you know, the memory of the space?

[This goes to understanding reciprocity in the PATTERN at work i.e., Pt = I.S. of an Ev].

PM
Yeah. Yeah. I've changed it physically. I've, I've changed [pause] I've physically changed it [indistinct] aaand [indistinct]. Uhm, if you look, if you look around you now, uhm [long pause] the dome wouldn't be there, if I hadn't been part of that, leading that team to make it happen, uhm, and its, its quite, its, its, sometimes you look at it and you think, yes, that's good but its, its, uhm, you get tired of doing things in the abstract, this is what the future animation is going to look like, and you think it'll never look like, because, it's always just simple things, you spend a lot of money grassing an area and putting a path down, and you think, people won't use that path because their nature will take them that way, straight across that field. And you go back six months later and there is a muddy path. Because that's human nature. You can try all, the only

way you're going to channel people is to actually put them in an alleyway and brick it up and say that's the only way you can go. You let people and they will naturally follow a course and it never, very rarely in my experience does it ever follow what an architect says or what its going to look like. Because its [indistinct] you put the pathway going round and so people walk straight across the middle. And I do it. And you think what a stupid place to lay out a path.

11. Interview question

When you are not in either of those three spaces, what kind of things change your mood?
[Here I want to see evidence of simulacrum. Can this person connect to this space 'remotely'?]

PM
Music, literature, people, uhm [long pause] but, but literature and music [long pause] uhhhm I mean I'm... I'm fairly passionate about, something like, Madam Butterfly, I will see every year and I will cry every single year. Despite the fact that I know the story, I know what's going to happen, it triggers that. And it...

Interviewer
Why do you think that is?

PM
Because its emotional, its' passionate, its [pause] powerful...

Interviewer
So, it gives you a sense of relief that you can actually journey beyond your...

PM
Yeahhhhhhhh, it takes you out of yourself and out of your... it takes you out of that space and into a different area, into somebody else's space that's directed it, and thought about it. And you think, my gosh, as a species we're capable of doing incredibly beautiful things [pause] as well as genocide on earth on unbelievable scale. Not many species can do that. Or want to do that.

12. Interview question

By contrast, when you are in this space, what kind of things change your mood?

[Back to the Transformations. Did we skip anything]?

PM
Hmmm.

Interviewer
Either of the three. So, when you're not in the space you actually feel your music, and your literature. When you're in it, what kind of things change your mood?

PM
[long pause] That's quite tricky. It can be something that's intrusive, like a noise, or...

Interviewer
Is it a physical thing or do you think its an emotional thing?

PM
I think its, it's a bit of both, um, [indistinct] it could be something like someone tooting a horn or being a bloody pain in the arse, where their rationale doesn't seem to coincide with my rationale at all.

Interviewer
Do you ever find its when you need to do something, when you need to act, to have a prompt like that...?

PM
Not so much, no. It used to, uhm, and I think it changed when you kind of start to look at some of the work that's been done or get involved with some of the politics or politicians you realise how duplicitous things are, how people are, um, out for different [indistinct]. It's a game. Its more like a career path.

Interviewer
So, you saying that when you exit the game, for you, that's the way to get around it?

APPENDIX B — THE IMPORTANCE OF VISUAL SUSTAINABILITY

PM
Yeah.

13. Interview question
What never changes? [+] in each of these three. What's the one thing that never changes for you…?

[Back to the Invariance. Can these be refined?]

PM
The one constant is a sense of release.

Interviewer
What? That you're inhabiting these spaces?

PM
That you're free. That you're there.

Interviewer
That you're there?

PM
Yeah, that you're there. That you still feel part of it. And I think that is one of the sad things, is when you back to somewhere and you think, oh, I don't remember it like this.

Interviewer
And do you always, in these three spaces, feel its still part of you?

PM
Yeah.

14. Interview question
Can you enjoy this space even when you're not there?

[Back to simulacra. Or memory. Or both].

PM
Yeah [very definite response]. I enjoy it because I know its there.

Interviewer
You know its there?

PM
I'm not sure, if they suddenly decided they're going to cement over Brecon Beacons and put a Wimpy Estate there, I might have a few things to say about it. Yeah? But I can enjoy it for the fact that it is still there. And is still accessible.

Interviewer
So, for you its still the reassurance its still there, its not so much…

PM
It's a constant.

Interviewer
Beg your pardon?

PM
It's a constant.

Interviewer
It's a constant. Yeah.

PM
But… [indistinct].

Interviewer
These things in those three spaces, its because you can recall them, right?

PM
Hmm (affirmative).

Interviewer
Its not just that you know its there, that's the reassurance, but its…

PM
No, no they're part of…

Interviewer
…Because you recall all these things?

PM
They, they, they make part of me. They become part of me.

Interviewer
So, can you enjoy the spaces when you're not there?

PM
Yeah.

Interviewer
I think we've answered that.

15. Interview question
In what ways do you or have you experienced this space, when you are not physically there?

[Again, seeing whether simulacra plays a role. Or memory. Or both].

PM
I'm thinking about, I'm thinking about each of those spaces that are important.

Interviewer
What's come up. Tell me what's coming up?

PM
Uuuhm, [long pause]. The British Library. The design of it. The contents of it. The smell of it.

Interviewer
Tell me something about the design of it.

PM
I think it's the clean lines. And the [long pause] its not fussy. But its still beautiful.

Interviewer
Its next to a very fussy building though isn't it? The station.

PM
Yeah, the station, you can't get…

Interviewer
Very impressive but busy…

PM
Yeah. But that's Victorian Gothic for you. You've got, you know…

Interviewer
And you prefer the library architecture to…

PM
Yeah. Because, you go to Mumbai, you can see St Pancras station, you know its… and that's the arrogance of this Empire of ours.

Interviewer
But those things are transplanted there, but the origin is here though. There's a little bit of a…

PM
Yeah. It's importing our comfort zone.

Interviewer
Like one of those glass buildings, and you can go to Johannesburg and you'll see the same thing.

PM
Yeah.

Interviewer
Exactly the same thing. Regardless of how beautiful it is.

PM
Yeah.

Interviewer
Ok and any of those other spaces? In what way do you or have you experienced this space…?

PM
In what sense?

Interviewer
In the sense that you're thinking about them now. So, think about the second and third one. What comes up?

PM
Ahhhh, the Docks, brings up memories of family, my grandfather, and, you know, having the toy set. So, its real. But its, uhm, an amazing place, uhm, and that's partly down to my grandfather being a storyteller, I think. Uhm, Brecon Beacons has always been part of my life, because we, if it snowed, we'd go tobogganing up there. Because its only like a 50–minute drive from Cardiff. And we'd go there for picnics and go for walks and, so there's always, there's always two in particular, the Dock and the Brecon Beacons, and its, it goes back to sort of to the time when we were doing Cardiff Bay and Peter [indistinct]?, Peter [indistinct]? was the

APPENDIX B   THE IMPORTANCE OF VISUAL SUSTAINABILITY

minister, all he used to say was, I want people in the valleys all working in Cardiff. And you'd say, oh ok, but there's no buses. Well, we'll have to do something about that then. So, what if you subsidise the bus routes. But the people in the valleys, they don't want to go to go to the city, because, they only go to the city on Wednesday. So, what can we do about that? So (laughter) he says what do you mean. So, I said, um, cattle prodding them and loading them on to a train, taking them, you know, they haven't got the skills [indistinct] and people are living in the back. So, what do we do about that. Well, we'll start building some skill centres there. Well, we'll do that then. And you go, so why are we doing this when people don't want to go to there to work in the first place. Because I want people in the valleys to… and you go ok, ok.

Interviewer
This whole tobogganing thing. Is it the steepness of the hill that comes into your memory, or just the tobogganing experience?

PM
Just the fun. Just the fun.

Interviewer
You don't think of the steepness or…?

PM
No. Just the fun.

16.   Interview question
What kind of things remind you of your favourite urban space?

[This speaks to redintegration. How has this person been reminded/ gone back to memory and reconstituted or re–mixed memories]?

PM
[long pause] Its interesting… things, there's always new things to see. Not so much the Docks now. The Docks are just… houses there.

Interviewer
Yeah, but what kind of things in your every day life?

PM
Uhm…

Interviewer
Not just the space but your day, your routine, every day, a typical day, the first question…

PM
Yeah.

Interviewer
What kind of things during that day will actually remind you of one of those three spaces?

PM
Well, anything. Anything and everything.

Interviewer
So, there's no constant there, you could be walking along and…

PM
I… yes. Uhm, I could see something and that could trigger some memory off of something that you, you…

Interviewer
Is there any specific action that you take, like cleaning the sink or making food?

PM
No. It could be anything…

Interviewer
Yeah. The mind wanders.

PM
It wanders in so much as, you can think, wow, I can remember being in a meeting when it, that was discussed. It would be a good idea if we, what about if we did this. And you could go back twenty years later and look and think, Oh! So, I was kind of right then, or that was a [indistinct]. And the most important thing to remember is that nobody dies. All you do is you waste money. You don't kill anybody. I told

myself, is, you know, people talk about pressure. If, if you're a neurosurgeon and you get something wrong, that's pressure. If you do jobs like mine, and you spend a couple of million pounds and it doesn't work, its only paper, it doesn't matter. You think, oh, well what have we learnt from that. That it will fall down in five years, in ten years, and we can have another go. Its not as if you think, my gosh, I've got this [pause] zombie. How am I going to tell the family.

Interviewer
Have you ever looked at Greenwich mean time and that little set of buildings up there, and has that ever jogged your…

PM
The smell. When you go inside. Yeah, yeah. It has a very distinctive smell.

Interviewer
Reminds you of?

PM
Uhm.

Interviewer
One of those three places?

PM
Yeah, it might be the Docks because the Docks offices where highly polished wooden floor. Black floor. And it had a very distinctive smell to it. And… I don't know whether it was the polish or whatever, but it had that very distinctive, clean, rich, warm smell. Which the building that the clocks in, that has the clock, has that smell. And you think, ahh, it smells exactly like [pause] the Dock clock. When you look at it, I think, probably coz they've got, or used to have the same wooden floor, and the designs have got similar materials. And it was looked after.

17. Interview question
If you were to pick one word or phrase to describe your favourite space, what would it be?
[Could this describe visual sustainability. What is most dear to this person]?

PM
[Long pause]. Hmm. Probably tranquil.

Interviewer
Even the Docks?

PM
Yeah. [long pause]. Because. It was [long pause] each one of those spaces… indistinct… was organised, and did have a structure …[indistinct] did have a structure, uhm, and it was, nature and humans together, as opposed to being apart or in conflict.

Interviewer
So, the order settled you down, despite the noise or activity. You just felt that there was a presence of order…

PM
Yeah. And there was a structure to it, I mean, it was tranquil. To me I find that quite peaceful and tranquil.

Interviewer
That's an interesting observation to make, because most people would throw up their hands and say, whoa, its so busy and but you saw through that, you saw the structure behind that…

PM
You were part of that.

Interviewer
Yeah.

PM
You, you, that would be going on in any case. I am much more interested in [long pause] if you like, the space, and, how people live in it…

Interviewer
The physical stuff?

PM
I find, I, I, yeah, the physical space. And I enjoy people watching, and to see how people react.

Interviewer
But you realise that abstract space is right there besides that physical space?

PM
Yeah.

Interviewer
So how would you explain that, I mean the dichotomy between the two elements. Do you find it something that's jarring, or do you find…?

PM
No, I think that's why I like the three spaces, because it does bring, the… [long pause].

Interviewer
Reconciles the mental with the physical?

PM
Yeah, yeah. It gives you time to breathe, or it gives me time to breathe. It gives my mind time to switch off. Because, there are things there that I can be curious about, but also, you know, I… I, have been known to go into the British Library and ask for the book so I can find out something that I've just seen on the building, you know, because you think, that's interesting, and you think, I wonder why. And you find out.

18. Interview question
Ok, there is a last question. Its not on the paper, but, ok. I'm going to put you now into the Docks.

PM
Ok.

Interviewer
Tell me how you feel.

PM
[Pause] Uhh. Very peaceful [short, crisp recollection].

Interviewer
I'm going to put you into the British Library.

PM
Very peaceful [emphasis on peaceful as, enduring…]

Interviewer
I'm going to put you into the… [Brecon Beacons].

PM
Peaceful.
Tranquil.
There's no… [long pause] any surprises, or they're gentle surprises.

Interviewer
And if you were to go now, to get on the train and go to each of those spaces, you'd expect to find the same thing?

PM
Yes.

Interviewer
Have you ever been disappointed?

PM
No.

Interviewer
Not once?

PM
Not once, touch wood.

Interviewer
Even in the busy British Library area?

PM
I love it when its busy, because I'm really fascinated by people.

Interviewer
Where would you sit when you're at the British Library? Outside?

PM
Outside.

Interviewer
Not inside the library?

PM
No. I like to watch people's reactions.

Interviewer

Because they cross that little urban patch there...

PM

I mean on the weekend I went with someone to pick something up and went down Abbey Road. And, its just fascinating watching the tourists taking pictures of that bloody crossing. [Indistinct] You know, you think... amazing. Came all the way from Japan and to have their photograph taken stood on a zebra crossing. Human beings are fascinating creatures. *But those three spaces...* [emphasis added].

Interviewer

I wonder what that chap going back to Japan...? If I could interview him... I mean, he's probably saying the exactly same thing that you're saying...

PM

Yeah: I don't know what we were supposed to take a photograph of, but I did. [indistinct] stood on a bit of white paint on the road.

Interviewer

Ok, [interviewee's name], thanks so much.

APPENDIX B

THE IMPORTANCE OF VISUAL SUSTAINABILITY

YOUTUBE: LARRY AND JANET MOVE OUT

Transcript with comments

Janet
We moved to The Heygate in 1973.

[The Heygate, in this sense, is a Structural Invariant (Physical Use). Why? Because it never changes in the minds of Janet and Larry. It is simply The Heygate, and any feelings generated (Transformation) (Visual Use) are in the storytelling and not in the physical object or architecture]. - - the use is physical because, as a building complex, it is a background object that is defined by the couple, from which they transform (through their feelings) in their story-telling - - the housing complex and its architecture are invariant because they are never described with feeling i.e. in any sense of a transforming experience or interaction.
Hypothesis:
P-u is the use of something (normally an invariant) in defining an object or event;
V-u is how we feel about that use in being defined by that object or event (always a transformation)
Visual sustainability is an urban condition caused by high levels of P-u and V-u].
- -
[directly engaged with the camera].

Oh! it was lovely.

Larry
Lovely.

Janet
Knew all my neighbours...
['Neighbours' is a physical use here in the sense that they are objects in relation to this dwelling - - 'neighbours' are thus structural invariants because the word, in its recollection, signifies a use that surrounding dwellers provide to this couple].

[quickly shifts gaze away] - - [this is a sign of Transformation, whereas before (directly engaged with the camera) it was about the Physical Use].

Mary next door... we used to call her sweary Mary because she swore a lot.

Larry
No!
[as in, don't say that about Mary on camera].

Janet
And, but no, it was Irene first and then sweary Mary. Never mind it doesn't matter...

[what doesn't matter? it's memory fetched, of Sweary Mary, that doesn't].

Larry
It does...

[what does matter for Larry? not the accuracy of her recollection, but their loyalty to their friends, to remain true to what they were and are. So this is about being visually sustainable, carrying forward their memories into the future responsibly].

Janet
Everybody was friendly.
[memory adjusted; their individual 'holographic plates' resonating].

I mean I had five children; they were all friends with the other lads on the estate. Enid's children grew up with mine as well. So, it was a real community you know. Nearly everyone knew everyone else. I mean you weren't in each other's pockets, but you knew ... [slight pause]
... people.

[you knew... what? not necessarily people, but you just knew. 'Knew' is a destination here: a state of being, of visual sustainability...you KNEW you could depend on people; you knew all was right with the world; you just KNEW].

Larry
Everybody used to be out the back yard, and uh, talking to each other. I mean we had Len and Mrs. Hayes; and then there was Chris.

Janet
Chris, yeah.
[thoughtful yeah].

Larry
Yeh.
[confirmation yeah].

Janet
Well, I mean Flo….

Larry
Yeah.

Janet
She used to shout over to me from the window there didn't she…

Larry
You talked up to her…

Janet
"I'll be down in a minute!", you know. We'd shout each other back then but that, that, it was like that, you know - a lovely community - and now it's sad cuz we're all being scattered…
[closing down psychic state].

Larry
Hmph.
[reluctantly agreeing to close that psychic state: hmph and uh].

Janet
Uh.

[janet closing down the psychic state] - -
[From 1:40 to 2:40 the images, we the audience, are watching must be the memories they are fetching and engaging with; forming new memories as they act these out again. Its part of the continuous preparation of memory for action that is so visually sustaining fo us all in life, unique to each one of us. What Janet is recollecting is not technically speaking the same as what Larry is recollecting—the notes being played are different but the song (the psychic state) is the same. We in turn are forming our own memories of their memories].

Janet
No-one in the maisonettes wants to move. Can't blame people who lived in the tall blocks…when the lifts were breaking down etcetera….

[Janet's is a softer landing into feelings of alienation - she's tempering her feelings with her warm feelings towards people].

Larry
Yeah, the people who lived in the tall blocks were shut off, because me sister… she was living on the eleventh floor and had no lift for 18 months, because the council would not repair the lifts. I mean the last time they decorated around here, I mean any outside decorations, was 1974!

[Larry feels the alienation more at this point; Larry feels resentment towards the lift i.e., what is this object/ how does it make you feel].

Janet
Yeah!

Larry
You know, how did they expect…

Janet
Just never done nothing
.
Larry
To talk about paint you know, falling off, of the walls, and the walkways…

Janet
Yeah.

Larry
I mean that this, this property here was painted once…

Janet
Yeah, once in all the time we've lived here.

APPENDIX B — THE IMPORTANCE OF VISUAL SUSTAINABILITY

Larry
… in the length of time we've been here. That's the outside paint work now… painted once!

Janet
Yeah.

Larry
The council done it once and, uh, the last time they done it was just before the Silver Jubilee in 77… ah … and they didn't even get round to us… they ran out of money.

Janet
Yeah [chuckles] our block was the only one that wasn't done right?

Larry
Exactly, yeah, they ran, they ran, well that part of that block over there, and this block.

Janet
Yeah.

Larry
They ran out of money - they always do anyway.

Janet
Yeah.

Larry
So, the Council runs out of money regular!

Janet
[laughs].

Larry
[laughs out loud].

Janet
Just don't run them down too much… [hearty laugh].

Larry
I don't give a hang about…

Janet
[giggles].

Larry
Yeah.
[affirmation].

Janet
[giggles].

Scene change

Tim
I always thought that the council would have some difficulty, um, getting rid of Heygate, simply because Heygate was a very integrated scheme. Not only were the walkways integrated, it had a district heating scheme. If you cut off the district heating scheme—and I, I've heard that that's what happened, um, well, it is a sort of, um, sort of, wha—wha—moral blackmail but it's some form of blackmail to encourage people to go!

Scene change

Larry
We're supposed to put heaters in here and they never give no heaters. Ten days now,

and no water, no washing, you know, we, we, we're wiping down with... with... with wipes. That's what we're doing. You can't, you can't wash, you can't wash upstairs with...can you?

Janet
I feel sorry for the families still left on the estate. At least we're going today.

Scene change

Daughter
Those things mum? Those records?

Janet
It might be worth something. I don't know what they are… they're brand new. They've never been used.

Daughter
Why did you get them?

Janet
I don't know.

Daughter
Where did you get them?

Janet
I don't know. What music is it?

Daughter
Piano…Richard Clayderman.

Janet
I don't even know where they come from. Maybe they're your fathers?

Daughter
The Reader's Digest! I remember when Dad was sent all this Readers Digest stuff that they just wouldn't stop sending it.

Janet
I'll leave them here then. Somebody might want them.

Scene change

Tim
The area which we had to redevelop was mostly, um, very tall, very nasty tenement blocks. There were not enough qualified tradesmen, particularly bricklayers, to build the houses in enough quantity and indeed in enough time. And so, it was decided that you should have some form of what was called industrialized building.

Scene change

Larry
I even worked on this site – awkward [indistinct]. Just building those concrete walls and then dropping the slabs on. Building up, you know, like a pack of cards really… but it was the [indistinct] you know solid as well, uh, you know it was a quicker way, it's a quicker way of building.

Scene change

Tim
Many people didn't have their own flat. An awful lot, I think. They had a room, and they would share a bathroom and share a kitchen in a property. And our aim was to provide, quite clearly, to

provide the potential for a community. I mean architects can't actually create communities. I mean communities can occur in the most, um, u-u-unfortunate circumstances. Indeed, communities can come together by the very fact that that the, the environment is lousy, and they want to make it better. So no, we didn't, we didn't set out to create a community, we set out to provide a, a reasonable environment for particularly families, but the point being that, that children could play outside to grow up and not just be, as it were, um, restricted in early development.

Scene change

Janet
Some people look at the place and say, oh it was a dump. But it wasn't a dump when we moved here compared to what we had lived in before, wasn't it?

Larry
Yeah.

Janet
When you think [indistinct] Road, I mean some people have said ooh the old buildings was better but what, washing in a sink with a scrubbing board? and you don't want to go backwards you want to go forwards don't you. You should have lived here back in the early 70s... and knew the community.

Larry
It was a good community.

Janet
To knock it that they were slums, and the children could never come to anything living on places like that. I've got five children, one of them is a pharmacist and other one's an engineer, another one's a mechanic, you know, Sarah has been through university. My children come to something. We considered ourselves very fortunate to have a place like this. But, I mean, we are sad about leaving it even though we've got a decent place to move to now, there's still memories tied up here. My daughter was born here. You know, it, it's memories isn't it - that you've got to leave behind. And, you know, although it's a concrete jungle to some people, when I look out my kitchen window and I'm busy washing, you can see all the blossoms and it's just like being in the country when you look out of your window. I will miss that when I move. I'll miss that terrible.

Interviewer
What about you Larry, what will you miss?

Larry
Ohhh dear, I dunno.

Janet
Nothing really, will you?

Larry
What you mean nothing?

Janet
No, cuz you're not you're not as sociable as me.

Larry
Not as sociable as you?

Janet
You're sort of, sort of shy, reserved.

Larry
You're talking to the devil you would.

Janet
Go on, if I have to talk to him, I suppose I would. [giggles] No, but you are more, you don't make friends very easy, do you? You sort of shy really. He don't look it but he is.

Larry
I'm not shy.

Janet
You were shy when I met ya, what are you talking about, I brought you out of your shell.

Larry
You been on the bottle tonight?

Janet
No, not yet. [laughs]

Larry
[laughs].

Scene change

Janet
They were building opposite the Caf that I worked in and they used to come in for lunch. It was actually his brother-in-law that set us up. He said, uh, there's... there's a young man out there wants to take you out tonight. So, we went to see Summer Holiday, didn't we? Cliff Richard in the pictures. So yes, that's how we met, wasn't it? I was serving your breakfast even 'fore I married ya. [Laughs]

Scene change

Janet
[Receives telephone call] Hello, hello, hello, [laughs] extra stress in my voice? I know Dave [laughs]. Oh G*d I am stressed. Huh? The Council's just arrived to start shifting us out and your father's... [indistinct]. No, I've had plenty of tears since this morning Dave but yeah there's nothing you can do. At least I'm not some of the poor buggers that still haven't got nowhere to go.

Scene change

Janet
You didn't want to decorate your place, you didn't want new carpets. Because from 1997 we were told we'd be out by 2000.

Larry
That, that we had 3 years.

Janet
And it took ten years more on top of that. Everything was up in the air. I mean I wasn't sleeping. Every day... I, I was miserable weren't I dear [indistinct].

Larry
You are miserable!

APPENDIX B — THE IMPORTANCE OF VISUAL SUSTAINABILITY

Janet
I knew... well, you was miserable too!

Larry
[laughs].

Scene change
(Removal truck arrives).

Scene change

Larry
Ugh! [laughs] These things need drying out. What a battle... [indistinct].

Janet
That bed is to be fit in my house and now they can't, they're saying they can't take it.

Larry
[Indistinct].

Janet
Oh, look what [indistinct]. It was wedged up... under the drawer. It must have fallen out of the drawer all right... never been used...

Larry
[Sighs].

Janet
Oh, I dunno...such is life. How are we gonna carry these out?

Larry
And them eggs!

Janet
[giggles]. Yeah! Five eggs on the window

Larry
Fry the eggs for the... [indistinct] Council when he comes around.

Janet
Yeah! [giggles]. I left five eggs on the window.

Scene change
(Removers trying to move the bed).

Larry
You were supposed to move us. And you were supposed to have an electrician here. That was it... and dismantle the bed. It has to go... the bed has to go. It's your bed. Over a thousand pounds for a f*cking bed.

[(Stress) (Swearing) (Sadness) (Mourning) (Bruised hand) (Janet comforts Larry) (Larry is stooped over, tears from both)].

Janet
It's broken...you silly cow. He's broken his hand. It's burning. You might have to go to the hospital. You shouldn't have tried. [indistinct]. It's not our doing...they are moving us. Would do it...
[Taking Larry's hand].

Larry
They were going without the bed... they were going without the bed...

Janet
And I told you I wasn't leaving until they sorted it out didn't I? I got the bag in me hand.
[Picking up dog droppings].

Scene change

Tim

My understanding is that once the council decided that it was going to have this major redevelopment, it, um, had to in effect 'decant', decant... that lovely phrase... everybody and scatter them to the four winds. Not surprisingly, I think, it was the high blocks and the small flats were decanted more quickly because there weren't the families there. And then what happened was that they had to make use of those units in the short term. So, they put in their people desperate for housing. Those were people who had, inevitably, all sorts of problems; and also, they had no um, um, immediate links to the community so it is hardly surprising that it became, it, it got a less good reputation.

Scene change

Larry

They started moving families out and move people in... somebody... some people was coming in there for like…what was it?

Janet

Temporary housing.

Larry

Temporary housing. Right. And they were using it, like er, maybe six months, ten months, a year.

Janet

But I mean those tall blocks I mean you'd get them throwing chick fat out of the window dirty child's nappies and, I mean the likes of us would never treat a place like that you know. You'd find hypodermic needles around the tall blocks, you know, with children going around in the lift shafts. I mean, you had none of that years ago and that's how bad it went down in, I'd say the last seven years was the worse, wasn't it?

Larry

Hmm.
 [confirmation].

Janet

Last seven years. It just went deeper and deeper into disrepair and I think the council just thought let's let it go.

Scene change

Larry

[sighs]. Oh G*d.

(Kicks at something on his way out the front door)

Scene change

Council A

Reasons for moving …decant… Region… decant.
(Someone filling in a form)

Janet

Kicking us out.

Council A

Oh, not at all. They, they're improving the lives of the residents of SE17.

APPENDIX B — THE IMPORTANCE OF VISUAL SUSTAINABILITY

Janet
They've not improved the lives because I was dealt a dumb deal three times with cr*p property.

Council A
Right.

Janet
Yeah .

Council A
But then this new one…

Janet
Cracked walls. It was filthy dirty.

Council A
This new one, you're in East Dulwich hey? hey?

Janet
It was filthy dirty.

Council A
The lady from Grantham used to live there, didn't she, hey?

Janet
It was filthy dirty when I moved in there.

Council A
Margaret Thatcher used to live down there… hey? The lady from Grantham?

Janet
I'm not complaining… it was filthy dirty

Council A
I can see the, I can see the similarities, hey?... all you need is a big handbag and the pearls and yeah, it'd be a dead ringer for you.

Janet
Yeah.

Janet
But….

Council A
You've cleaned it up now.

Janet
It was the better of what we had been offered and that's the G*d's honest truth.

Council A
Okay.

Janet
Yeah.

Council B
Okay. So, is that a thank you then?

Janet
No! I'm not thanking you cuz you're still pushing me out. I'd stay here. You think I'm gonna thank you?

Council A
I tell you - that the regeneration project is going to enhance the lives of the res….

Janet
How was it gonna enhance the lives? You promised us better homes. Where were they built? You're trying to get rid of your rubbish.

Council A

No.

Janet

You bloody are.

Council A

No... I refute that - on camera!

Scene change

(loading the van)

Council C

This is the [indistinct] one. It's the termination of tenancy.

Janet

Yes.

Council C

Saying that you're giving up this tenancy. We will hand that in, and it releases the 4800 pounds.

Janet

But if I sign this now, you'll boot me out before my bird's sorted.

Council C

Your bird?

Janet

Bed. Where's the proof that if my bed doesn't get in that place that you're gonna compensate me?

Council C

What you would do…

Janet

I want proof…. otherwise, I'm not signing that.

Council C

How can, how can I… well don't sign it, you don't get your 4800 quid.

Janet

We've spent more than that trying to move. I've lost more than that as well...

Council C

Well, you lose a lot more if you don't get your money...

Scene change

Janet

Where do I sign... here?

Janet

Sign me bloody life away.

Council C

now, now.

Scene change

(loading the van).

Larry

The bowl of fruit goes last, ain't that right Lad? It's always the bowl of fruit. They might want that when they get down there…. locked up. That's it. That's it… all ready... all ready.
(Leaving the house for good through the front door).

Council C

So, let's see your Chaplin impression.

APPENDIX B — THE IMPORTANCE OF VISUAL SUSTAINABILITY

Larry
Have you given him the keys?
(To Janet)

Council C
I'm pushing me luck.

Council A
She wants to do it when she's gone through the door.

Janet
Yeah.

Council A
Come on…

Janet
Goodbye house.
(Talking about a Turkish good luck charm on the door)

Council A
She's got a lucky Turkish thing.

Janet
Is it lucky? I'm leaving my home?

Council A
We can have the keys now and you can have your eggs back. Gi, give us our keys! Thank you very much and best of luck in your new home. Best of luck in your new home. It's been a real pleasure. If your bed doesn't work… call us.

Janet
Come on!. She don't want to come… come on babe…
[Trying to get the dog to move].

Council A
Yeah. Come on. You gotta move on.

Janet
She, she don't wanna go… she, come on! We've gotta go!…come on!

Council A
Come on, that's it, that's it, that's it. Thats it!

Janet
Come on. Keep going
[is she talking to the dog, or herself?].

Council C
That's it, keep going, keep going.
[is he talking to the dog, or Janet?].

Council B
She knows she's not going for a walk she knows it's a … I bet she cr*pped on my leg. In protest.
[he knows what it is, couldn't say it, then changed the subject with poorly disguised humour].

Janet
Cheerio anyway.

Council C
Take care. You'll hear from us in a couple of weeks.

Janet
Right.

Council A
We will call you.

Janet
And I'll call you too if…

Council A
I know.

Janet
… my bed don't get in.

Council A
Yes, oh yeah, well, actually we'll call you in a couple of hours.

Council B
Take care.

Council C
Bye Lady, enjoy your new home.

(scene of the dog).
(Council workers move in, start boarding up).

Scene change
(One year later)

Larry
This is a tiger room. She never gets rid of any of the tigers - everything is in here and downstairs. I thought she'd get rid of some of them, but she didn't. And the famous bed.

Janet
We all got stressed and falling out and upset over the move. I mean you can't say that, you know, if I hadn't moved she'd still be with me. You can't say that because she, she was suffering from arthritis, but she was still quite lively until we moved.

Larry
This is Lady's spot. That's where she lies. In the in that corner and I just put a bit, bigger square around, that's it where she's here, she's lying, so that's it. and I put her ashes in there. And, uh, Jan [Janet] got a flower, a white flower, cuz she was, the dog was, Lady was white, uh.

Scene change

Larry
We moved from [indistinct] estate on to the Heygate in 1973. But something was built, you know, uh, and occupied with, you know, in, in the seventies, you know, its a…

Janet
Well, they're not old are they, not old [firstly, 'not old' is Form; but secondly, 'not old' is Dynamic Form—involves qualia, qualia-in-memory].

Larry
Hmpf!

Janet
There was nothing said about, well you'll only be [pause] twenty-eight years in this place. Thirty years.

Larry
Thirty odd years.

Janet
Yeah!

Scene change

APPENDIX B — THE IMPORTANCE OF VISUAL SUSTAINABILITY

Tim

It was normally assumed that the buildings would last at least 60 years and that was the basis on which, um, that money was borrowed by the Council. We always assumed it would last, in a structural sense, rather longer but clearly they would, um, dissolve over time. We didn't expect them to remain in excess of 60 years, we expected it to develop. It's obviously disappointing that after, what, almost less than 40 years, it's [pause] no longer occupied and is about to be [pause] demolished.

Scene change

Larry

I think it will be 2020 before there'll be anything built on here... [indistinct]... and occupied. I'll be dead.
[Signifies no interest in the new buildings even before they have even been built. He wants nothing to do with the new development].

Janet

Yeah. We'll probably won't see it.

Larry

I think the bones will be stripped by then. We'll be pushing up daisies!

Janet

End of an era!

Larry

[Laughs].

Janet

Isn't it! End of an era!
[loud proclamation of an achievment, of a treasured life on Heygate. So those memories are clear and valuable to them. End of an era - repeated twice - here signifies a willingness to
remember their old home].

Larry

We'll be pushing up daisies by then.
[repeated: Larry has had enough of these negative memories].

[pushing up daisies - repeated twice - here signifies a willingness to forget the new buildings even before they have even been built. He wants nothing to do with the new development].

Janet

Let's just hope they don't move us out of this place before we kick the bucket.

[Both laugh. "This place" is not a sign of home, just 'this place'].

Oh no... I don't wanna move again. No. Unless [emphasised] they redone Chearsley, I'd move back.

[Janet is also avoiding talking about the proposed new development on Heygate; preferring instead to recall a former estate. This suggests a lack of visual sustainability in her life at 'this place'].

Larry

No
[The suggestion here is that 'home' for Larry was the Heygate].

Janet

Oh, I would.

Larry

No

[Larry covers his eyes. This act suggests he's thinking of his old home again and his body language suggests a wish to be private with whatever specific thoughts he just fetched and with which he is now engaging].

Janet

Oh, I'd move back on me own then.

[Laughs. The suggestion here is not to leave Larry but a willingness to leave "this place". Virtual action kicking in here as she prepares to act. Because 'this place' has no meaning for Janet, except for the memory of Lady, the dog. And the dog's death is, in a way, a metaphor for the funeral at having died when they were moved out].

Larry

[Stays quiet. Sense of resignation].

[END]

APPENDIX C THE IMPORTANCE OF VISUAL SUSTAINABILITY

APPENDIX C

THE SOUND OF DATA

In future research I hope to look at how these data is reflected as sound. The idea of data as sound resonates with the work of Iannis Xenakis (Xenakis and Kanach, 1992; Something Rich and Strange: The Life and Music of Iannis Xenakis, 2022). Xenakis has demonstrated how music is a form of language which conveys certain emotions. In the same way, sound through interaction type belongs to that reflection pool which is the invisible city. The discordant, chaotic sound (Figure 57 on page 223) is unapologetic because it describes *alienation in no uncertain terms. The reaction I have received when playing this sound back to people has always been the same: "That alienation sound is maddening! Oh my [expletive]! Hold a constant beat!", or "Could you please turn it down, the dog doesn't like it". But that is exactly the point. It is meant to be uncomfortable and alienating. The genius of Xenakis is conveyed through his professionally produced music but these sounds derived from interaction types simply intend to convey the data i.e., what we *see*, especially when we are alienated. For the study area, we are, quite literally, the sound being made. This future research will be structured around the idea that if alienation is sound, then my digital tapestry represents an orchestra, *based on the following conditions:

- The regular background beat equates to one of two things. In a fixed position, for example, standing or sitting on a bench, it equates to a heartbeat of 110 beats per minute. The other analogy is that the beat represents a walking pace of 110 steps per minute.
- The notes are arranged as follows:
  WHOLE 4 seconds; HALF 2 seconds; QUARTER 1 second; EIGHTH 0.5 seconds; and SIXTEENTH 0.25 seconds and accurately represent the data in length and timing.

In Figure 56 on page 222, it can be seen how each zone is sequentially represented for approximately 60 seconds. This digital tapestry was intended to represent only the MIX of interaction types and therefore excludes SIM. To understand what the sound may be like with SIM included, the following sound from the interactions in Block 1.12 provides a sense of that effect (Figure 58 on page 223). This video produces somewhat different melodies for each zone, from a selection of the same notes applied randomly to each interaction across the study area. In this case, the notes I have used are different from Figure 56 on page 222 and the sound produced is therefore be quite different. However, it is the representation of the sound we produce that is important.

*See definition of alienation on on page 79.

*Excerpt from my preprint: *Joyful vs joyless expenditure: Relevance, real estate, and the voice of urban data* (2023, p.4).

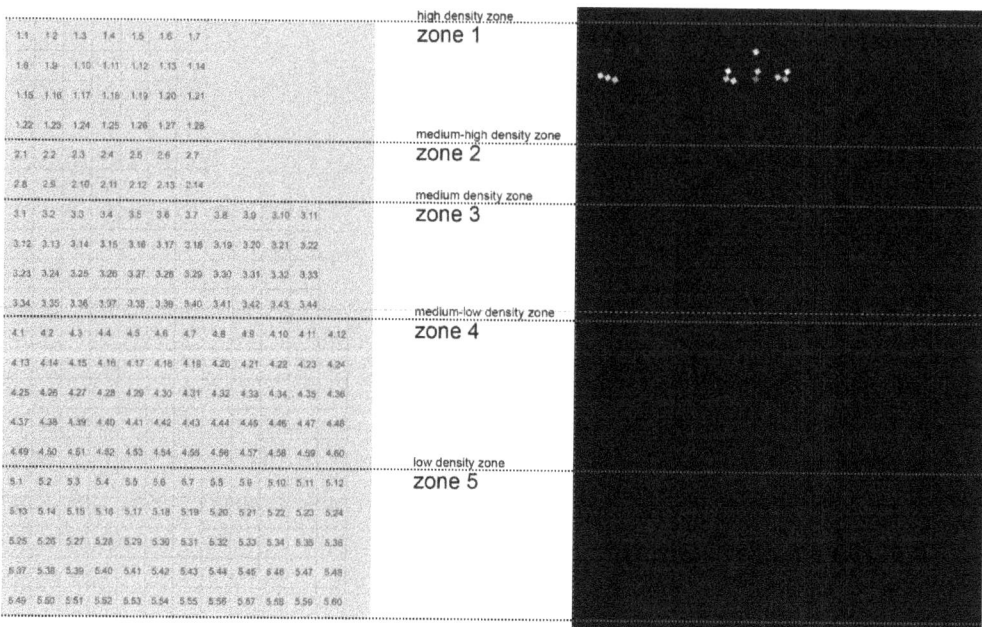

Figure 56. Digital tapestry with sound: The sounds made along the transect between zones 1 and 5 (video watch at https://doi.org/10.6084/m9.figshare.24996428.v1.

In this example, what we hear is the temporal sounds of transient groups of a people, as they individually engage with their surroundings. At around the 50 second mark, the effect of the first of several SIM interaction types can be heard. The video recording has been omitted due to the University of Hertfordshire's ethics requirements. The preliminary conclusion is that the sound is less important than the realisation that it's *we* who are making that sound. And, for alienating conditions, that does not bode well for cities that ignore the importance of visual sustainability in urban design strategy.

Figure 57. Alienation produced in sound form: low entropy; low complexity (sound).
Hear sound at https://doi.org/10.6084/m9.figshare.24996347.v1.

Figure 58. Block 1.12: urban sound with SIM interaction type (sound).
Hear sound at https://doi.org/10.6084/m9.figshare.24996326.v1.

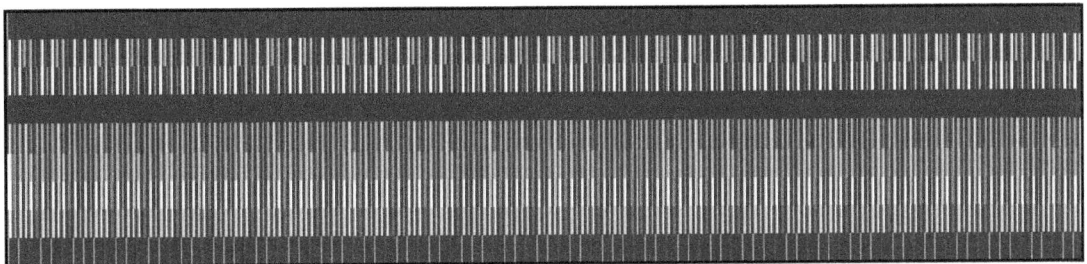

Figure 59. The sounds we make Zone 3. High entropy; high complexity (sound).
Hear sound at https://doi.org/10.6084/m9.figshare.24996377.v1.

www.ingramcontent.com/pod-product-compliance
Lightning Source LLC
Chambersburg PA
CBHW040949020526
44118CB00044B/2817